CONTENTS

THE VICTORIA HISTORY OF HAMPSHIRE

BASINGSTOKE REINVENTED
1800 to 1925
FROM AGRICULTURAL TOWN TO MANUFACTURING CENTRE

Written by Bob Applin, John Ashworth, Jennie Butler, Bob Clarke, Bill Fergie, John Hare, Janet Hird, Andrew Howard, Michael Jahn, Barbara Large, Lesley Mason, Jean Morrin, Mary Oliver, Roger Ottewill, Derek Spruce and Joan Wilson

Edited by JEAN MORRIN

VICTORIA COUNTY HISTORY

Hampshire

First published in the United Kingdom in 2025

by The Hobnob Press,
8 Lock Warehouse, Severn Road, Gloucester GL1 2GA
www.hobnobpress.co.uk

on behalf of the Institute of Historical Research, School of Advanced Studies,
University of London

A Victoria County History Publication

British Library Cataloguing in Publication Data
A catalogue record for this book is available from the British Library

ISBN   978-1-914407-92-5

Typeset in Minion Pro 11/14 pt.
Typesetting and origination by John Chandler

*Front cover images: View of Basingstoke from the Holy Ghost Chapel (the Liten) c. 1830 (old print); and
c. 1925 (postcard).*

Back cover image: Burberry Shooting Coat, 1887.

LIST OF ILLUSTRATIONS

Figures

Maps

Tables

FOREWORD

T HE IDEA OF a national series of town and parish histories for every county in England was first mooted at Queen Victoria's Diamond Jubilee in 1897 and the Victoria County History (VCH) was dedicated to her. In 2012, Her late Majesty Queen Elizabeth II agreed to the rededication of the project to mark her own Diamond Jubilee.

Hampshire was the first county to publish a history of each of its parishes in red book volumes (1912) but these contained only leading families, the Church of England and local charities. In 2008 Hampshire later became the first county to undertake a complete revision of a parish in the modern VCH style which includes the social, economic and religious history of the ordinary people. This volume is the sixth in the new series to be completed in Hampshire. It follows Mapledurwell (2012), Steventon (2016), Basingstoke, a Medieval Town, c.1000-c.1600 (2017), Cliddesden Hatch and Farleigh Wallop (2018) and Dummer and Kempshott (2022).

Basingstoke Reinvented 1800 to 1925: From Agricultural Town to Manufacturing Centre considers the emergence of Basingstoke as a southern industrial town in the second half of the 19th century. Thomas Burberry, founder of the famous fashion house, invented gabardine. Wallis and Steevens developed from a local company supplying agricultural machinery into a producer of road rollers. Thornycroft moved to Basingstoke in 1898 and produced lorries for the military and civilian markets. All relied on the railways for the supply of raw materials and the export of finished products.

This project has been undertaken entirely by volunteer historians, its costs met by book sales, donations and grants. Help and support is much needed to enable the work which remains to be done to complete the parishes in the Basingstoke area and, ultimately, the rest of the historic county of Hampshire. I am sure this volume will not only interest people living locally, now and in the future, but also appeal to a much wider audience and encourage research in other southern towns concerning local industrialisation.

I welcome this refreshing addition to the history of Hampshire, and I commend this delightful book to you.

Nigel Atkinson

Nigel Atkinson Esq
HM Lord-Lieutenant of Hampshire

ACKNOWLEDGEMENTS

M OST OF THE Hampshire VCH team have contributed to this book. Some have written sections and others, including Sarah Gould and Diane Kelly, have helped with editorial work.

We have profited from research and publications done previously on Basingstoke by the late Barbara Applin. The late Mike and Josie Wall helped with research. Debbie Reavell of Basingstoke Heritage Society has generously shared her considerable knowledge of Basingstoke's past with us. Ian Hird created spreadsheets for analysis of 1921 census.

Such a study is very much dependent on the unsung backing of a variety of Record Offices. The staff of the Hampshire Record Office have been very supportive throughout a project which has been largely dependent on material in their care. John Hollands of the Willis Museum helped with source material. Hampshire Cultural Trust provided access to their Thornycroft archive and allowed us to use their photographs. The Thornycroft Society invited us to read their records, mainly of apprenticeship and pupils, at Pensdell Farm, Cliddesden. The Museum of English Rural Life in Reading gave us access to the Wallis and Steevens archive and were very helpful.

Guidance from Adam Chapman and Ruth Slatter at VCH central office at the Institute of Historical Research, University of London has been invaluable. Jonathan Dollery has drawn the excellent maps of development in Basingstoke.

We are also grateful for financial support. The Victoria County History Trust financed travel to the National Archives in 2022 to study the then newly released 1921 census. They also financed Jon Dollery to draw maps three and four. We are supported by Basingstoke and Deane Borough Council who donated £500 towards our publishing costs.

We are grateful to John Chandler and Louise Ryland-Epton of Hobnob Press for agreeing to publish this Short, now that the University of London press no longer offer this service.

PREFACE

BASINGSTOKE HAS GONE through several periods of considerable change from the growth of the cloth industry in the 15th and 16th century[1] to its dramatic expansion since the 1960s which is still underway. This book covers the period when the town was transformed from a market town serving north-east Hampshire into a manufacturing centre producing goods for the national and international markets. The main new industries were factory produced clothing and engineering. The breakthrough in clothing was led by Thomas Burberry, founder of the famous fashion house. His development of gabardine led to a flourishing business supplying military and wealthy sporting customers. Wallis and Steevens developed from a local company supplying agricultural machinery into a producer of road rollers, threshing machines, trucks and pumps which were sold worldwide. Thornycroft moved to Basingstoke in 1898 and produced lorries for the military and civilian markets. All relied on the railways for the supply of raw materials and the export of finished products.

Between 1861 and 1911 Basingstoke's population grew by almost 150 per cent, as the town benefited from the new opportunities. Under the leadership of a number of prominent Nonconformists, the town grasped both the opportunities of technological innovation such as the treadle sewing machine and new manufacturing opportunities like gabardine and steam engines.

The study of this industrialisation contributes to a debate about how far manufacturing developed in southern towns after its initial establishment in the north of England and Scotland. For example, Calne, Chippenham, Gloucester, Guildford and Reading also benefited from the railways which assisted their local industries.[2]

Basingstoke grew rapidly to accommodate the new factories and provide housing for the workforce. Much of this housing survives in what are now conservation areas but most of the industrial and religious buildings of this period of expansion were demolished in the 1960s and afterwards when Basingstoke was redeveloped as a London overspill town (Map 3).

The book begins in 1800 with the agricultural and market town and considers its transformation by the early 20th century. A final date of 1925 allows the impact of, and recovery from, the First World War to be assessed. Physically the town's appearance had then reached a new stability which it was to retain until its later 20th century transformation.

1. Hare, *Medieval Basingstoke*.
2. *VCH Glos*. IV, 183–8; J. Brown, *The English Market Town*, (Ramsbury, 1986), 86; *VCH Wilts* IV, 199, 221–2, 224, 227; https://www.dennissociety.org.uk/history.html (accessed 20 Sept. 2024).

INTRODUCTION

Landscape

Basingstoke parish lies on the dip slope of the upper chalk, known as the Seaford Chalk Formation, of the North Hampshire Downs at a point where it slips below the younger rocks of the Thames Basin (to reappear as the Chiltern Hills to the north). It is part of the area labelled Hampshire's 'Northern Slope' (Map 1).[1]

The most prominent feature in the north-east of the parish and most heavily populated part in the 19th century was the valley of the river Loddon. This rose near the western boundary of the parish at a height of 300ft at West Ham and flowed eastwards onto the impervious beds of the London Basin just beyond the eastern edge of the parish at about 260ft. It then continued north to join the Thames at Wargrave. Erosion of the Loddon valley revealed springs in the chalk that fed the river from West Ham eastwards. The water supply from those springs in the vicinity of St Michael's church provided a year-round supply that enabled the core of a settlement to start there which in due course developed a secondary settlement on the high ground around the Market Place at about 300ft.[2] A small south bank tributary of the Loddon runs from Black Dam, a fishpond fed by springs. The pond supplied

Map 1. Geology map early 20th century.

1   R. Mudie, *Hampshire.* Vol. 2, *The Northern, Eastern and Southern Slopes, and the New Forest* (Winchester, 1839), 1.
2   Hare, *Medieval Basingstoke,* 2.

Hackwood House, home of Lord Bolton, which lay just beyond the eastern boundary of the parish in Old Basing.[3]

The low watershed at Worting at about 400ft, to the west of Basingstoke, led to the upper Test valley which became a major route to the south-west. Much of the area to the north of the Loddon valley rises to between 300 and 400ft, with the highest point being at Winklebury Camp which is just over 400ft. To the south of the town the undulating chalk downland is between 300 and 550ft above sea level with 535ft on Winchester Road and 435ft on Cliddesden Hill. There are some surface deposits of clay with flints which influenced local land use.

In 1786 the agricultural landscape had been transformed by the enclosure of 3,500 a. of the parish.[4]

Boundaries

B ETWEEN 1800 AND 1925 the shape of Basingstoke parish changed little. Any adjustments to the boundaries were relatively minor. In 1800, the boundaries of the parish and borough of Basingstoke (Map 2) were the same as those shown on the map prepared for the duke of Bolton in 1762.[5] At the time the total area was 3,970 a. with most of it being rural.[6]

Shortly after the implementation of the Municipal Corporations Act 1835 the boundaries of all municipal boroughs were reviewed by commissioners. They confirmed that the borough and parish were coterminous, and that the area was nearly 4,000 acres. The urban portion occupied only 5 per cent of the area so the commissioners suggested reducing the urban boundary to include only the town and its immediate hinterland, but this did not happen, and Basingstoke retained its existing boundaries. A traditional perambulation of the boundaries took place in 1855. Civic dignitaries walked the 'eighteen miles, two furlongs and thirty-five poles' over two days.[7]

There were minor additions of 66 a. and 136 a. resulting from the implementation of the Counties (Detached Parts) Act of 1844 and the Divided Parishes and Poor Law Amendment Acts of 1876 & 1882 respectively,[8] increasing it to 4,172 a. Such changes were relatively uncontroversial. This was not the case, however, when it came to the adjustment of the boundary with the parish of Eastrop (Map 2), a small

3   HRO, 54M98/E/B1/34. With town development a roundabout on the ring road has been named after Black Dam ponds to which it is adjacent. Basing and Old Basing were used interchangeably until the late 20th century when Old Basing became the official name of the parish.

4   HRO, 5M52/E69.

5   Hare, *Medieval Basingstoke*, 25.

6   HRO, 23M72/P1/1, 2.

7   HRO, 148M71/1/5/5; *HC,* 20 Oct. 1855.

8   OS Map, 1:10560, sheet 18, revised 1894 but surveyed 1871.

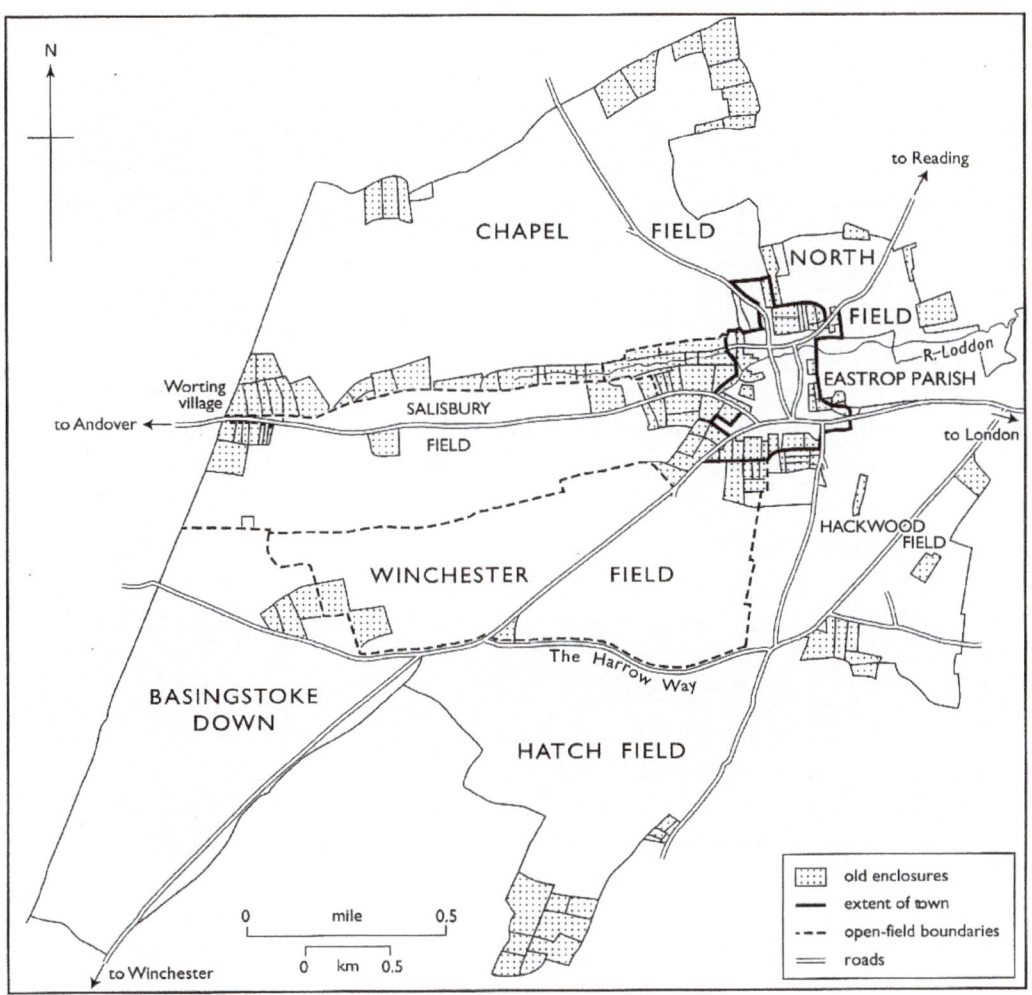

Map 2. Basingstoke parish in 1788. © Derek Spruce.

parish adjoining the east of Basingstoke, divided into four parts. The development of housing during the 1880s in the central part of Eastrop, which bordered Basingstoke, converted it into a suburb of the town, and created pressure to adjust the boundary. Basingstoke borough argued that the residents of Eastrop were enjoying the benefits of public services, such as paving, sewerage and education, but were not contributing to the cost. Their opponents argued unsuccessfully to retain Eastrop's distinctive identity.[9] Consequently, in November 1891 the urban portion of the civil parish of Eastrop, comprising 23 a., was added to the municipal borough of Basingstoke, increasing its area to 4,195 a.[10] Although part of the borough, it was not added to the parish of Basingstoke and this part of Eastrop retained its civil parish status until 1932. Between 1891 and 1925 no further adjustments were made to Basingstoke's boundaries.

9   *HBG*, 20 Dec. 1890.
10   OS Map, 1:10560, sheet 18; *Census Report Hants*, 1901, 41.

Landownership

I N 1840 THERE were ten owners who each held more than 100 a. although most of this was leased out. Lord Bolton owned the most land. His family had acquired through marriage the Paulet long-standing lands in the town.[11] Nine of Lord Bolton's tenants rented 540 a., Thomas Penton, who rented 249 a. of South Ham farm, farmed the most land. Eleven other people held long leases from Bolton for 623 a., a total of 1,653 a. or 29 per cent of the parish. Richard Eyles was the second largest landowner with 449 a. of which he farmed 122 a. at Skippetts End. He leased 282 a. at Bury Farm to Ann Hyde and by 1851 he was living there himself, farming 401 a.[12] Other substantial owners were the assigns/devisees of Augustus Hankey (290 a.), William Apletree at Goldings with 125 a., George Paice with 214 a., and Revd Workman with 104 a. Then there were the institutional holders whose ownership represented past prosperity and wealth: Merton College, Oxford, had held 200 a. from the 13th century; Winchester College 121 a. from the 15th and Pembroke College, Oxford, 276 a., which had been bought from the descendants of a wealthy clothier in 1745. Some of the surrounding gentry held land in the town such as G.P. Jervoise of Herriard, W.P.J. Long Wellesley, the earl of Portsmouth and W.L. Sclater.[13]

Enclosure and the break-up of the existing pattern of landholding helped urban development. A field of land could be given a street plan and subdivided into lots which were then sold freehold to individual purchasers for industrial and residential use.[14] Changes in landownership began before 1840 with the break-up of the earl of Dartmouth's estate. He had inherited the great estate in Basingstoke that had formerly belonged to the Blundens, a successful family of clothiers and maltsters in the 17th century but little remained in his hands by 1840. It was probably sold off after 1806.[15] West Ham farm was sold by the earl of Dartmouth's executors to John Hasker in 1818 (d. 1821), then to Christopher Lefroy by 1840 and eventually passed to the Thornycroft company.[16] Fifteen acres of land north of the town were sold to the GWR in 1847 for its station and yards by the trustees of the late Charles May.[17]

In 1908 the 103 a. Down farm north of Kempshott and south of Worting Road was bought by Homesteads Limited from the governors of Queen Mary's school

---

11 The Paulet family of Old Basing were marquesses of Winchester (1551–1689) and dukes of Bolton (1689–1794). The dukedom became extinct in 1794 on the death of the sixth duke.

12 *Census*, 1851.

13 HRO, 21M65/F7/13/1 and 2.

14 For example, HRO, 10M57/SP56.

15 HRO, 31M91. The land tax of 1806 shows him as a major land holder but with subsequent entries crossed through.

16 HRO, 63M83/A1/4; 21M65/F7/13/1 and 2.

17 HRO, 10M57/E77; below, Settlement, for further development of South View.

for development with bungalows and smallholdings.[18] It was named the Kempshott Village estate despite the objection of Dummer with Kempshott parish council that it was not within its boundary but part of Basingstoke.[19] Homesteads Limited was one of several companies involved in plotland developments across south-east England from the first decade of the century into the interwar period at a time before the advent of effective planning legislation after 1945.[20] The first building permits were given in 1909,[21] and development then proceeded steadily until interrupted by the outbreak of war, resuming in the early 1920s.

The Goldings estate provides another example of change. It had been held in the later 18th century by Francis Russell, a wealthy lawyer, surveyor and administrator, in whose time the house probably underwent major expansion.[22] It was held by William Apletree and his family in 1840 until at least 1878.[23] Subsequently it was owned by Samuel Field, a wealthy retired solicitor, in 1881[24] and then by the Lefroy family.[25] In 1921 it was bought by the borough council; the house became council offices and the spacious surrounding park a greenspace memorial to those who died during the First World War.[26]

Population

BETWEEN 1801 AND 1921 the population of the parish of Basingstoke grew from 2,589 to 12,415 or by 380 per cent. This rapid growth was not constant and slowed in the aftermath of the arrival of the railway in the 1840s and 1850s, as the town lost its role as a vital stopping point on the main coach route from London to the west country. Rapid growth resumed in the 1860s and remained consistent until at least 1911, reflecting the town's emergence as an industrial centre, based on mass manufacturing of clothing and engineering (Table 2). Those enterprises, combined with the drift to the towns following the increased mechanisation in agriculture, led to a doubling of the population from 4,654 in 1861 to 9,793 in 1901 (Table 2). This contrasted dramatically with neighbouring, albeit smaller, market towns like

18 HRO, 10M57/SP274; *HBG,* 12 Sept. 1908.
19 *HBG*, 14 Nov. 1908.
20 D. Hardy and C. Ward, *Arcadia for All: the Legacy of a Makeshift Landscape* (1984); Kempshott History Group publications at https://kempshotthistory.org.uk, including M. Wolstencroft, *Kempshott Village: the early years, 1900–1920* (2019).
21 HRO, 58M74/BP454.
22 Below, Built Character.
23 *White's Dir.* (1878), 133. Isabella Apletree, widow, held it in 1875 (HRO, 12M/49/C1).
24 *Census*, 1881.
25 *Kelly's Dir.* (1903), 50.
26 https://www.basingstoke.gov.uk/content/page/44210/Basingstoke%20Town.pdf (accessed 1 Nov. 2023); below, Social Hist., The First World War and its Impact.

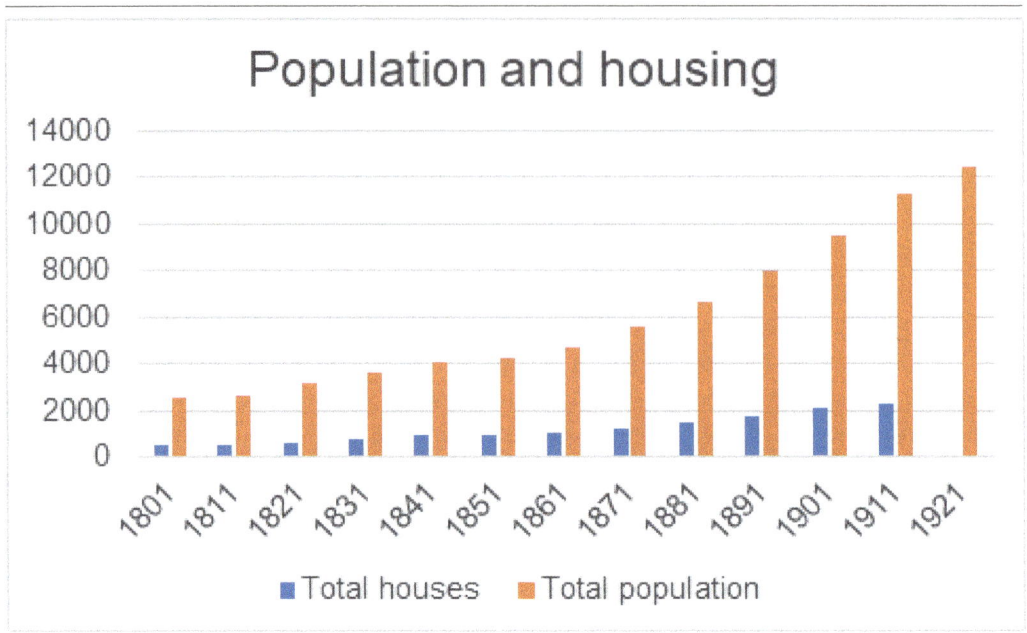

Table 1. Population and housing 1801–1921.

.

Year	Population of Parish			Increase	% Increase
	Male	*Female*	*Total*		
1801	1239	1350	2589	---	---
1811	1253	1403	2656	67	2.6
1821	1499	1666	3165	509	19.2
1831	1718	1863	3581	416	13.1
1841	1933	2133	4066	485	13.5
1851	2050	2213	4263	197	4.8
1861	2273	2381	4654	391	9.2
1871	2662	2912	5574	920	19.8
1881	3156	3525	6681	1107	19.9
1891	3733	4227	7960	1279	19.1
1901	4543	4967	9510(a)	1550	19.5
1911	5332	5927	11259(a)	1749	18.4
1921	5936	6479	12415(a)	1156	10.3

Note

a. Until 1891, the parish and municipal borough of Basingstoke were co-extensive. From 1901 to 1921, the municipal borough included the surviving urban portion of the civil parish of Eastrop and the combined populations were 1901, 9,793; 1911, 11,540 and 1921, 12,723.

Table 2. Comparative population increase by decade.

Odiham and Overton, which declined during this period.[27] In 1881, 40 per cent of the population had been born in Basingstoke, with another 30 per cent born in Hampshire. The counties bordering Hampshire contributed another 12 per cent and a further 2.5 per cent came from the rest of south-east England. This late growth generated a considerable demand for housing and with it a transformation of the urban area and in the town's appearance.[28] Although the growth rate slowed between 1911 and 1921, Basingstoke at 10.3 per cent still had the second highest increase for a Hampshire urban area after Southampton (11 per cent).[29]

Settlement

I N 1800 THE shape of the urban area of Basingstoke had changed little since the medieval period. Its two core elements were the upper town or Top of the Town, east and west of the Market Place, and the lower town around St Michael's church (Fig. 1), to the north of the upper town.[30] Church Street (Fig. 2) and Wote Street

Fig. 1. St Michael's church in 2023. © Barbara Large.

were the main streets linking the two. Major change only came later in the 19th century and early 20th century. The urban area expanded rapidly to accommodate

27 *Census*, 1861–1901.
28 Below, Settlement and Built Character.
29 *Census Report Hants*, 1921, ix.
30 Hare, *Medieval Basingstoke*, 79–83.

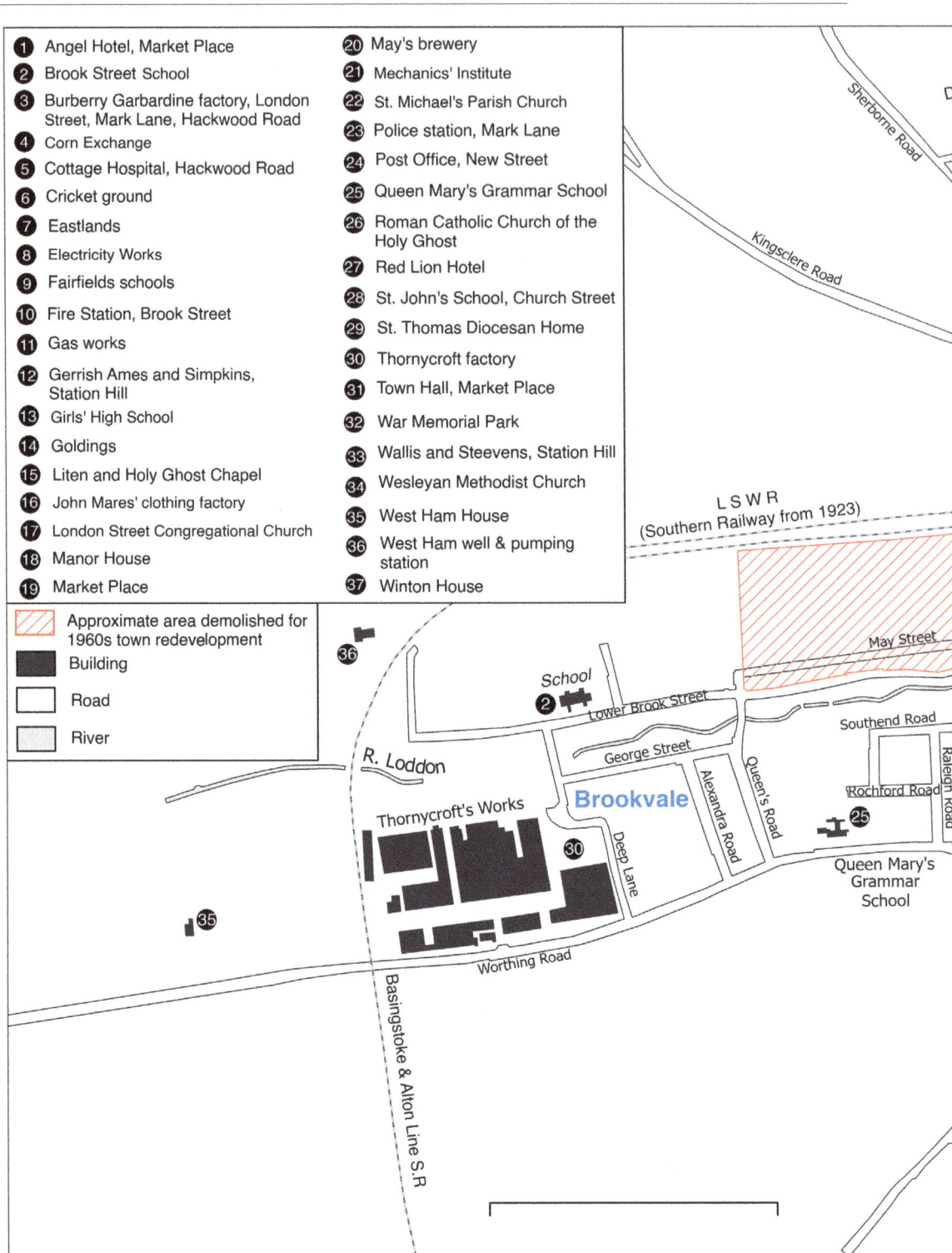

1 Angel Hotel, Market Place
2 Brook Street School
3 Burberry Garbardine factory, London Street, Mark Lane, Hackwood Road
4 Corn Exchange
5 Cottage Hospital, Hackwood Road
6 Cricket ground
7 Eastlands
8 Electricity Works
9 Fairfields schools
10 Fire Station, Brook Street
11 Gas works
12 Gerrish Ames and Simpkins, Station Hill
13 Girls' High School
14 Goldings
15 Liten and Holy Ghost Chapel
16 John Mares' clothing factory
17 London Street Congregational Church
18 Manor House
19 Market Place
20 May's brewery
21 Mechanics' Institute
22 St. Michael's Parish Church
23 Police station, Mark Lane
24 Post Office, New Street
25 Queen Mary's Grammar School
26 Roman Catholic Church of the Holy Ghost
27 Red Lion Hotel
28 St. John's School, Church Street
29 St. Thomas Diocesan Home
30 Thornycroft factory
31 Town Hall, Market Place
32 War Memorial Park
33 Wallis and Steevens, Station Hill
34 Wesleyan Methodist Church
35 West Ham House
36 West Ham well & pumping station
37 Winton House

Approximate area demolished for 1960s town redevelopment
Building
Road
River

Map 3. Basingstoke town centre in 1925. © Hampshire VCH.

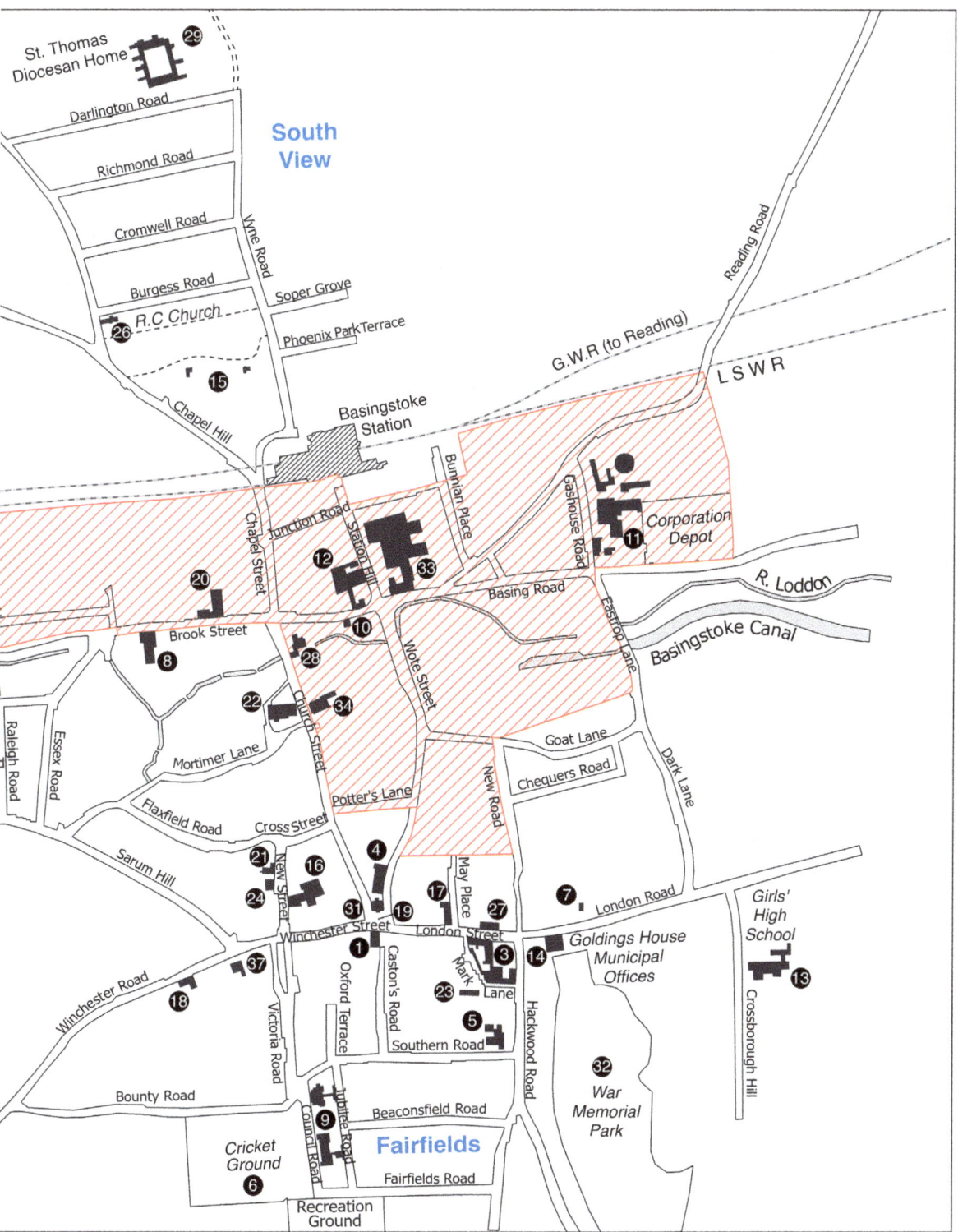

The map of 1930 has been coloured to show the growth of housing during this period. From 1872 this is based on the Ordnance Survey 6 inch maps, with the date being that of the survey not of the publication. It shows the main changes but cannot hope to be comprehensive of all individual houses or rebuilding during the period 1762-1930, and should not be taken as evidence of the function or date of any specific house.

1762. This shows the core of the town as it had existed since the Middle Ages (1). This shows the built up street line in 1762, but some of the buildings would have been rebuilt by 1830.

1851. Change had been largely piecemeal. The station (2) represented a focus of future growth with some new housing nearby (3).

1872. At the end of the decade of fastest population growth (1861-71), expansion had taken place in north-east near the station (3), in south-west (Flaxfield Road and Sarum Hill) (4) and in piecemeal infilling. But signs of growth were also seen in the layout of future estates, where roads had been planned and located but houses had not yet been built. This was the case with both South View (with plots in south, west and east auctioned in 1869) (5) and Longcroft/ May Street (6).

1897. Individual buildings had been built in South View but this was incomplete. May Street had been built. South of this, a new estate was developed by Alfred Tyrell, after his purchase of the land in 1870 (Southend, Rochford and Essex Roads) (7). There were new estates to the South in the Fairfield area after the council gained permission to issue long leases in 1882 (8), and to the East (Chequers Road) (9).

1909. May Street had been extended, when expansion of the railway sidings south of the railway proposed in 1899, necessitated demolition of some houses which LSWR agreed to compensate by building addition-al houses. A new estate had been established at West Brookvale (George Street, Alexandra Road, Queen's Road, and Lower Brook Street) (10), and one between Rochford and Worting Roads (11).

1930. Most developments were in the west, with extensive ribbon development along Worting Road (12). Council houses had been built, particularly in the Kingsclere Road-Sherborne Road estate (13).

Sources: 1762 HRO, 23M72/p1/2 (reproduced in Hare, *Basingstoke, a medieval town,* 8-9; 1851 Archer-Davis map of Basingstoke (1851) HRO, 45A21/1, see '*Making of Basingstoke*' 13 & 109. The date given for OS maps is that of the surveying not of the publication. The latter are the 6 inch maps (XVIIINE) for 1872, 1897, 1912, 1933.

Market Place and London Street, providing the main route from London to the south-west. Alleys linking the streets to the back yards survived. In the 19th century the Market Place was enlarged.[32] In the historic streets there was some infilling, change of use and building enhancements but no fundamental redevelopment.

In the post-medieval period this area had grown in importance as a staging post for east-west traffic, reaching a peak in the early 19th century. When the railway undermined the stagecoach trade the inns became small hotels and public houses or were converted to other uses, such as the Crown in Winchester Street which became a coach building works.[33] East along London Road from London Street were Goldings and Eastlands houses and the War Memorial Park (1921), formerly park land of Goldings.[34]

32   Below, Economic Hist., Markets.
33   *Census,* 1851.
34   HRO, 148M71/1/5/166.

Fig. 2. Looking down Church Street c.1900.

Towards the end of the 19th century the need for street improvements in the town centre became evident, resulting in the widening of Victoria Street. This stimulated the development of housing on the remaining open land immediately south of the town centre. In 1899 the Victoria Park estate was offered for sale with 30ft plots on Victoria Street and 15ft plots 'for the erection of artisans' dwellings' on Oxford Terrace (Map 4).[35] New Street developed from the 18th century, north of Winchester Street.[36] The Mechanics' Institute (1861) and John Mares' factory (1894)[37] were sited in New Street.

This area was hardly affected by town redevelopment from the 1960s and the medieval street pattern was largely preserved in 2024.

Lower Section of the Town Centre

This lay around St Michael's church in Church Street and to the south of the river Loddon. The northern end of Church Street joined Brook Street where May's Brewery,

35 HRO, 53M75/Z1; *HBG*, 8 Oct. 1898; 22 Apr. 1899 and subsequent issues.
36 Stew Lane was renamed New Street by 1783; *BG*, 4 Feb. 2024.
37 Below, Social Hist., Institutes and Reading Rooms; Economic Hist., The Clothing Industry.

already a major business in 1800, expanded by 1850.[38] New Road from the 19th century provided an additional link between the upper and lower town. In 1834 the gas works opened on Gashouse Road between the Reading and Basing roads (Map 3). By the 1890s a few shops such as Basingstoke Co-operative Society opened in this area.[39] East of Brook Street, along Reading Road, Totterdown was a very poor area with slum housing.[40]

Expansion of the Town: the Coming of the Railways

The arrival of the London and South Western Railway (LSWR) in 1839 to the north of the existing town attracted residents, industry and commerce. The area around the railway station had been essentially rural and included the Liten burial ground and the Holy Ghost chapel, both dating from the Middle Ages (Fig. 26).[41] The physical impact on the landscape, with the moving and levelling of large volumes of chalk to form platforms and sidings, and the smoke and noise generated by this new form of transport transformed the area. The arrival of the Great Western Railway (GWR) link from Reading in 1848, together with its associated station and ancillary buildings, intensified the physical impact (Fig. 9).[42] The railway was a magnet for a number of industries which exemplified Basingstoke's emergence as a significant manufacturing town. From the 1850s Wallis and Steevens' ironworks, and, from 1878, the clothing factory of Gerrish, Ames and Simpkins dominated Station Hill, immediately south of the station (Fig. 17).[43] The railway also created demand for licensed premises. The Great Western Hotel north of the station and the Junction Hotel to the south (the Station Hotel from 1906) were built in the late 19th century.[44]

A good train service to London was frequently mentioned by promoters of new housing developments. The first advertisements for freehold building land on the South View estate in 1869 referred to the 18 trains daily reaching London in little over an hour.[45]

Expansion of the Town: Housing

Industrial enterprise and the resulting population increase led to the need for more housing. The latter required land. Already by 1762, the town was edged by old

38 Stokes, *Basingstoke*, 109. Brook Street was demolished in the 1960s and its site lay under Churchill Way in 2024.
39 Below, Economic Hist., Retailing.
40 Below, Public Utilities, Water Supply and Sewerage.
41 Baigent and Millard, *Basingstoke*, 170; Hare, *Medieval Basingstoke*, 83–8.
42 Below, Railways. The route of the GWR was still used in 2024.
43 Below, Economic Hist., The Clothing Industry.
44 HER 71528. The Station Hotel was demolished in 1975. The Great Western Hotel closed in 2018.
45 *RM,* 12, 19 June 1869.

Map 5. Sarum Hill and Flaxfield Road early 20th century.

enclosures, providing potential for building expansion, as reflected in some later housing developments, such as in Longcroft, later May Street (Map 4). The Enclosure Act of 1788 converted common field rights into individual holdings.[46] Private ownership allowed the sale of land for buildings. Usually the landlord would sell off a field or strip of land in lots for others to develop, often after establishing the necessary street plan.[47] From early on stratified areas of housing could be distinguished, as in the contrast between Sarum Villas and Western Terrace in 1872 (Maps 4 and 5).

From the 1860s the lack of adequate working-class housing was highlighted by the press, the borough council, the church and the magistrates.[48] With the arrival of Thornycroft in 1898 the problem became much worse. In 1921 of the 889 of their employees[49] living in the borough just over half came from outside Hampshire.[50] Thirty-five per cent of Wallis and Steevens' 206 employees came from outside Hampshire as did 70 per cent of GWR and 40 per cent of LSWR employees.[51] Development began with Newtown (Lower Brook Street and May Street), Essex Road estate (East Brookvale) and along Flaxfield Road and Sarum Hill (Map 5). Three new areas of the town: South View, north of the railway, mainly for middle class occupation; Fairfields, south-west of the town centre; and the predominantly working class, West Brookvale, west of the centre, developed in the later 19th century and beginning of the 20th (Map 4). All three are now conservation areas.[52] But the housing and factories in the area between the upper town and the railway station were largely swept away in the 1960s by Churchill Way, the main road serving the redeveloped town, and by Alençon Link (Map 3).[53]

North of the Town Centre: South View

The South View Estate developed on rising land to the north of the railway line beginning in 1869. Forty desirable plots in Sherborne, Vyne and Burgess Roads were auctioned on behalf of the ironmonger John Burgess Soper. He had acquired the land two years previously from the May family.[54] As later maps show, the process of development was slow and piecemeal with the construction of a succession of larger

46   HRO, Q23/2/7/1–2.
47   For example, HRO, 10M57/SP56.
48   HRO, 10M57/SP244; 46M74/PZ5.
49   These figures include those of the workforce recently laid off by the four companies.
50   *Census*, 1921.
51   *Census*, 1921. The clothing companies, employing mainly local women, had less impact on housing demand.
52   https://www.basingstoke.gov.uk/conservationappraisals (accessed 24 July 2023).
53   M. Hughes, *The Small Towns of Hampshire* (1978), 40.
54   HRO, 10M57/SP122; D. Reavell, *South View* http://southviewbasingstoke.wordpress.com; this early expansion of settlement and that in Newtown below is clearly shown on OS 1:1250, sheet 12.8 (1873). View map at https://maps.nls.uk/view/105982906 (accessed 11 July 2024).

houses (Map 4). Eight more plots on Burgess Road were auctioned in 1892, advertised as in a bracing situation with charming views. They also overlooked the new public gardens on the same road recently purchased by Basingstoke corporation.[55] From the 1880s Phoenix Park Terrace and in the 1890s and 1900s Cromwell Road, Soper Grove, Burgess Road and Vyne Road were developed. Properties in Soper Grove were advertised in 1902 as let mainly to railway workers at 8s. per week.[56] Beyond South View by 1911 there were 50 inhabited houses in Coronation Road off Reading Road, many built by F. Trinder.[57]

Fairfields, South of the Upper Town Centre

Development took place on higher land south of the built-up area. In 1879 the first section of the new Cottage Hospital was opened on the corner of Hackwood Road and Southern Road. The cattle market moved in 1870 from near the Market Place to a site in Fairfields.[58] From the 1850s housing slowly developed along Winchester, Cliddesden, Hackwood, Beaconsfield, Fairfields and Jubilee Roads.[59] Castle Road and Wallis Road were built in 1900.[60]

In 1888 the Basingstoke school board opened the Fairfields schools in Council Road.[61] Fairfields was also an area with open spaces including May's Bounty cricket ground from 1855 and Castle Field recreation ground for local children, south of Fairfields schools.[62] In the 1920s individual tennis courts were let to local businesses.[63]

Newtown and Brookvale, West of the Town Centre around Worting Road

Development began in 1869 on land at the west end of Brook Street where 180 plots 'for the erection of large or small houses' were offered for sale on meadow land along the Loddon valley.[64] The area which became known as Newtown comprised May Street (formerly Longcroft) and Lower Brook Street.[65] In 1870 Alfred Tyrell, from Hadleigh in Essex, bought a large plot of land in the west of the town and laid out

55   HRO, 10M57/SP223. The same sale offered plots in Vyne Road and Soper Grove.
56   HRO, 10M57/SP252.
57   *Basingstoke and District Dir.* (1911), 41–42; *HBG,* 24 May 1902; for example, HRO, 58M74/BP246.
58   Below, Economic Hist., Fairs and Markets.
59   OS Map, 1:2500, sheet 18 (1894).
60   HRO, 58M74/BP 97.
61   Below, Social Hist., Education.
62   https://www.basingstoke.gov.uk/content/page/33813/Conservation%20Area%20 Appraisal%20for%20Fairfields.pdf (accessed 25 July 2023); below, Social Hist., Education, Fairfields schools.
63   HRO, 148M71/1/5/193.
64   HRO, 10M57/SP125.
65   Demolished 1960s.

Essex, Southend, Rayleigh, Rochford and Solbys Roads for housing.[66]

Thornycroft works (Map 3) on Worting Road, west of the town centre opened in 1898, with its own sidings south of the railway, and became the largest employer in the town. In response West Brookvale developed as a rectilinear group of streets between Queen Mary's school and Thornycroft. [67] From 1899 John Mares, clothing manufacturer and the owner of the Worting Road Estate, built three new roads, Queen's Road, Alexandra Road and George Street, and auctioned plots for working-class houses with some middle class villas.[68] The prospectus for the Worting Road Estate in August 1900 showed there were 205 plots 'of various sizes suitable for the immediate erection of dwelling houses, cottages, shops, etc', some of which had already been sold, and in some cases built on.[69] In February 1901 Thornycroft bought 15 plots of land on Alexandra Road for the erection of eight blocks of four double tenements to provide accommodation for 64 families.[70] By 1903 the whole of the estate had been sold for building and there were 146 houses in Queen's Road, Alexandra Road, George Street and Deep Lane.[71] In 1901 May Street had 187 houses and Lower Brook Street had 62 houses.[72] In 1899 the LSWR agreed to build 14 new houses on land in Lower Brook Street to replace housing demolished when the station was enlarged.[73] Development of the remaining vacant plots then continued more slowly during the following decade. In 1912, for example, an application for 20 houses on George Street was submitted on behalf of Thornycroft.[74] In 1921 Thornycroft employees were especially numerous in Brookvale: Lower Brook Street (42), May Street (61) and Worting Road (89).[75]

Brookvale school opened in 1909 for 200 local children.[76] King George V playing fields adjacent to Thornycroft opened for sports in 1922.[77]

Industrial Housing

Wallis and Steevens built houses for their workforce from 1900 as it was difficult to find affordable cottages. They purchased 32 a. of land at Cliddesden, just south of the

66   HRO, 10M57/SP167.
67   https://www.basingstoke.gov.uk/content/page/64348/Brookvale%20West%20CAA.pdf (accessed 24 July 2023).
68   *HBG*, 4 Mar. 1899; HRO, 10M57/SP244.
69   HRO, 23M72/E18; HRO, 54M74/BP64, 65, 66; 63M83/A5/1.
70   *HBG*, 20 Apr. 1901, 31 Aug. 1901.
71   *HBG*, 7 Feb. 1903.
72   *HBG*, 31 Aug. 1901.
73   *HBG*, 7 Jan. 1899, 28 Jan. 1899.
74   HRO, 58M74/BP570.
75   *Census*, 1921.
76   Below, Social Hist., Education.
77   https://www.basingstoke.gov.uk/content/page/64348/Brookvale%20West%20CAA.pdf (accessed 10 Oct. 2023).

Basingstoke and Alton Light Railway, for £2,000 to build 15 pairs of substantial but affordable cottages. Each cottage had a 1/6 a. garden with a shared field behind.[78]

Burberry housed some workers over his Winchester Street shop. In 1871, after the creation of his first factory there were two servants and 20 boarders all described as draper's assistants, and ten years later there was a housekeeper with two general servants and 27 others.[79] Interestingly, these generally came from a distance, with only a minority from Hampshire: in 1871, four out of 22, and in 1881, eight out of 30. In 1911 39 shop workers were sleeping in the dormitories above the shop, supported by a housekeeper and four domestic servants.[80]

Thornycroft was still expanding accommodation for workers in 1919 when it purchased 36 a. of the former West Ham Estate. The company used West Ham House as a boarding house for up to 40 of their students called 'pupils', and apprentices.[81]

Fig. 3. Cranbourne Lane council houses in the 1960s.

Council Housing

The borough council established a Housing of the Working Classes Committee in 1898 to consider the provision of public housing, although no housing was built until 1914. At a town council meeting in February 1899 the mayor (H.M. Julian) observed

78   MERL, TR WAL, AD1/1; HRO, 58M74/BP128; *Cliddesden*, 20.
79   *Census*, 1871, 1881.
80   *Census*, 1911. Below, Economic Hist., the Clothing Industry.
81   Below, Economic Hist., Thornycroft; Social Hist., Thornycroft Works School.

Fig. 4. Basingstoke c.1830 showing thatched roofs, St Michael's church and the old town hall.

that 'There was great difficulty in obtaining houses in the town, and tenants were afraid to make complaints as to insanitary conditions lest they should be turned out of their houses'.[82] However, some councillors objected that council housing would reduce the value of their rental property and a temporary check to economic growth in 1907 caused further delay. In 1912 a large increase in the Thornycroft workforce and sanitary officers' reports of overcrowding led to renewed demand for council housing, and an enquiry from the Local Government Board as to what action was being taken.[83] A crescent of 28 houses in Cranbourne Lane, south of the town centre, were the first council houses to be built in the town (Fig. 3). Rents were between 6*s*. 6*d*. and 6*s*. 9*d*. which was too high for the poorest local people.[84] A further 135 council houses were completed between 1920 and 1922 in Kingsclere and Sherborne Roads, followed by 74 houses in Merton Road in 1926. [85]

Built Character

I N THE UPPER town, two-storey timber-framed buildings with wattle and daub infill were still the norm in 1800 and, despite a history of fires, for example in 1392 and 1656,[86] thatched roofs were evident on the fringes if not in the very centre

82 *HBG*, 11 Feb. 1899; *HO*, 26 Apr. 1913.
83 *HO*, 20 Mar. 1912, 15 Mar. 1913.
84 *HO*, 11 July 1914. Demolished 1965 for road redevelopment. Stokes, *Basingstoke,* 129.
85 Stokes, *Basingstoke*, 129–30; HRO, 148M71/1/5/210.
86 Hare, *Medieval Basingstoke*, 7–16; Baigent and Millard, *Basingstoke*, 75, 78–9.

(Fig. 4).[87] From 1815 thatch was banned as a roofing material for new buildings within the area covered by the Paving Act. Many cottages were still thatched in *c.*1830 but when rebuilt, tiles or slates had to be used.[88] From 1815 the pavement commissioners also required the removal of bow windows and projecting signs had to be refitted flush to the walls. On 9 September 1815 George Windsor, an edge tool maker, and 11 others whose premises had projecting signs denoting their trades, were ordered to follow this new requirement. Townspeople were prosecuted if they did not comply.[89]

Plots were narrow and totally occupied by properties which extended to the roadside. The brick-built almshouses dating from 1608 at the eastern end of, and set back from, London Street represented a rare, and expensive, departure from the more usual timber framing. These almshouses have a symmetrical façade of one storey with eight windows. The walls are painted brick with a stoop tile roof and central gable commemorating the founder.[90] In the timber-framed buildings, brick infilling had replaced wattle and daub panels as a first step towards modernisation. In 2024 at least two fully timber-framed buildings survived on the south side of London Street.[91] Four houses had their upper façades enhanced with mathematical tiles (which mimicked brickwork) or brick with refenestration in the 18th century.[92]

In 1800 Basingstoke did not appear prosperous, the upper town area containing some poorer properties. Even worse were some dwellings in the low-lying part of the town in Totterdown (Reading Road) and Brook Street.[93] In 1871 Ballard described some of the housing for the poor as totally unfit for human habitation being damp, dilapidated, and unventilated. Particular examples were ten low thatched cottages in Totterdown Dell, 12 houses forming Ford's Buildings in Brook Street and some very badly built cottages on the west side of Church Square.[94]

However, from the mid-19th century civic pride and increasing wealth resulted in some individual buildings being built or enhanced, mainly in Victorian Gothic or Classical styles.

87   In 2023, 26 and 26A London Street still showed timber-framing.

88   HRO, 148M71/1/5/7/1, 39.

89   HRO, 148M71/1/5/7/1, 31–2.

90   HER 69; NHLE, no. 1339724, Deane's Almshouses (accessed 9 July 2024); Baigent and Millard, *Basingstoke*, 708–9. For history and modern usage, W. Fergie, 'Sir James Deane Almshouses, Basingstoke, 1608', *HFC Newsletter,* 75 (Spring, 2021), 5–8.

91   23, 25, 25A, London Street, NHLE, nos 1092591 23, 25, 25A London St.; 1264317, 26, 26A, London Street, (accessed 9 July 2024). Hare, *Medieval Basingstoke*, 7–16.

92   23, 25 London Street in 2023.

93   Totterdown was the old name for Reading Road from its junction with Basing Road to the railway bridges.

94   Ballard's Report upon the sanitary condition of Basingstoke, Medical Department of the Local Government Board, 28 December 1871; Stokes, *Basingstoke*, 118.

Top of the Town: Winchester Street, Market Place and London Street

The only civic building of any note in the town in 1800 was the town hall in the Market Place, which was built in 1657.[95] Although it had Classical detailing it still conformed to the medieval model of a first floor meeting room above an open ground floor trading area.

Its replacement, the surviving 1832 town hall, designed by Lewis Wyatt, consists of five bays and was built in the Classical style with some Italianate influence and an open ground floor.[96] Built of brick with stucco and mouldings over, it was the largest and most impressive civic building in the town (Fig. 5).[97] The corn exchange (the Haymarket Theatre from 1951) was built 1864—5 in Classical Italianate style with yellow brickwork and seven bays.[98] At the same time the previously open ground floor of the town hall was enclosed for conversion into office accommodation.[99] In 1887 John May spent £2,000 to build a large clock tower on the town hall.[100] The lesser

Fig. 5. Town hall with clock tower in the 1890s.

95 Baigent and Millard, *Basingstoke*, 463. For earlier halls see Hare, *Medieval Basingstoke*, 11, 19.

96 The Willis Museum moved to the 1832 town hall in 1984.

97 *White's Dir.* (1859), 487; Pevsner, *North Hampshire*, 162; NHLE, no. 1230876, town hall with attached drinking fountain (accessed 2 Oct. 2024); W. Fergie, 'Basingstoke's New Town Hall – Architect: Lewis William Wyatt (1777–1853)', *HFC Newsletter*, 68 (2017), 25–7.

98 Pevsner, *North Hampshire*, 163; HER 2159, 2157; NHLE, no. 1092590, Haymarket Theatre (accessed 28 Sept. 2024).

99 *P.O. Dir.* (1867), 482.

100 *Kelly's Dir.* (1923), 58.

market was built in 1884—5 with a five bay decorative façade, a low block parapet and central raised feature with pediment over. It has a large cornice moulding and carved and coloured fruit ornament.[101]

From the mid-19th century, individual commercial and religious properties were rebuilt or improved to enhance the town centre as industry developed. In London and Winchester Streets the most impressive commercial buildings reflected the wide range

Fig. 6. London Street c.1920 showing Congregational church on right.

of architectural styles prevalent at the time and the ease of transporting building materials by rail. In London Street these developments included the High Victorian Classical façade of the London and County Bank (later National Westminster Bank) built in 1864. It was designed by Frederick Chancellor, with three storeys of yellow brick walling and Bath stone dressings, under a parapet and high chimneys.[102] The Red Lion was significantly enhanced c.1860, by the addition of a third floor and new façade with eight windows, to the original 16th century coaching inn. The addition of this third storey created one of the tallest buildings in London Street. Prior to that its timber framing, still evident in the interior, may also have been evident on the exterior.[103] In 1892 Burberry opened a shop with a factory behind, adjacent to the almshouses at the east end of London Street. The shop's grand frontage to London Street in the Classical style and with a rusticated ground floor, still survived in 2024 as the Gabardine Bar, although the factory to the rear had gone.[104] The Congregational

101   NHLE, no. 1278226, Lesser Market (accessed 15 July 2024).
102   HER 2124; NHLE, no. 1092580, National Westminster Bank (accessed 15 July 2024).
103   HER 2126; NHLE, no. 1339723, Red Lion public house (accessed 15 July 2024).
104   HER 68488.

Fig. 7. Winchester Street c.1910.

(from 1972 United Reformed) church (Fig. 6) of 1801 became a building of note in 1860 by the addition of a full height neo-classical Doric portico of five bays, built by G.B. Mussellwhite.[105]

In Winchester Street later development included the neo-Tudor gable with town badge of the Hampshire Bank in 1894 (the Maidenhead Inn, 2024), and Burberry's Emporium. The latter was a redevelopment dating from 1905 designed by Cooper and Howell of Reading with cast iron colonnade and stucco details, following a fire which destroyed the existing timber-framed building. It was the largest retail enterprise in the upper town (Fig. 7).[106]

Lower Section of the Town Centre

Buildings were more spaced out than in the upper town with large exemplars such as St Michael's church and Chute House. The Blue Coat school was rebuilt on Cross Street in 1862.[107] The area was mixed residential and business. Housing on Lower Church Street, Church Lane and Church Square was mainly occupied by professionals and those living on their own means. For example, in 1901 among the ten heads of household in Church Square, there were two doctors, two music teachers, a Wesleyan

105 Pevsner, *North Hampshire*, 160; HER 2125; NHLE, no. 1230843, United Reformed
      Church (accessed 15 July 2024); below, Religious Hist., Independents/Congregationalists.
106 Pevsner, *North Hampshire,* 164–5; HER 72129.
107 Demolished in 1960s.

Fig. 8. Goldings in 2023. © Bill Fergie.

minister and two living off their own means.[108] Wote Street and Church Street retained their appearance until the 1960s. One significant building at the bottom of Church Street lost to town redevelopment was the Wesleyan Methodist Church (Fig. 47). In 1875 a new chapel had been built there and then replaced with this larger very striking Gothic building in 1905.[109]

Substantial Individual Houses

A few individual and relatively grand houses for wealthy citizens were built from *c.*1800 in the upper and lower town. Some pre-dated the industrial development of the town. Chute House, the former rectory, was built in 1773, adjacent to St. Michael's church at the bottom of Church Street.[110] It was red brick with five bays and two storeys until extended *c.*1890. The rectory was followed, later in the 18th century, by a fine pair of town houses in Cross Street. At the bottom of Church Street, Brook House, Queen Anne House and Bedford House were further large residences of this approximate date.[111] Brewery House, a Georgian house with a double bowed front was built *c.*1800 in Brook Street, reflecting the prosperity of

---

108 *Census*, 1901.
109 Below, Religious Hist., Wesleyan Methodists.
110 HER 2106; NHLE 1092620, formerly known as the Parsonage House (accessed 15 July 2024). Used as offices in 2024.
111 All were demolished in the 1960s. Queen Anne House and Bedford House were developments of earlier houses.

May's nearby brewing business.[112]

On London Road, the Georgian mansion known as Goldings started life as two 17th century timber-framed houses on the road frontage. In the mid-18th century the more easterly of the two houses was given a major facelift with a red brick Georgian street elevation incorporating two fine Venetian windows at ground floor level. In *c*.1795 the complex was greatly extended to the rear in fashionable yellow brick and the street frontage of the eastern house was wrapped up in matching yellow mathematical tiles (Fig. 8).[113] Eastlands was built opposite, *c*.1800, with a Tuscan porch of three columns.[114] Both were two-storeyed substantial houses with pleasure gardens. In 1921 Eastlands had large tennis and croquet lawns.[115] Richard Wallis, brother of the owners of Wallis & Steevens, and a corn and seed merchant who in 1867 had lately erected a mill, lived there in the 1870s, and promoted the building of the British Infants' school.[116]

Winton House, built on the south side of Winton Square, Winchester Road and at the western edge of the upper town *c*.1800, was a three-storey classical town house. It was a symmetrically fronted, red brick seven-bedroom house of five bays with a porch of pairs of Tuscan columns. It had large gardens including a tennis lawn.[117] By 1917 it was owned by a doctor who held his surgery there.[118] The nearby Manor House on Winchester Road overlooking the cricket ground (Fig. 24) in Bounty Road was built in 1897 for John Mares, clothing manufacturer. Built in Queen Anne Revival style it had four reception rooms and ten bedrooms,[119] its grounds extended to 4.5 a. and included three tennis courts in addition to fruit, vegetable and rose gardens. This was the last of the grand residences built within the town centre (Fig. 24). [120] When Mares died in 1930 the house was sold.

North of the Railway Station

The first station was designed in 1839 for LSWR by Sir William Tite, the architect of many railway stations for the company. It was replaced and enlarged in 1903—4

---

112 For a photograph, see HRO, 138A08/3. Demolished in 1960s. Site in 2024 under Victory roundabout.

113 HER 2122; NHLE, no. 1092579, Golding Ho. (accessed 15 July 2024); Pevsner, *North Hampshire*, 162; W. Fergie, 'Goldings – Nos 3 and 5 London Road, Basingstoke: the Anatomy of a Building', *HFC Newsletter*, 83, 2025, 16; W. Fergie, 'The Sir James Deane Almshouses, Basingstoke, 1608', *HFC Newsletter*, 75 (Spring, 2021), 7.

114 NHLE, no. 1278437, Eastlands (accessed 15 July 2024); HER 2120.

115 HRO, 10M57/SP290; NHLE, no. 1092588, Winton Ho. (accessed 15 July 2024).

116 TNA, ED 103/117; HRO, 12M49/A7/5/11.

117 Pevsner, *North Hampshire*, 165; NHLE, no. 1092588, Winton Ho. (accessed 15 July 2024); HER 2152. Winton House was still standing in 2024 and housed commercial offices.

118 HRO, 32M71/E5.

119 HRO, 149A10/B10; the Manor House in 2024 has been divided into offices.

120 HRO, 159M88/988.

Fig. 9.   LSWR station in 1915.

after the doubling of the track (Figs 9 and 11). North of the railway in Burgess Road the Roman Catholic church of the Holy Ghost was built in 1903 in Gothic Revival style with flint walls and a red tile roof. It was the work of the parish priest, also an architect, Alexander Scoles.[121]

South View Estate

The Victorian and Edwardian South View estate included terraced properties mainly in Phoenix Park Terrace and Soper Grove, semi-detached houses in Burgess and Richmond Roads and detached housing in Cromwell Road.[122] The estate contained some substantial residences. South View House had a central tower, croquet lawn and vineyard. Hillside, Vyne Road, was the residence of John Burgess Soper and after his death in 1895 it was offered as a private residence or as a 'Hunting Box' (Fig. 34).[123]

Darlington Road became the location for St Thomas Home for 'Friendless and Fallen Women'. Designed by A.R. Barker, it was built 1874—8, mainly in Queen Anne Revival style. A large quadrangle linked five residential houses for residents to a large commercial laundry (Fig. 28).[124] In 1885 a fine chapel by Henry Woodyer in the emerging Arts and Crafts style was added to the complex. [125]

121 Pevsner, *North Hampshire*, 160; below, Religious History, Roman Catholics.

122 https://southviewbasingstoke.files.wordpress.com/2014/04/a-short-history-of-south-view-pdf1.pdf (accessed 21 Aug. 2023); Reavell, *South View*.

123 HRO, 10M57/SP226, SP238.

124 Revd R.F. Bigg-Wither, *History of St Thomas Home. The Winchester Diocesan Penitentiary* (1887).

125 Pevsner, *North Hampshire*, 167–8; NHLE no 1278440, St Thos Ho. (chapel), (accessed 15

Fairfields Area

South of the Upper Town, All Saints' Church was built from 1915 to 1917 to the design of Temple Moore. Its tower, surmounted by a shingle roofed turret, made a particularly impressive contribution to the local townscape.[126] Nearby lay Fairfields board (later primary) schools by Charles Bell, two-storey buildings constructed in 1887—8 in red brick with flints in Queen Anne Revival style (Fig. 27).[127] Victorian and Edwardian housing built in this area was mainly two-storey red brick terraces. More spacious middle-class terraces, detached and semi-detached houses were built on higher ground on Cliddesden Road.[128] This followed the Treasury's permission in 1882 for the corporation to grant building leases on Fairfields.[129]

West Brookvale

In West Brookvale the social hierarchy is apparent in the three groups of housing: small two-up-two-down terraces found in George Street (Fig. 10) and Deep Lane; shorter terraces of paired houses with bay windows in Lower Brook Street, Queen's Road and Alexandra Road with larger detached and semi-detached and three-storey villas in Worting Road. All are brick, usually orange/red with grey slate roofs and

Fig. 10. *George Street c.1910 showing the Working Men's mission hall. Courtesy of Alastair Blair.*

July 2024); below, Social Hist., St Thomas Home, Darlington Road.
126 Below, Religious Hist., All Saints.
127 Pevsner, *North Hampshire*, 163.
128 https://www.basingstoke.gov.uk/content/page/33813/Conservation%20Area%20
       Appraisal%20for%20Fairfields.pdf (accessed 11 Aug. 2023).
129 HRO, 148M71/1/5/67; *RM*, 18 Nov. 1882.

built around a planned street layout and common building line with rear gardens.[130] In 2024 it was a Conservation Area, designed to preserve the social character of Basingstoke at the beginning of the 20th century.[131]

Transport and Communications

Roads

Basingstoke's location at the junction of several turnpikes and the extensive stagecoach activity made it 'a very great thoroughfare.'[132] The pattern of coaching routes in the early years of the 19th century is shown in Table 3.

The servicing of stagecoaches was a round the clock activity with a number of the coaches to London arriving between midnight and five in the morning. In 1828 the Royal Mail coach left the Angel every night at half past midnight.[133] Road improvements shortened journey times. Stagecoach traffic grew strongly after 1800, peaking in 1828. Then most coaches, including the mail coach, travelled the 18 miles between Basingstoke and Andover in 2¼ to 2¾ hours. Some light coaches were given a 1½ hour schedule, where previously it had taken three hours. After the railway's arrival in 1839, the long-distance coaching trade almost ended. By 1844 only one stagecoach to Reading still operated.[134] However, Richard Wallis acted as a carrier for places to the west of Basingstoke, including Whitchurch, Andover and Salisbury, which were not reached by rail until 1854–7.[135] Inns dependent on long distance coaches were seriously hit, with innkeepers and coach masters losing their livelihoods.[136] Loss of employment following the collapse of the coaching trade was not immediately offset by the benefits of being a railway hub.

Destination/Year	services per day 1828	services per day 1839
LONDON	10	1
Salisbury	2	1
Exeter	3	3
Exeter/Plymouth	3	
Southampton	6	7
Weymouth	1	1
Barnstaple	1	
Reading	1	1
Total	27	14

Table 3. Coaching routes early 19th century

130 Brookvale West Conservation Area. https://www.basingstoke.gov.uk/content/page/64348/Brookvale%20West%20CAA.pdf (accessed 24 July 2023).

131 https://www.basingstoke.gov.uk/content/page/64348/Brookvale%20West%20CAA.pdf (accessed 24 July 2023).

132 E. Mogg, *Paterson's Roads, Being an accurate description of all the cross roads in England and Wales,* 18th edition (London, 1826), 573.

133 Sadler's *Dir. Hants* (1784), 63–4; *Pigot's Dir.* (1828), 9.

134 *Pigot's Dir.* (1844), 12.

135 He also used the canal for places such as Odiham and London to the east (see below).

136 Below, Economic Hist., Inns.

Year	No. of Local Routes	Services per week	Places with one carrier per week
1828	9 {long distance}	15	4
1844	7	9	7
1852/3	7	11	4
1855	11	21	7
1859	10	18	7

Table 4. Carrier services for selected years.

For goods traffic, in 1828 there were seven firms running 31 wagons per week to London and 21 to Taunton, Salisbury and the West Country. Other carriers served towns within 15–17 miles of Basingstoke. There were nine routes and 15 services to Reading, Andover, Farnham, Winchester and Alton and other places they passed through.[137]

Although the railway revolutionised long distance transport, short distance distribution of goods still depended on horse drawn vehicles until well into the 20th century and their trade increased (Table 4), with inns providing various complementary services.[138]

Carriers brought horticultural produce into town for sale and acted as agents for country people, purchasing goods on their behalf and delivering them to their homes. They also carried passengers. Some trades people delivered to villages using their own wagons or carts, examples being a coal merchant delivering from Basingstoke wharf to Lady Bolton at Hackwood House in 1839 or Alfred Milward taking his wares to potential customers.[139] Initially trading was with adjacent market towns, including Newbury, Reading, Alton and Winchester, and by 1844, there were also weekly local carriers to Overton.

In spite of a small decline between 1855 and 1859, only the service to Monk Sherborne ceased, and two others reduced their frequency. The service to Andover had ceased shortly after the rail link opened in 1854. After 1859, however, the number of local routes almost tripled and the services increased by over 500 per cent to 1920. Increases between 1875 and 1898 meant that many villages not previously served joined the network.[140] Services to Newbury and Alton, two larger towns without direct rail links to Basingstoke, continued throughout the 19th century. After 1920 there was a steady decline associated with the growth of bus services.

137 *Pigot's Dir.* (1828), 9.
138 Hants Museum Service (HMS), WOC5226.538.1 DPAAPE; HMS, WOC5226.946 DPAARV54.
139 Stokes, *Basingstoke*, 113.
140 These included Mortimer, Silchester, Hartley Wespall and Ramsdell, which now enjoyed at least eight services per week, with three of them on Saturday.

Most carriers started from an inn in Basingstoke, with some being consistently favoured, such as the Feathers in Wote Street, cited in every directory from 1828. In 1911, 16 carriers started from there.[141] Others that were well used included the Wheatsheaf, Rose and Barge.[142] Wednesday, as market day, saw most departures, especially for places with one service a week. After 1890 many services also departed on Saturdays.[143] By the late 19th century some carriers experimented with a steam powered van made by Wallis and Steevens.[144] After 1918 when many army surplus motor vehicles became available there was a widespread move to these.[145]

From 1871 struggling Turnpike Trusts such as the Basingstoke to Aldermaston (1877) were wound up. Under the provisions of the Local Government Act 1888, the newly established Hampshire County Council took over the maintenance of main roads.[146] After the First World War these were gradually tarmacked and traffic volumes through Basingstoke grew so much that the town centre was often gridlocked. By the early 1920s the foundations of a motorised urban bus network had been laid. In 1923 there were daily bus services from Basingstoke to Aldershot and Newbury.[147] In 1926 the Venture bus service began and became the major bus company serving the town.[148]

Basingstoke Canal

The Basingstoke Canal, approved initially by Act of Parliament in 1778, but not completed until 1794 owing to problems raising finance, was the first 'agricultural waterway', carrying for example, corn, timber, manure and peat and serving a rural rather than an industrial area.[149] From the outset it was rarely very profitable.

Description of Route
The canal ran for 37 miles from Basingstoke to a junction with the Wey Navigation, which provided a link of three miles to the Thames at Weybridge and from thence to London. It followed the contours of the land.

The canal basin in Basingstoke, most of which lay within Eastrop, is shown on Map 6. Only the western end and much of the wharf was within Basingstoke parish. In 1799 £200 was spent to add a warehouse, saw pits, coal pens and an accompanying

---

141 *Kelly's Dir.* (1911), 59.
142 The Barge became popular by 1911.
143 Below, Economic Hist., Inns.
144 Wallis and Steevens steam van no. 7106. Used by J.C. King, carrier at Weston Patrick, from Jan. 1910.
145 Robert Applin, pers. comm., Nov. 2013.
146 www.turnpike.org.uk/English, (accessed 6 Sept. 2024).
147 *Kelly's Dir.* (1923), 61.
148 https://www.basingstokegazette.co.uk/memory_lane/1307303.twenty-years-of-stagecoach/. (accessed 6 Sept. 2024)
149 18 George III, c. 75; 33 George III, c. 16; Vine, *London's Lost Route*, 34–5, 40, 52–4.

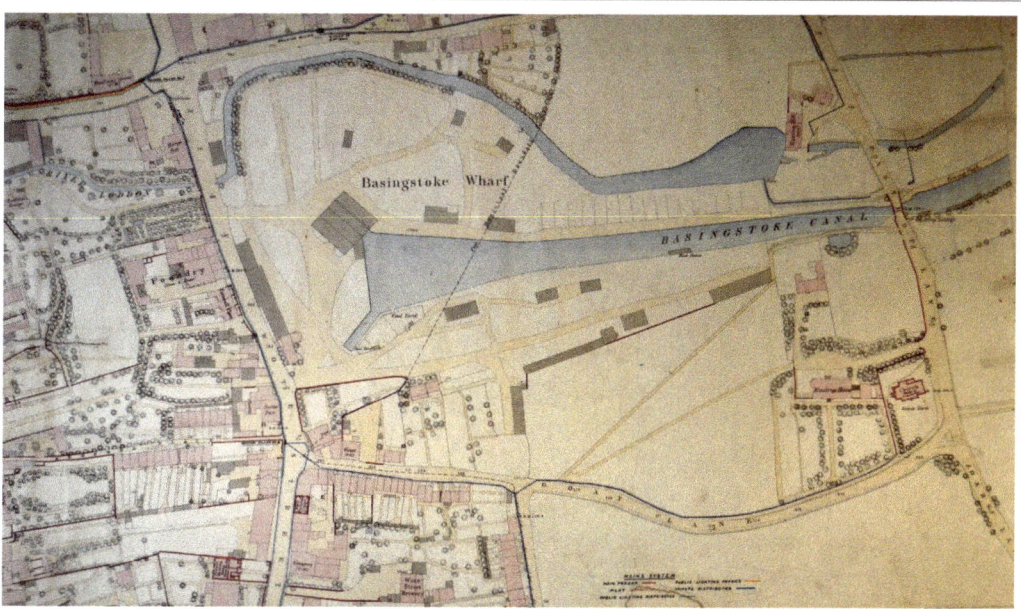

Map 6. Canal basin and urban part of Eastrop, 1877.

house. Further facilities were added, including two power cranes and other conveniences for loading and unloading barges, an extensive timber wharf and six thatched cottages with gardens.[150]

Finance and Administration

Raising funds to build the canal was particularly challenging. The capital sum required of £86,000 was subscribed by 154 investors. Thirty-six per cent of the shares were owned by investors from London. Twenty-three per cent, accounting for 31 per cent by value, were owned by people from the Basingstoke area but over half of these were owned by three local peers and a gentleman.[151] A prime mover was the earl of Dartmouth who owned an estate in Basingstoke but was also the proprietor of the very profitable Birmingham Canal Navigation.

Few tradesmen in Basingstoke bought shares, possibly as the minimum subscription was £100, and those that did quickly found that it was not a sound investment. By 1800 £100 shares were being sold for £30 and by 1834 they were valued at only £5.[152] On 4 June 1866 an application was made to the Court of Chancery for the winding up of the Company.

Initially meetings of the Canal Company were held in Basingstoke with the first clerk, Charles Best, being also the town clerk of Basingstoke. He continued with the company until 1816 assisted in later years by a deputy clerk based in London. Charles

150 HRO, 13M48/63/19.
151 Lords Dartmouth, Portsmouth and Rivers and Mr Newton of Litchfield.
152 Vine, *London's Lost Route*, 129.

Headeach, a Basingstoke solicitor, became clerk in 1827 and remained in post until his death in 1866.[153] Frederick Bushnell, listed as a timber and coal dealer in 1859, became the wharf and traffic manager between 1859 and 1871.[154]

Traffic

During the lifetime of the original company to 1869, tonnage only exceeded 30,000 tons in three years during the 1830s when the canal carried construction materials for the railway. Once the railway opened it drew business away, Basingstoke wharf trade falling by 25 per cent.[155] Toll income was rarely above half the original estimates and rates had to be cut to compete with carriers in the 1820s. After the railway opened in 1839 competition increased and tolls had to be cut by 50 per cent in 1844.[156] The company had hoped that onward wagon trade would be a significant feature in its trading, but an 1827 report suggested that this was not fulfilled.[157] During the Napoleonic Wars onward trading with Southampton, Winchester and the West Country was temporarily boosted when the sea route was threatened by French privateers. However, in peacetime canal traffic bound for Andover, Alton and Alresford found it difficult to compete with carriers using the turnpike roads from London and in 1822 the canal users obtained an abatement of 1s. 8½d. a ton for goods bound for these towns.[158]

In 1794 barges left Basingstoke every Thursday at 8.00 a.m. for London and boats from Messrs Sills and Sons of Hambro Wharf, Upper Thames Street, left on Thursdays on the day's tide. The cost was 12s. per ton.[159] The journey time was three to four days.[160] After a period of mismanagement, the Canal Company ceased trading in its own barges in 1804 and trade was continued by private traders. Charles Bagnall with various partners was active from c.1814. In 1827 John Richard Birnie became the chief carrier, operating a fleet of 12 barges. He took out a 21–year lease on Basingstoke Wharf but became bankrupt in 1832 owing £60,000.[161] His business was taken over by R. Wallis & Co. by 1844,[162] but in 1854 they described themselves as corn and coal merchants with an office near the railway station and no mention of the canal.[163]

Building the railway gave a temporary boost to freight carriage on the canal which peaked in 1838 with over 33,000 tons of building material carried via the

---

153 Vine, *London's Lost Route*, 50, 92.
154 *White's Dir.* (1859), 494; *P.O. Dir.* (1867), 483.
155 Vine, *London's Lost Route*, 106.
156 Vine, *London's Lost Route*, 108.
157 TNA, RAIL 1019/6.
158 Vine, *London's Lost Route*, 92.
159 *Universal British Dir. of Trade*, Vol. 1 (1792), 168.
160 *RM*, 9 Dec. 1799.
161 Vine, *London's Lost Route*, 92–4.
162 *Pigot's Dir.* (1844), 12.
163 HCT, PPAARU81.

Wey navigation.[164] In 1840 a pitched market at the Wharf saw 300 tons of cheese sold but this traffic was soon lost to the railway. In 1850 the committee of the Canal Company recommended applying for an act to sell the canal.[165] This was postponed owing to an upturn of traffic in the 1850s to the Aldershot area for building the new military camp.[166] In 1867 the canal was mentioned with the railway as increasing communications with London[167] but by 1875, the canal was described as 'disused'.[168]

Although a boat house is shown on an 1877 map there is no evidence of pleasure boats operating from Basingstoke. However, there are records of barges being hired for group outings as far as Greywell tunnel.[169]

Disruption to Traffic

The economic basis of the canal had been poor from the start, but it was also beset by disruption. Between 1800 and 1840 reports to shareholders listed 23 cases of disruption to navigation, the longest being two months.[170] Droughts between 1800 and 1803 necessitated only half loading of barges.[171] Freezing conditions resulted in ice blockages with the canal closed for extended periods. In addition, the deep cuttings and tunnel in Greywell parish, east of Basingstoke, gave repeated trouble. There were landslips, as in 1794 and 1804,[172] and a partial collapse of the tunnel in 1813 and 1835.[173] It was also blocked for a period of years between 1871 and 1884.[174]

Sewage Issues

Early in the 19th century the company obtained the pavement commissioners' agreement to divert the stream (later in a barrel drain) that ran down Wote Street. This was to enhance water supplies by directing it into the canal basin instead of the river Loddon, but a problem arose when adjacent houses began to empty effluent into it. Blockages caused sewage to stagnate in the canal leading to complaints from residents.[175] In 1873 the newly formed Urban Sanitary Authority asked the canal's then owner, William St Aubyn, to remove the sewage. He counter claimed that the Authority was responsible for separating the sewage from the stream and took legal action. The Authority had to pay damages and arrange a temporary solution by

164 Vine, *London's Lost Route*, 114.
165 Vine, *London's Lost Route*, 122.
166 Vine, *London's Lost Route*, 123–31.
167 *P.O. Dir.* (1867), 481.
168 *P.O. Dir.* (1875), 27.
169 A. Attwood, *An Illustrated History of Basingstoke* (Derby 2001), 75; Vine, *London's Lost Route*, 149.
170 TNA, RAIL 1019/6.
171 TNA, RAIL 1019/6
172 Vine, *London's Lost Route*, 41; TNA, RAIL 1019/6.
173 TNA, RAIL 1019/6.
174 Vine, *London's Lost Route*, 184.
175 Ballard Report 1871, 1; HRO, 145M71/1/7/1; TNA, MH 10683, 10684.

building a retaining tank which required regular emptying.[176] The situation was not completely resolved until the borough council built a new sewage works in 1880 on Swing Swang Lane.[177]

Later Years

The company went into liquidation in 1869. There were no offers to buy it, forcing the liquidator to manage it himself until 1874.[178] Between 1874 and 1895 the canal had four owners interspersed by three periods of liquidation. In 1895 the canal profited briefly after it was bought by Sir Frederick Hunt JP. He replaced small scale brickmaking at Up Nately with a much larger enterprise, the Hampshire Brick and Tile Company. Bricks were transported from a quay on the canal at Up Nately. Production peaked at 13,500 tons in 1899—1900.[179] However many bricks developed faults owing to imperfections in the clay. This, combined with a major breach in the canal at Woking in September 1899, resulted in both the canal and the brick companies going into liquidation in July 1900.[180]

Carriage of foodstuffs and general merchandise to Basingstoke ceased in August 1900 but a few barges reached the town, mostly with timber for White's yard and sand for Wallis & Steevens. The last barge tying up at Basingstoke was recorded in February 1910.[181] In a final attempt to pass a barge to Basingstoke in autumn 1913 the aptly named *Basingstoke* carried a token cargo of foundry sand for Wallis & Steevens. It only reached Old Basing wharf after the dry bed from Up Nately was refilled with water.[182] After the First World War, the canal basin was filled in.[183]

Railways

The construction of the railways and the town's emergence between 1840 and 1854 as the junction for three routes facilitated the transformation of Basingstoke's economy.

In 1834 an Act was passed for constructing a railway from Nine Elms, Lambeth (Surrey) to Southampton which became the London and South Western Railway (LSWR).[184] On 10 June 1839 the line was opened from Nine Elms to Basingstoke and from Winchester to Southampton. The Basingstoke to Winchester section was completed on 11 May 1840 and until then passengers had to travel that section by

176 L. Rosenthal, 'Owners of the Basingstoke Canal 1870–1880', *Surr. and Hants Canal Soc. Newsletter* (July 2009).

177 L. Rosenthal, 'Owners', 16; below, Public Utilities, Sewerage.

178 Vine, *London's Lost Route*, 138.

179 Surr. and Hants Canal Soc., ledger H4.

180 Vine, *London's Lost Route*, 143–4.

181 Vine, *London's Lost Route*, 174.

182 T. Harmsworth, 'Last attempt to get to Basingstoke', *Basingstoke Canal Society Newsletter* (Autumn, 2000), 10–12.

183 The site of Basingstoke Wharf in 2024 was under Festival Place shopping centre.

184 4 and 5 William IV c.88, 25 July 1834. Work commenced in October 1834.

coach.[185] The line was extended from Nine Elms to Waterloo in 1848.[186] The LSWR extended its operations westward, opening a line to Andover on 3 July 1854 and onwards to Salisbury in 1857, and Exeter in 1860.[187]

On 1 November 1848 the GWR opened its line from Reading. This was broad gauge and incompatible with the narrower track of other companies until a third rail, laid in 1856, enabled mainly standard gauge goods trains to travel from the south coast to the industrial midlands and the north. Previously goods had been transferred from standard to broad gauge wagons in a tranship shed.[188] Since the lines were run by different companies originally there were two distinct but adjacent stations with the GWR terminus lying immediately north of the LSWR station.[189] The station in 2024 includes the footprint of both.

Basingstoke's industrial expansion during the second half of the 19th century was due primarily to the railways. The railway facilitated a substantial increase in the transport of goods, with coal from the Somerset coalfield and raw materials for industry being important items.[190] The LSWR quickly became the principal goods carrier, displacing the roads and canal. It issued a detailed tariff in 1845[191] showing that it was cheaper to bring coal to Basingstoke from Southampton rather than London. Much coal, however, was brought direct from the north or Wales. Extensive sidings were developed to the east of the LSWR and GWR stations by the LSWR. They were expanded by the LSWR, especially to the west of the station after 1875 when the bridge over Chapel Street was

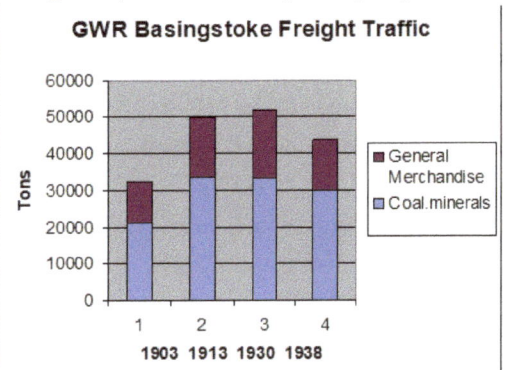

Table 5. Basingstoke freight traffic.

widened to take four tracks (Fig. 11).[192] A massive goods shed was built in 1903.[193] Between 1914 and 1954 a mile long branch served Park Prewett Hospital.[194] In 1901

185 R.A. Williams, *The London and Southampton Railway*, Vol. 1, (1968), 38–40.
186 R.A. Williams (1968), 158–61.
187 R.A. Williams (1968). 72–3, 85–6, 91–2.
188 V. Mitchell & K. Smith, *Woking to Southampton* (1988), 42. Broad gauge trains ceased to run in 1869.
189 HRO, 10M57/P86. The GWR station was demolished in 1932 when GWR Reading trains ran into platform 5 of the LSWR station as they still did in 2024. V. Mitchell & K. Smith, *Woking to Southampton*, Midhurst, 1988, 42–3.
190 Below, Economic Hist., Industry.
191 HRO, 10M57/TR10/1.
192 V. Mitchell & K. Smith (1988), 43.
193 V. Mitchell & K. Smith, *Basingstoke to Salisbury*, (1991), 5.
194 D. Smith, (1986), *Park Prewett Hospital*, 91–99.

Fig. 11. Railway sidings in 1872 and 1909.

a Basingstoke to Alton line was built as a Light Railway.[195] The line ran at a loss resulting in closure in 1916 after which the rails were lifted and sent to the Western Front. In October 1921 reopening this line was considered. The proposal was not supported, but in 1924, following a public campaign, the line was re-laid by the newly formed Southern Railway.[196] It was still unprofitable and closed for passengers in 1932 and freight in 1936.[197]

Detailed statistics for each company's freight traffic, covering similar periods, are not available. However, Table 5 based on GWR data, shows the importance of coal and coke deliveries.[198] The LSWR is likely to have handled more general merchandise.

Substantial growth in passenger traffic resulted in the LSWR station being replaced in 1850—1 and expanded in the 1870s. The present station was built in 1903.[199] Initially, in 1839 there were five trains a day in each direction with a second class fare of 7s. Carriages were conveyed for 26s. plus 25s. for two horses.[200] By 1856

195 M. Dean, K. Robertson & R. Simmonds, *The Basingstoke and Alton Light Railway* (1998). After closure, a siding into Thornycroft's motor works was retained.

196 www.friendsofaltonstation.org.uk/community/friends-of-alton-station-8100/basingstoke-railway (accessed 1 Oct. 2019). Southern Railway was established in 1923 following the merger of the LSWR with the other south coast railway companies. It lasted until nationalisation in 1948.

197 Stokes, *Basingstoke*, 71.

198 GWR traffic dealt with at stations and goods depots 1903–38, National Railway Museum, G2/116/1.

199 V. Mitchell & K. Smith (1991), 10.

200 HRO, 9M49/Z230/4.

Department	Number
Carriage and Wagon. Examiners & Oilers	27
Engineers Gangers & Lengthmen, Signals & Telegraph	55
Locomotive. Engine shed. Cleaners, Drivers (31), Firemen 30,	92
Traffic. Station master, Inspectors, Clerks (15), Carters, Checkers, Guards, Porters (passenger & goods 38), Shunters (28), Signalmen (21)	151
	Total 325

Table 6. LSWR Staff 1921.

there were nine trains a day to London with the fastest taking one hour 15 minutes and the cheap Parliamentary train three hours. The frequency of trains to Waterloo had increased by 1897 to three times this figure.[201]

There were 35 railway employees living in Basingstoke in 1851,[202] by 1911 this had increased to 313.[203] GWR employees were small in number, with between 32 and 40 in the years 1903 to 1930.

Data for LSWR staff in 1921[204] are shown in Table 6.

Communications: Postal Services, Telegraph and Telephone

Robert Cottle, chief magistrate and five-times mayor of the borough, became the town's first postmaster in 1808.[205] Operating out of a small shop in Winchester Street, two hatches in the wall enabled customers to deliver/collect their letters while remaining on the roadway.[206] Mail was put into a postbag at 10.00 p.m. and delivered to the Angel Inn in Market Place (Fig. 12) where the stagecoach driver would sort them into the different towns he was passing through.[207]

Following the introduction of the penny post in 1840 and the coming of the railway, the volume of post rapidly increased.[208] Cottle's office received and despatched

---

201 V. Mitchell & K. Smith (1988), 40. Under the 1844 Act companies had to provide one train each day stopping at all stations for a fare of not more than one penny per mile to enable the less well-off to travel. *HBG*, 30 Oct. 1897.

202 *Census*, 1851.

203 *Census*, 1911.

204 TNA, AN 82/93. The 1921 census summary for Basingstoke lists 254 male 'railway workers' (*Census Report Hants*, 1921), 68, but this would have excluded those living in the villages around.

205 http://www.basingstokegazette.co.uk/memory_lane/11800552.changes_to_the_Royal_Mail/ (accessed 22 Mar. 2017)

206 *HBG*, 21 Mar. 1925; *White's Dir.* (1859), 491.

207 http://www.basingstokegazette.co.uk/memory_lane/11800552.changes_to_the_Royal_Mail/ (accessed 22 Mar. 2017)

208 https://www.history.ac.uk/sites/default/files/file-uploads/2019–06/railway_history_26.01.14.pdf (accessed 11 Sept. 2024).

Fig. 12. Market Place and Old Angel Café (formerly the Angel Inn) on George V Coronation Day 1911. Courtesy of Alastair Blair.

mail several times a day and money orders were granted and paid from 9.00 a.m. to 6.00 p.m.[209] By 1844 letters arrived from, and were despatched to, London twice a day by rail and once a day to and from other parts of Hampshire and the south-west of England.[210] A small post office opened in Worting in 1847.[211]

When Cottle retired in 1859 at the age of 71 his business passed temporarily to C.J. Jacob and then to the Misses Curtis who had previously worked with Cottle. The Misses Curtis opened a savings bank in 1861 and a telegraph office in 1870 at 26 Wote Street.[212] Pillar boxes were erected on Winchester Street, Sarum Hill and Church Street.[213]

When the parcel post began in 1883, the increased workload caused the sole surviving Miss Curtis to retire. New larger premises were built at 23 Wote Street to specifications laid down by the Postmaster General and constructed by Joseph Tigwell, whose son became the local postmaster.[214] Sunday deliveries were introduced

209 *HBG*, 21 Mar. 1925.
210 *Pigot's Dir.* (1844), 10.
211 https://sites.google.com/site/ukpostofficesbycounty/home/england (accessed 21 Mar. 2017).
212 *HBG*, 21 Mar. 1925; https://sites.google.com/site/ukpostofficesbycounty/home/england (accessed 21 Mar. 2017).
213 *P.O. Dir.* (1875), 29.
214 *HBG*, 21 Mar. 1925.

and later an additional weekday delivery making four a day.[215] Several smaller post offices operated for a time, such as Essex Road, 1889—1906; Chapel Street, 1895—1904; and Flaxfield Road (Map 5), which opened in 1902.[216] During the First World War, women were employed as postal workers for the first time.[217] By 1911 there was a telephone exchange at 63 Wote Street.[218] Phone numbers were advertised in a 1915 trade directory but there were no private numbers, nor for any of the three major companies: Burberry, Thornycroft and Wallis and Steevens. The very few (21) that had numbers were largely selling services: a vet, builders, public houses and hotels, solicitors, police, the Conservative Association, Percy Fisher, leather manufacturer, Lanham drapers and St Thomas Diocesan home.[219]

In 1925 the Wote Street post office was replaced by purpose-built premises in New Street, with serving counters, spaces for writing telegrams, a telegraph room, a telephone exchange and a sorting office.[220]

Basingstoke had its own newspaper from 1878 when John and Sidney Bird established the *Hants and Berks Gazette,* the first newspaper to be printed in the town.[221]

215 http://www.basingstokegazette.co.uk/memory_lane/11800552 changes to the Royal Mail (accessed 22 Mar. 2017).

216 https://sites.google.com/site/ukpostofficesbycounty/home/england (accessed 21 Mar. 2017).

217 http://www.basingstokegazette.co.uk/memory_lane/11800552.changes to the Royal Mail (accessed 22 Mar. 2017).

218 BT Archives, Holborn, London/POST 74/58.

219 *Kelly's Dir.* (1915), 57–62.

220 *HBG,* 4 Apr. 1925.

221 Known as the *Basingstoke Gazette* in 2024. https://www.basingstokegazette.co.uk/aboutus/ (accessed 2 Aug. 2024).

ECONOMIC HISTORY

'BASINGSTOKE CONTAINS NO manufactures, but is a place of very great thoroughfare, and is situated in the centre of a rich agricultural district' was reported in 1837.[1] Before the 1850s any goods produced in Basingstoke were mainly sold locally. Villagers could sell their crops and livestock at the town markets and purchase goods in return, whether imported products or those produced in the workshops of the town.

After 1840 Basingstoke was transformed by the construction of the railways and the town's emergence as the junction for three routes. Raw materials were brought in easily, and manufactured goods were exported to other parts of the country and overseas. The second half of the 19th century witnessed the development of large industrial units in the companies of Wallis and Steevens, an engineering firm, Burberry and a group of related companies who manufactured clothing, and in 1898 Thornycroft, a major engineering company, moved to Basingstoke. The town's population grew more rapidly than neighbouring towns or the country at large, doubling between 1861 and 1901[2] and there were dramatic changes in the patterns of employment. In 1851 Basingstoke had a working population of 1,673 of which 286 (17.1 per cent) were engaged in agriculture, 316 (18.9 per cent) in domestic service and 73 (4.4 per cent) in dressmaking and millinery. The remaining 998 were involved in various trades and services.[3] By 1901 the employed work force had risen to 4,612; 3,195 were males, with agriculture, including market gardening, having fallen to 154 or only 4.9 per cent. More men were now engaged in engineering and machine making (283 men or 9 per cent), in the railways (313 men or 9.9 per cent) and in clothing and tailoring (241 or 7.6 per cent).[4] New houses were built to accommodate the growing population giving employment to the building and allied trades, which occupied 17.7 per cent of the male work force.[5] But above all employment opportunities for girls and women were transformed. In 1901 the clothing sector occupied 41 per cent of employed females (589), while by contrast, female indoor servants (411) made up only 28 per cent. Lower proportions of servants among working women were also found in northern textile towns.[6]

1   Parl. Paper, 1837 (238) *The Report of the Municipal Corporation Boundaries Commissioners*, 25 Apr. 1837.
2   Above, Introduction, Population.
3   *Census,* 1851.
4   *Census Report Hants*, 1901, 94–5.
5   *Census Report Hants*, 1901, 94.
6   *Census,* 1901; R. Pope (ed.), *Atlas of British Social and Economic History since c.1700*

By 1921 the working population had risen to around 5,800, of which 2,400 were engaged in manufacturing. Many now worked in large factories, in the engineering firms of Thornycroft and of Wallis and Steevens; the clothing firms of Thomas Burberry, of Gerrish Ames and Simpkins, or of John Mares; or in the railway companies of LSWR or GWR. Farming and market gardening had increased to some 300 employees but was a very small proportion of the workforce, the remainder were employed in various service trades or professions. The main forms of employment for men were engineering and metalworking (877) and transport (592, of which 254 were railway employees).[7]

Agriculture

From Open Field Farming to Enclosure

In 1800 Basingstoke's urban area occupied only a small percentage of the parish, near to the Loddon valley.[8] In 1840 buildings occupied 4 per cent of the parish compared with 83 per cent arable land, 2.5 per cent common, 8 per cent meadow and common.[9] Until 1788 farming was carried out on scattered strips within six large open fields.[10] Then in 1788 a local Enclosure Act swept away these open fields and created compact holdings.[11] Two examples of these new post-enclosure farms can be seen in a survey carried out in 1797 for the second earl of Dartmouth of his lands in the south of England.[12] Lord Dartmouth had inherited the Blunden lands in Basingstoke via his grandmother to become the second largest landowner there. The largest of his four farms in Basingstoke, West Ham (338 a.), formed a compact unit straddling the Loddon Valley. The 20 a. of meadow adjacent to the Loddon were twice the value per acre of the arable land on the chalk. The house on Worting Road 'suitable for a genteel family of moderate fortune' and farm buildings cost an estimated £1,200.[13] The three largest fields, all over 75 a., are not shown as subdivided and the notes in the survey indicate that timber for temporary fences was provided free from the earl's woodland at Ellisfield. Minching's (135 a.), in contrast, was less coherent being four scattered units with the farmhouse and cottages located a mile away in the town. During the same period, seven new large farmhouses, including West Ham, were built at the centre of compact new farms at a distance from the town.

(London, 1990), 158–9.

7   *Census Report Hants,* 1921, xxix.

8   Parl. Papers, 1835 (116), *First Report of the Commissioners appointed to enquire into the Municipal Corporations of England and Wales. Report of the Town of Basingstoke.*

9   HRO, 21M65/F7/13/1, tithe apportionment.

10   Hare, *Medieval Basingstoke,* 23–9; HRO, 23M72/P1/1 and 2.

11   HRO, Q23/2/7/1–2.

12   Staffs. RO, D3074/G/1/1.

13   Staffs. RO, D3074/G/1/1; HRO, 63M83/A1/4/5.

Although the 1840 tithe survey differentiates between arable and meadow it does not give a breakdown of the crops grown. These were recorded in the parish summaries of agricultural returns from 1866 (Table 7). The profile in 1866 shows an established rotation system with cereals, fodder crops (mostly turnips) and temporary grass for grazing and hay. There was very little permanent grass.[14]

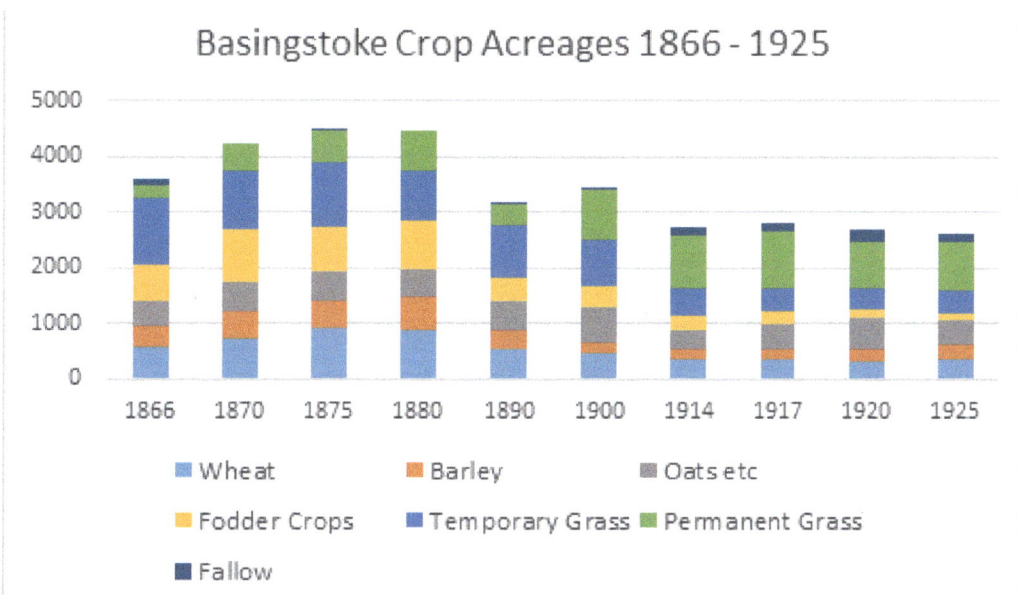

Table 7. Basingstoke crop acreages 1866– 1925.

Agricultural Depression

From 1875 British farming underwent a severe depression, prompting changes, which lasted beyond 1925 (Tables 7 and 8). Independent evidence of the downturn in Basingstoke comes from data given to Parliamentary bodies. In 1848 George Harriett, chairman of the Basingstoke Agriculture Protection Society, made no mention of hardship for farmers but concentrated on improving the terms of leases to encourage improved practices.[15] The picture in 1894 was very different when Hugh Raynbird, auctioneer and land agent to Lord Bolton for 40 years, gave evidence to the Royal Commission on the agricultural depression.[16] On his 14,000 a. Hampshire estate rental income had peaked in 1877 at almost £11,000 with arrears of only £821. By 1892 the rental income had fallen to just under £7,500 and arrears totalled £4,227. In 1866 only 140 a. were managed directly by the estate. By 1892 tenants could not be found for 2,734 a.[17]

14   TNA, MAF 68/27, 28.
15   Parl. Papers (1848), 285–91.
16   Parl. Papers (1894), *First Report of the Royal Commissioners on Agricultureal Depression,* 177–82.
17   TNA, MAF 68/1382.

Oats for feeding animals overtook wheat after 1900. At the same time permanent grass overtook temporary grass suggesting that farmers had little option but to let land revert to the cheapest form of farming. Cereals remained the main crops grown but their acreage was much diminished and root crops almost disappeared after being significant in the years 1865 to 1890. Land farmed declined from 4,572 a. in 1875 to 2,690 a. in 1925, a 41 per cent fall in 50 years.[18]

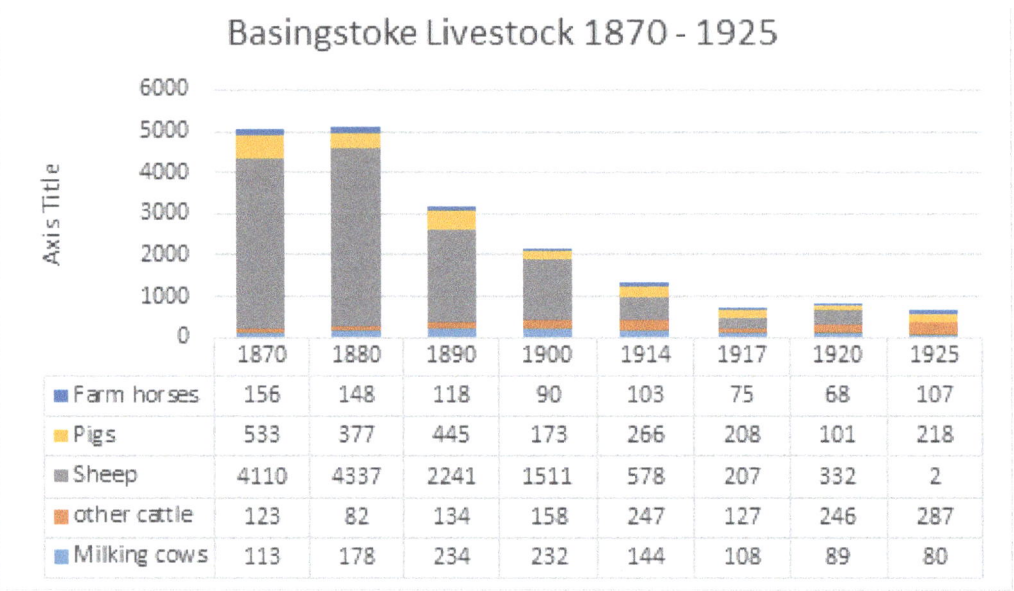

Basingstoke Livestock 1870 - 1925							
	1870	1880	1890	1900	1914	1917	1920	1925
Farm horses	156	148	118	90	103	75	68	107
Pigs	533	377	445	173	266	208	101	218
Sheep	4110	4337	2241	1511	578	207	332	2
other cattle	123	82	134	158	247	127	246	287
Milking cows	113	178	234	232	144	108	89	80

Table 8. Basingstoke livestock 1870–1925.

Table 8 displays the relative numbers in the various categories of animals and shows the huge decline in animals kept owing to the complete disappearance of sheep. The major decline in sheep numbers ending in a return of two in 1925 reflects an increase in land being laid down to permanent grass and a small increase in cattle numbers. However, these were not milking cows, which reached their peak of over 230 in 1890 and 1900, but store and beef cattle. The decline in farm horse numbers was due in part to the lower requirement when much land was put down to permanent pasture but also to the introduction of tractors at the end of the period.

Table 9 shows the decline in the price that farmers could obtain for their wheat crops in the face of foreign competition in the last quarter of the 19th century. The fall in profitability at a time when inflation was stable explains why farmers reduced the amount of grain they grew.

Industrial growth and mechanisation also produced a decline in the agricultural work force. The first census of 1801 recorded 362 people chiefly engaged in agriculture, only three fewer than in trade, manufacturing and industry. In 1881 the

18   TNA, MAF 68/242, 413, 638, 1268, 1838, 2636, 2807, 2972, 3242. These figures are slightly inflated as they are based on farmers' returns and some included land outside the parish.

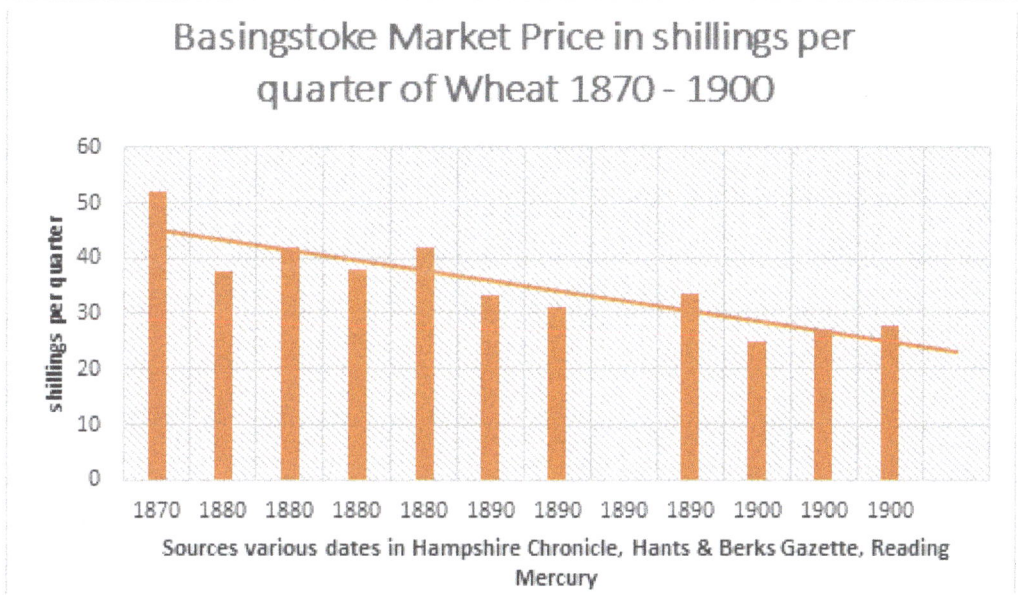

Table 9. Market prices for wheat 1870–1900.

number had fallen to 157 or 8 per cent. By 1901 that number was only 88 or 3.25 per cent[19] of male employees and 11 of those were recorded as working in market gardens or nurseries although many more temporary part-time workers would have been used.

Throughout the period from 1800, farm workers were among the most poorly paid as there was an oversupply of labour, increasing mechanisation and little alternative employment before the arrival of the railway industry *c.*1840. Across southern England workers protested in the Swing riots of 1830. Within Basingstoke the only recorded protests were at the isolated Down Grange farm, the home of Mrs Cassandra Hankey where 50 labourers armed with sticks assembled on 19 November. Mrs Hankey gave them money. Three days later 150 men returned, broke into the blacksmith's forge and took three sledgehammers to break up a winnowing machine.[20] The army arrested the rioters. Twenty-one men, including six from Basingstoke, were committed to the county gaol for riotous assembly on 27 November.[21]

Alternative Agriculture: Poultry

As the farming recession deepened and income fell, new initiatives occurred throughout England such as large-scale poultry farming.[22] In Basingstoke this was

19   *Census*, 1801, 1881, 1901.
20   J. Chambers, *Hampshire Machine Breakers: the story of the 1830 Riots* (1996), 25, 30, 31, 43, 56–7, 67, 152; HRO, 8M62/27.
21   Chambers, *Hampshire Machine Breakers*, 56.
22   P. Brassley, 'British Farming between the Wars' in P. Brassley, J. Burchardt and I. Thompson (eds), *The English countryside between the wars: regeneration and decline*

a response to the growing demands of the town and its good rail communications to wider markets. Plots of up to 20 a. were marketed at Winklebury from 1901 as suitable for poultry and market gardening.[23] A similar initiative took place at nearby Kempshott.[24] A developer, Homestead Estates of Poole, marketed plots suitable for poultry farming.[25] S.G. Hanson bought Old Down farm in 1908 and started large scale egg farming there in 1911 and his book, *Commercial Egg Farming*,[26] attracted considerable attention nationally.[27] In 1924 there were 11,000 poultry in Basingstoke.[28] The number of poultry farms listed in Kelly's trade directories rose from six in 1915 to 15 in 1923 and 24 in 1939.[29]

Market Gardening and Plant Nurseries

Alternative employment was also provided by market gardening. Thomas J. Edney started trading in Basingstoke in the 1870s as a house furnisher but in the late 1890s he became a fruit grower and market gardener. By 1903 he was running nurseries in Winchester Road. George Cooper advertised as a nurseryman based in Wote Street and Hackwood Road in 1907,[30] claiming the business had been established in 1826. In 1911 three nurseries were listed in Basingstoke and some market gardens were established in the Winklebury/Kempshott area; in 1923 five were listed.[31]

Industry

T HE CLOTH INDUSTRY which flourished in Basingstoke in the 15th and 16th centuries had declined by the late 17th century. Brewing and malting then became the major industries and were flourishing in 1800. From *c*.1850 Basingstoke was transformed into an industrial town mainly through the development of new clothing and engineering businesses.

(Woodbridge, 2006), 194.

23 D. Reavell in *BG*, 22 Nov. 2022; *HBG*, 28 Dec. 1901; *HO*, 17 May 1913.

24 J. Hussey, *The Rise and Demise of Egg Farming in Kempshott*, (2018). https://kempshotthistory.org.uk/wp-content/uploads/2022/08/The-Rise-and-Demise-of-Egg-Farming-in-Kempshott-Web.pdf, (accessed 26 Oct. 2023); above, Introduction, Landownership.

25 D. Hardy and C. Ward, *Arcadia for All: the Legacy of a Makeshift Landscape* (1984); Kempshott History Group publications at https://kempshotthistory.org.uk, (2019).

26 S.G. Hanson, *Commercial Egg Farming (1913)*.

27 *Nantwich Guardian*, 13 Feb. 1917; *Coventry Herald* 17 Feb. 1917.

28 TNA, MAF 68/3188.

29 *Kelly's Dir.* (1915), 58–62; (1923), 63–7 (1939), 45–7.

30 *HBG*, 15 June 1907.

31 *Kelly's Dir.* (1903), 51–4, (1923), 63–9.

Brewing and Malting

May's Brewery in Brook Street was the biggest brewery in Basingstoke and the surrounding district (Fig. 13). It was part of the move at the end of the 18th century towards brewing on an industrial scale as well as the introduction of the tied house system. In 1802 it brewed about 8,000 barrels a year, rising in 1857 to about 10,600. May's were also maltsters who used fine local barley but later, profiting from the rail links, also purchased barley in the best national markets.[32] At the same time, it increased the number of its public houses to 63, with 23 in Basingstoke itself. It owned a small steam vessel which was used to transport beer along the Basingstoke Canal to outlets connected with the new military camp at Aldershot.[33] The company continued to dominate the local market. In 1912 of 43 public houses in the town, 24 were owned by, or leased to, May's Brewery. In 1920 it bought the Kingsclere brewery and its public houses.[34] When the Hartley Row Brewery was put up for auction in 1921, May's bought six of their public houses.[35]

Fig. 13. May's Brewery c.1860.

Basingstoke hosted three other breweries. The Pear Tree Brewery in Flaxfield Road was owned by the Barrett family of Farnham, who were also maltsters.[36] The Wote Street Brewery which produced about 1,700 barrels annually was bought by the Barretts in 1878. The Barretts closed the Pear Tree Brewery, moved their operations to Wote Street and in 1889 amalgamated this with the Lion Brewery, Farnham, to form the Farnham United Breweries.[37] Adams' Victoria Brewery in Victoria Street was run by Sarah Ann Adams, the widow of the founder, and her sons. At Sarah's death in 1898, the brewery

---

32   HRO, 10M57/SP95; *Slater's Dir. Hants* (1852–53), 12; *Harrod's Dir. Hants* (1865), 607.
33   HRO, 10M57/SP95.
34   K. Osborne, *Hampshire Hogsheads* (1996), 59.
35   HRO, 50M63/B47/12.
36   *Pigot's Dir.* (1844), 10–11; *P.O. Dir.* (1855), 16; *Harrod's Dir. Hants* (1865), 607.
37   *St James's Gaz.*, 23 Oct. 1889.

and its public houses were sold to Crowley's of Alton. Apart from the brewers there were seven maltsters in 1844 including William Curtis and Luke Redgrove of Church Street.[38] A malthouse in Church Street was still standing in 1875.[39]

The Clothing Industry

In the late 19th century, the town's clothing industry was transformed from a workshop and home-based, or domestic industry, catering for the townspeople and those of the rural hinterland, to factory production for the national and international markets. This was the initiative of a remarkable group of Victorian entrepreneurs led by Thomas Burberry, the inventor of gabardine and founder of the famous fashion house. Under him the town acquired three different long-standing clothing companies: Gerrish, Ames and Simpkins; John Mares; as well as Burberry.[40] He and his associates saw the potential of technological innovation to allow the mass manufacture of garments. The railways would both allow the cheap import from the north of England of cloth and coal, and the cheap and quick distribution of manufactured goods. At the same time the development of the treadle sewing machine (for which Burberry became an agent for the Singer Manufacturing company) and multiple cutting of the cloth allowed tailoring to shift to factory production. They also showed themselves well aware of the value of marketing and of the differing clothing demands of particular groups in the wider society. Different factories concentrated on the 'off the peg' mass market, the middle-class bespoke trade, the expensive outdoor market and military needs. Burberry handed over sections of his business to those with whom he had been working, so that a succession of independent Basingstoke companies emerged from his efforts. Gerrish and Ames were former employees and John Mares was his nephew.[41] This small group of entrepreneurs were also part of a wider network linked by their religious Nonconformity. Burberry himself also remained active in the selling of goods within Basingstoke.[42]

Thomas Burberry

Thomas Burberry was born in 1835 near Dorking (Surrey), the son of a Nonconformist

---

38　*Pigot's Dir.* (1844), 11.

39　HRO, 10M57/SP153.

40　Despite the importance of the clothing industry, it is poorly served by its documentation. The Burberry 19th century records were probably all destroyed in the Winchester Street fire of 1905, and its later archives are inaccessible to outside scholars. The John Mares, and Gerrish, Ames and Simpkins archives have not been located and were probably destroyed with the closure of these companies.

41　*HBG*, 19 Apr. 1879; *White's Dir.* (1878), 134–6.

42　Below, Retailing.

farmer[43] and set up shop in Basingstoke in 1856.[44] He was already well-established as a draper in 1868, when he started a clothing factory behind his shop on the north side of Winchester Street,[45] and by 1871 he was employing 80 hands.[46] His description in the directories had changed from linen draper in 1867 to wholesale and retail draper and clothing manufacturer in 1878.[47] During this period he established a 'steam cutting factory' for making working men's clothes on Station Hill.

Gerrish, Ames and Simpkins

In 1878 Burberry disposed of his 'steam factory' on Station Hill to two of his employees, George Ames and William Gerrish, previously draper's manager and valuer respectively, and an additional partner, the company being known subsequently as Gerrish, Ames and Simpkins (Fig. 17).[48] This company produced mass off-the-peg clothes for sale beyond Basingstoke, and was described in 1885 as a 'wholesale clothing manufacturer',[49] employing nine men, 200 women and twelve boys in 1881.[50] During the First World War the firm expanded, buying Morley Hall in Hackney,[51] and producing a range of weatherproof garments known as 'Blizzardeen'.[52]

Thomas Burberry and Gabardine

After the disposal of his Station Hill factory, Burberry continued to develop a factory in New Street. He added a boot and shoe department, millinery and dressmaking departments, a cutting room for men's clothing, a machine room for special clothing, and the shops on the ground floor.[53] Burberry worked with John Mares, who was described in 1881 as a draper's assistant, but by 1889 had become a partner.[54] In the 1880s, they advertised for tailoresses, 'good machinists accustomed to the general

43 ODNB, Thos Burberry (1835–1926), men's outfitter (accessed 2 Oct. 2024).
44 Daily News, 7 Apr. 1926. B. Shurlock, 'Would Thomas Burberry (1835–1926) of Basingstoke have succeeded without his Strict Baptist ethos?', HFC Newsletter, 79 (Spring, 2023), 10–13; ODNB, Thos Burberry.
45 BG, 23 Oct. 2000. Also, below Retailing.
46 Census, 1871.
47 Kelly's Dir. (1867), 483; White's Dir. (1878), 134.
48 Opening date provided in funeral notices and obituaries of William Gerrish, HBG, 27 Apr. 1907; HC, 27 Apr. 1907, and in advertisements referring to disposal of stock by Burberry (HBG, 28 Sept; 5, 12 Oct. 1878). The references to the disposal of the clothing factory are on 5 and 12 Oct. William Simpkins was a draper from Henley on Thames where he remained. His interest was probably financial, although his son moved to Basingstoke and later became a director of the firm.
49 Kelly's Dir. (1885), 596.
50 Census, 1881.
51 VCH Middx. X, Hackney (1995) 99, 101.
52 J. Tynan, 'Military Dress and Men's Outdoor Leisurewear: Burberry's Trench Coat in First World War Britain', Jnl of Design History (2011), 149.
53 HBG, 19 Apr. 1879.
54 Census, 1881; Kelly's, Dir. (1889), 45.

Fig. 14. Burberry's Hackwood Road factory shortly after it opened in 1892.

trade',[55] and were dependent on the treadle sewing machine which was transforming the British clothing industry from the 1870s to the 1890s.[56]

Burberry is best known for his long-term development of the gabardine, a waterproof textile. Hitherto, the only commercially manufactured waterproof clothing was the Macintosh rubberised rainwear. But this was impermeable and therefore uncomfortable to wear during any energetic activity.[57] Burberry sought to produce a cloth that was weatherproof, yet breathable, and suitable for those who enjoyed the country pursuits of hunting, fishing, riding and walking. Gabardine looked back to the loose shepherds' smocks of the chalklands where the oil from the sheep's wool had helped to waterproof the fabric.[58] He registered gabardine (and the 'self-ventilating weatherproof') as a trade mark in 1879 and patented it in 1900.[59] It had already gained approval at the International Health exhibition in South Kensington in 1884,[60] and in 1888 he had patented his 'Improved materials specially adapted for the garments of sportsmen'.[61] During his quest to find a cotton substitute for the

55   *RM,* 14 Apr. 1883.
56   A. Godley, 'Singer in Britain: the diffusion of sewing machine technology and its impact on the clothing industry in the United Kingdom, 1860–1905', *Textile History,* 27 (1) (1996), 59–76.
57   M. Rose and M. Parsons, *The neglected legacy of Lancashire Cotton: industrial clusters and the UK outdoor trade,* (Lancaster Univ. Management Sch. Working Paper 2005/25), 7.
58   *Daily News,* 7 Apr. 1926.
59   Burberry's Ltd, *Burberry's of London: an Elementary History of a Great Tradition* (1987).
60   *ODNB,* Thos Burberry.
61   M. Coatts, *The Burberry story* (Victoria and Albert Museum, no pagination, 1989).

original linen 'gabardine', Burberry worked closely with the Manchester Chamber of Commerce, who tested weatherproof fabrics for him, and with the Pandora Mills of Farnworth, Lancashire, for fabric development. The new cloth was triple proofed: in the raw material, in the yarn and after weaving, and was especially tightly woven. It was often used with a waterproofed woollen cloth lining. The cloth was woven in Farnworth and then made into clothes in Basingstoke. Only after Burberry's became a public company did it acquire the Pandora Mills in 1920.[62]

The development of gabardine opened up the opportunity to tap into the wealthy country gentry and elite metropolitan Victorian society and their sporting activities (Fig. 15). By the mid-1890s Burberry was advertising his gabardine 'Yeoman' overcoat and gaiters as 'the perfect outfit for exposure in all weathers'.[63] A London base was needed for this

Fig. 15.   *Burberry Shooting Coat, 1887.*

new market. From 1889 his son, Arthur took orders in an hotel in Piccadilly in the West End. In 1891 Burberry opened a store in London's fashionable Haymarket[64] and extended it in 1913.[65] Subsequently the rise of the motor car opened up a further new affluent market.[66] Between 1900 and 1914, the company went international, opening shop branches in New York, Buenos Aires, Paris and Montevideo.[67]

Although in the long run this enlargement of the company's markets led to a decline in Basingstoke's importance within the company and the eventual closure of production there in 1957,[68] this was not yet apparent. Burberry now reorganised his works in the town separating the gabardine and sporting production from the rest

---

62   Rose and Parsons (2005), 7–8.
63   *Bucks Herald*, 4 Apr. 1896.
64   *Burberry's Ltd* (1987).
65   Coatts, *Burberry story.*
66   Coatts, *Burberry story.*
67   *ODNB,* Thos Burberry.
68   *BG,* 4 Feb. 2000.

of his activities. In 1892 he opened a grand new shop and offices in London Street with a factory behind, between Mark Lane and Hackwood Road (Fig. 14),[69] known as the Hackwood Road factory. In June 1892, he dissolved the partnership with Mares[70] and in 1894 sold the New Street factory to Mares for £3,000. In 1895 the Burberry company continued to have its headquarters in Winchester Street, but by 1899 it had been divided with the local retail company remaining in Winchester Street, and the headquarters for the sporting and gabardine business in London Street.[71]

Burberry successfully broadened his market to the armed forces. He developed the Tielocken, the predecessor of the trench coat, in 1895.[72] In 1901 he designed a new service uniform for British officers, and although these were produced at the officers' expense by their own tailor, many chose Burberry.[73] During the First World War Burberry's produced an estimated half a million trench coats for combatant officers.[74]

The company, and its London manager R.B. Rolls, showed an early grasp of the value of celebrities, whether the military or explorers and pioneers. Burberry's clothes were worn in the Arctic and Antarctic by Shackleton, Scott, Nansen and Amundsen, and were taken on Mount Everest in 1922 and 1924.[75] They were also used by aviators like Alcock and Brown, the first to cross the Atlantic in 1919.[76]

Thomas Burberry died in 1926 having converted Burberry's into a public company in 1920 with his two sons among the directors.[77] His legacy dominated the town until its 20th century transformation: the three factories, the memorial garden and the new range of shops which replaced his Emporium after the 1905 fire.[78] Burberry also had interests in shops in Reading, Alton and Cheltenham[79] and factories in Reading and Winchester.[80]

John Mares

John Mares headed his own company from 1894, concentrating initially on bespoke work and made to measure tailoring, with many shops over a wide area, including Wales, sending orders to Basingstoke.[81] Significantly in 1907 it was one of the few

69   *BG*, 4 Feb. 2000; 'sole manufacturers of Gabardine…', *Bennett's Business Dir. for Hampshire,* (Birmingham 1925).
70   *London Gaz.*, 1 July 1892.
71   *Kelly's Dir.* (1895), 51; *Kelly's Dir.* (1899), 53.
72   https://www.burberryplc.com (accessed 17 Nov. 2023).
73   Coatts, *Burberry story*.
74   Burberry's Ltd (1987); Tynan, 'Military Dress', 148.
75   Rose and Parsons (2005), *ODNB,* Thos Burberry.
76   Coatts, *Burberry story*.
77   *ODNB,* Thos Burberry.
78   Below, Retailing.
79   *HA*, 7 May 1884; *London Gaz.*, 31 Mar. 1893; *RM*, 18 Nov. 1893.
80   https://www.hampshirechronicle.co.uk/news/18750530.discovery-site-burberrys-winchester-factory/ (accessed 17 Nov. 2023); HRO, 19M65/B482.
81   A. Attwood in *BG*, 24 Oct. 1997.

Fig. 16. Design for John Mares factory extension in New Street 1910. HRO, 58M74/BP 500.

companies in the Basingstoke directory stating its telegram address, probably because swift ordering of clothing and measurements would be an important part of the operation.[82]

Mares fostered a dramatic expansion of the business and its buildings and bought and sold land for housing.[83] He added new offices and a small warehouse in 1897, and more offices and workrooms in 1902.[84] He bought up extra land on the New Street frontage between 1902 and 1905,[85] and in 1903 added the major building which dominated New Street until its demolition in the 1960s (Fig. 16). On the ground floor were offices and buying rooms with workrooms for tailors and cutters on the first floor.[86] After the Burberry fire of 1905 some rebuilding of a range on the edge of the site was needed where it abutted Burberry's site. Later, an extra floor was added to the main building, providing further workshops.[87] Such growth reflected the company's expansion beyond made to measure products. In 1907

82 *Kelly's Dir.* (1907), 58.
83 In 1899, Mares put in an application to build 21 houses of varying sizes in Worting Road. HRO, 58M74/BP64, 65, 66. They survive in 2024; above, Introduction, Settlement.
84 HRO, 58M74/BP222.
85 HRO, 58M74/BP222, 260.
86 HRO, 58M74/BP260; for the buildings see R. Brown, *Basingstoke's Pictorial Past* (1987), 18, 45. It appears on the 1909 revision of the 25–inch OS map (1910 XVIII 8).
87 Illustrated in R. Brown, *Basingstoke's Pictorial Past*, 45. This addition had been made by 1930 (see illustration in 'Mares Limited, Basingstoke', *The Outfitter*, 15 Feb. 1930.

a 'peltinvain' raincoat department was set up and in 1910 this was followed by a ready-to-wear department.[88] By 1920 John Mares Ltd was described in the directory as 'wholesale clothiers'.[89] John Mares became a private limited company in 1908. The founder died in 1930, leaving a company whose products were known 'in every quarter of the globe'.[90]

The Impact of the Clothing Industry

The impact of the three factories on the town was considerable. By 1901, the clothing trade was a significant employer of male labour (211) but its impact on women was much greater. These trades now occupied 41 per cent of all employed women. Significantly domestic service, that traditional source of so much women's labour, in 1921 occupied only 20.5 per cent of the female workforce, compared with 40.8 per cent in Alton and 33.5 per cent in Andover.[91] In the aftermath of war, women's work had become more diversified but the makers of textile goods and articles of dress provided 33 per cent of female employment.[92] The large number in the clothing industry was transformative. Winifred Rutley recalled a room in 1909 in Burberry's factory with 300 sewing machines there. In 1921, Burberry's gabardine factory employed over 300 workers.[93] In 1930 Mares was described as employing hundreds.[94] Not all of the 738 clothing workers in the 1921 census would have been employed by the three factories. Tailors' and drapers' shops would employ some and there were also outworkers.[95] Some of the latter were employed by subcontractors who installed a few sewing machines in a converted dwelling house and produced for the larger factories.[96]

The industrial growth required an influx of labour. Burberry had shown an appreciation of this by setting up a dormitory above the shop in Winchester Street which may have served both his manufacturing and retail businesses.[97] The factories absorbed girls from the town and villages around, when they reached their fourteenth birthday and could leave school. Winifred Rutley of Overton joined Burberry's as an apprentice in 1909, receiving a weekly wage of 3s. and 2s. 6d. for the railway fare. All three clothing companies objected to the 1909 Trade Boards, arguing essentially that payment by results allowed them to act more flexibly and paternalistically in the interests of their workers, and that their conditions were not the same as those

88　*The Outfitter*, 15 Feb. 1930.

89　*Kelly's Dir.* (1920), 61.

90　'Mares Limited, Basingstoke', *The Outfitter*, 15 Feb. 1930.

91　*Census Report Hants*, 1921, xxxvi.

92　*Census Report Hants,* 1921, 68.

93　*BG*, 4 Feb. 2000; Mrs J. Griffiths (née Winifred Rutley) *One Woman's story,* (1979), 39.

94　*The Outfitter*, 15 Feb. 1930.

95　Outworkers are referred to in Gerrish's obituary, *HBG,* 27 Apr. 1907.

96　For example, Griffiths (1979), 40.

97　Above, Introduction, Industrial Housing.

in London.[98] During the First World War, Burberry's reputation was attacked in Parliament for its opposition to the trade unions, to the regulations imposing minimum wages of the Trade Boards, and its traditional dependence on cheaper female labour.[99]

Engineering

Two major companies transformed the Basingstoke economy from the second half of the 19th century as their products were sold worldwide. Both suffered in the depression after the First World War but recovered by 1924.

Wallis and Steevens

Wallis and Steevens began as an agricultural machinery producer but diversified into road rollers and other machinery for the home and overseas markets. In 1843 Francis and Charles Wallis, who were Quakers, took over George Caston's ironmonger's shop[100]

Fig. 17. Wallis & Steevens and Gerrish, Ames & Simpkins factories on Station Hill. Courtesy of Alastair Blair.

98   Univ. of Warwick, MRC, Digital collections, work in the sweated trades, 1910s–1920s (accessed 28 July 2023); Trades Union Congress MSS.292C/239.35/7/40; 35/7/7; 35/12/137. (accessed 28 July 2023).

99   S. Weston, 'Branding Burberry. Britishness, Heritage, Labour and Consumption', unpublished PhD thesis 2016, Goldsmiths, Univ. of London, 107–9. It is not clear how far the opposition was directed at the London East End of the company's operation and how far at Basingstoke.

100 *Pigot's Dir.* (1844), 11.

Fig. 18. Wallis and Steevens top shed c.1892. Hampshire County Council. Provided by Hampshire Cultural Trust, 2025.

and foundry in the Market Place and began casting ploughs and other agricultural implements for the local market.[101] Francis Wallis died in 1848 and was replaced by his younger brother, Arthur (1830–1900) who, in 1856, started the North Hants Ironworks at new premises on Station Hill (Fig. 17), south of the station. Proximity to the railway remained essential to the success of the firm. He and a new partner, C.R. Haslam, used the railway to bring in raw materials and for shipment of machines. In 1862 Charles James Steevens joined the company as a partner and it became known as Wallis and Steevens, retaining this name after Steevens' retirement in 1882.[102]

Their machines were exhibited at agricultural shows in the United Kingdom and overseas, for example in 1857 at Salisbury, where their hand-worked bench drilling machine was highly commended.[103] The company also manufactured steam engines with a 36–inch steam-driven threshing machine exhibited at Leeds agricultural show in 1861. Portable engines of 4 and 8 hp were sold to threshing contractors by 1867.[104]

---

101 Wallis and Steevens deposited their archive at the Museum of English Rural Life, University of Reading [MERL]. R.A. Whitehead was commissioned by the Wallis family in 1978 to write a history of the company. R.A. Whitehead, *Wallis and Steevens. A History* (The Road Locomotive Soc., 1983), which gives a detailed technical history of the company's products. Some of their machines are preserved in Milestones Museum, Basingstoke, together with Thornycroft vehicles.
102 Whitehead, 9–10, 19.
103 Whitehead, 12.
104 Whitehead, 12.

In 1873 the company won a bronze medal for an 8 hp portable steam engine at the Universal Exhibition of Manufacture in Vienna.[105]

From the 1870s during the agricultural depression, Wallis and Steevens diversified beyond farming machinery. They manufactured their first self-propelled traction engines and sold castings to the LSWR. They provided generators to the private electrical market, such as Siemens Brothers and the British Museum.[106] They sold road locomotives to fairgrounds and steam engines to the new electricity generation industry.[107] They supplied the British Empire and the wider overseas markets including a flour dresser and bone mill to the Cape of Good Hope and a threshing machine to Bogotá, South America.[108] Other overseas business expanded. The company exhibited at the Paris Exhibition of 1881.[109] Portable engines, threshing machines and traction engines were sold to Austria, Turkey, Germany, Russia and New Zealand.[110] A range of products were supplied to France, India, Australia, Brazil and Russia.[111]

One special market was the British colonies in South Africa where from 1878 to 1894 Herbert Wallis sold machinery, produced in Basingstoke, to the diamond mining industry. For example, in 1882 nearly £10,000 worth of tipping trucks, elevators and pumps were dispatched to E.W. Tarry of Kimberley.[112] In 1892 Wallis and Steevens' wagons won a gold medal at the Kimberley Exhibition.[113] Some products were shipped through Crown Agents but many were supplied by Wallis and Steevens using the Union Steam Ship Company, Southampton, which sailed to the Cape of Good Hope.[114] The risks involved were exposed in 1891, when £1,341 worth of trucks were claimed on insurance after the SS *Nubian* sank.[115] Expansion of this business ceased in 1894 with the death of Herbert Wallis in Johannesburg, but trucks and winding engines were supplied for the next 40 years.[116]

A major technical innovation in 1891 secured the company's success when a 6 hp traction engine was converted to a road roller which was able to consolidate chalk rubble surfaces for use by the new bicycles and motor cars with iron and solid rubber tyres (Fig. 18). This demand for road rollers was encouraged by the creation of new councils under the Local Government Act, 1894, with duties to maintain roads.[117]

105 MERL, TR WAL AC1/2–19.

106 Whitehead, 18.

107 Whitehead, 18, 21.

108 MERL, TR WAL AC/5, 133, 326–8, 429, 700.

109 MERL, TR WAL AC1/2–19.

110 For example MERL, TR WAL AC/23, 61, 91, 278–80, 156, 399–400.

111 Whitehead, 19.

112 MERL, TR WAL AC1/23, 504–6, 496.

113 Whitehead, 18.

114 MERL, TR WAL AC1/10, 13, 24, 579.

115 MERL, TR WAL AC1/10.

116 For example, MERL, TR WAL AC1/10, AD1/1.

117 MERL, TR WAL AC1/9, 10.

Wallis and Steevens floated as a public limited company in 1897 to secure future investment and expansion beginning with new sheds and an enlarged foundry.[118] The company continued to expand. The balance sheet value more than doubled from £70,941 in 1896 to £151,640 in 1913.[119] The company employed 82 men and seven boys in 1881.[120] By 1912 it employed 234, including three women and 31 salaried staff.[121] Their apprenticeship scheme ensured the transmission of skills in-house.[122]

Immediately before the First World War, road rollers, steam wagons and steam tractors were the main product lines although the supply of parts and accessories for machines and production of agricultural machinery remained valuable. Some of the Wallis family had ceased to be Quakers and a few had joined the Church of England before the company started producing cast iron cases for mortar bombs in 1915. Several rollers were sold to the War Office.[123] After the First World War a new paint shop, a showroom and more sheds were built.[124]

Fig. 19. Wallis and Steevens Advance roller, 1924. Milestones museum © Jennie Butler.

118   MERL, TR WAL AD1/1; HRO, 58M74/BP34, 58M74/79.
119   MERL, TR 21 HC AC7.
120   *Census*, 1881.
121   MERL TR WAL AD2/2, 3: Response to Board of Trade Census, 16 Mar. 1913.
122   Whitehead, 46–7.
123   Whitehead, 34–5.
124   HRO, 58M74/BP730, 732, 844; MERL, TR WAL AD1/1.

They were benevolent employers, apart from providing some houses they built a large dining room and sanitary facilities at their factory.[125] The company also supported leisure activities with contributions to works' football, cricket, shooting clubs and a band.[126]

Immediately after the war there was a brisk demand for steam tractors and rollers, but the tractor orders declined. By 1921 the works was substantially overmanned and unprofitable. This was tackled by a combination of short-term working, lay-offs and wage reductions. In 1922 the board reduced the wages of all men and senior boys by 15s. a week and other boys by 3s. 6d. a week. Despite this, the board found enough money to pay a 5½ per cent dividend to preference shareholders and a 5 per cent dividend on other shares.[127]

In 1924 Wallis and Steevens made a great innovation with the Advance series road rollers which ensured their success for decades (Fig. 19). They facilitated tarmac road surfacing, essential for the new pneumatic tyres, by consolidating the hot road surface as it was laid. They were also very manoeuvrable and made even surfaces relatively quickly.[128] Initially Advance rollers were steam-powered and these remained popular in overseas sales, especially to India, the Dutch East Indies, and Siam (Thailand).[129] But they were easily converted to run on petrol and diesel for the home and overseas markets.[130]

Thornycroft

A major boost to the economy of the town came when the Thornycroft Steam Wagon Company moved to Basingstoke in 1898. Originally boat builders in Chiswick, Thornycroft diversified into building steam-powered lorries and vans, demand for which was growing. The original workshops in Chiswick were inadequate for expansion. After examining several options, the company chose Basingstoke for its new factory as the town was served by good road and rail links.[131] The company purchased 16 a. of land in Worting Road where a siding could also be built to connect the works to the proposed Alton Light Railway.[132] In 1898 they built new workshops and offices on this land (Fig. 20).[133]

There is no information about the number of people Thornycroft employed at

---

125 MERL, TR WAL AD1/1; HRO, 54M74/BP147, HRO, 58M74/BP244; above, Introduction, Industrial housing.
126 MERL, AC1/50, 127.
127 Whitehead, 35.
128 HRO, 37M85/5/WO/174.
129 MERL, TR WAL AC1/27.
130 HRO, 37M85/5/W O/174; MERL, TR WAL AC1/1, 19, 27, 54. Wallis and Steevens operated in Basingstoke until 1981, moving to Daneshill in the 1960s when their Station Hill factory was demolished.
131 HBG, 6 June 1946.
132 HBG, 30 July 1898, 6 June 1946.
133 HRO, 58M74/BP38.

Basingstoke in the early years, but its impact can be seen in the growth of employees' pay. Weekly payments in November rose from £221 4*s.* 1*d.* in 1904 to £893 18*s.* 5*d.* in 1912, despite an apparent reduction between 1906 and 1908.[134]

In 1899 Thornycroft supplied steam-powered lorries to the Army in South Africa during the Boer War.[135] The company first entered a vehicle in the War Office trials in 1901, which won first prize, and in 1909 the company was awarded the first and only prize.[136] In 1900 other customers for its steam-powered lorries included Chelsea Borough Council, the Wholesale Co-operative Society, Bentley's Yorkshire Brewery, Vaux Brewery in Sunderland and the Northampton Brewery.[137]

Thornycroft became a major bus manufacturer during the Edwardian period. London's first steam-powered bus was a Thornycroft double-decker.[138] The first of its petrol-driven vehicles was introduced in 1902.[139] In 1905 Thornycroft supplied buses to customers in Britain and overseas countries including India.[140] In 1906 its customers for buses included companies in London, Manchester, and Nottingham as well as the Great Eastern Railway and LSWR.[141] In 1904 John I. Thornycroft & Co Ltd bought the Thornycroft Steam Wagon Company for £86,493 18*s.* 9*d.*[142] Thornycroft also built a number of motor cars. These were aimed at the upper end of the market. Princess Christian, the third daughter of Queen Victoria, took delivery of several Thornycroft cars from 1905 onwards.[143]

Following the introduction of the War Department subsidy scheme, Thornycroft stopped making cars in 1913 to concentrate on lorry production.[144] During the First World War Thornycroft produced almost exclusively J-type lorries and chassis for the War Office. Exceptionally, a small handful of J-type lorries were supplied to private operators and around 120 X-type lorries to the India Office from 1916.[145] The War Office chose the Thornycroft lorry chassis for fitting with anti-aircraft guns. By the end of the war, Thornycroft had supplied some 5,000 lorries to the War Office to carry ammunition and mobile anti-aircraft guns and as general transport vehicles.[146]

During the war, Thornycroft's Basingstoke factory was one of the first in England to employ women on motor vehicle construction. By the end of the war women were

134 HCT, Thornycroft Archive, 208/1/1 and 2.
135 N. Baldwin, *The Illustrated History of Thornycroft Trucks and Buses* (1989), 7.
136 HCT, Thornycroft Archive, 1/18, *History and Present Position of the Company*, n.d.
137 HCT, Thornycroft Archive, 222/1.
138 *HBG*, 6 June 1946.
139 Townsin, *Thornycroft*, 12–13.
140 *Commercial Motor*, 16 Nov. 1905.
141 HCT, Thornycroft Archive, 222/1.
142 Abridged prospectus in the *Globe*, 11 July 1904.
143 R. Twelvetrees, *Thornycroft Road Transport Golden Jubilee* (1946) 6; HCT, Thornycroft Archive Box 222.
144 Townsin, *Thornycroft*, 19; *Commercial Motor*, 9 May 1912, 12 June 1913.
145 HCT, Thornycroft Archive, 222/1.
146 Thornycroft & Co, *Half a Century of Thornycroft Progress* (1919), 47.

Fig. 20. Thornycroft factory c.1915.

more than 35 per cent of the workforce. This factory also made a large number of
motors for boats. It also manufactured some of the first Stokes trench mortars and
many thousands of shells. It made 3,010 depth charge throwers for the Admiralty for
use against German submarines. Their manufacture was largely done by women. The
Ministry of Munitions sent representatives from firms in other parts of the country to
the Basingstoke works to see how women were employed there.[147] The rapid growth of
the company before and during the war required an influx of workers into the town.
Analysis of the 1921 census returns shows that this company employed more workers
not born in Hampshire than the other large firms.[148]

Thornycroft took great pride in educating their workforce of pupils and
apprentices. Pupils[149] paid 300 guineas to train for three years as engineering
managers within the company and the wider world. Apprentices served from age 16
to 21 and were trained as fitters, machinists, and patternmakers. Thornycroft trained
its workforce on the job but in 1920 opened a works school where apprentices were
paid to study half a day a week and pupils two half days a week.[150] In 1921 West
Ham House housed 11 engineering pupils and four engineering apprentices, aged

---

147 *Half a Century of Thornycroft Progress,* 44, 51, 93.
148 *Census,* 1921; 46 per cent only were born in Hampshire compared with 58 per cent for all
       11 companies analysed.
149 Pupils were students from wealthy families. Below, Social Hist., Education.
150 TNA, ED 74/3; below, Social Hist., Education.

17 to 23.[151] They were supported by a master and servants. The pupils came mainly from southern England with one from York. Two apprentices were from Essex and Monmouthshire. The other two came from Chicago (USA), and Cairo (Egypt). Thornycroft had agreements with governments of countries such as Egypt to train apprentices who would later work on exported vehicles.[152] In 1921 there were 55 apprentices and 17 pupils.[153] In addition the company provided a 16 a. playing field adjoining the works with football and cricket pitches, a bowling green and tennis lawns.[154]

Thornycroft, in common with other manufacturers, suffered immediately after the war. The government established an organisation to repair and sell surplus war vehicles at Slough. Reconditioned J-types sold for around one quarter the price of new ones.[155] The market became saturated with second-hand lorries. There was general economic uncertainty resulting in cancelled orders and falling demand

Fig. 21. Thornycroft factory c.1950.

from India and Australia. This led to a surplus of unsold stock. In November 1920 Thornycroft discharged some 700 employees, including the entire night shift of over 300.[156] Those staff reductions had a significantly detrimental impact on the

151 West Ham house built by the earl of Dartmouth; above, Agriculture.
152 *Census*, 1921; apprenticeship register held by Thornycroft Society at Cliddesden.
153 *Census*, 1921.
154 *HBG*, 31 May 1919; *HA*, 20 Dec. 1919.
155 Townsin, *Thornycroft*, 28.
156 *HBG*, 6 Nov. 1920.

prosperity of the town. Employees' pay totalled over £7,700 in the week ending 6 November 1920 but the following week this had been slashed to £4,462.[157] The following January further cuts took place, and it was proposed to close the factory for two days each week.[158]

The impact on employment was reflected in the June 1921 census. The company remained by far the largest single employer with 611 recorded within the borough, just over twice as many as John Mares, the next largest company. But in addition, 278 were recorded as unemployed but formerly employed by Thornycroft.[159] The reports to the Annual General Meeting (AGM) in 1922 and 1923 explained that the sales of motor vehicles had been adversely affected by competition from countries with depreciated currencies, by the sales of surplus War Department vehicles and by the 'heavy depression in trade'.[160] However, things appeared to have picked up by 1924. At the 1924 AGM Sir John Thornycroft reported that there had been a 40 per cent increase in vehicle sales and in 1925 a further 50 per cent increase (Fig. 21).[161]

Building

The town's builders catered for a range of demands from town and country. Benjamin Thorne was responsible for the restoration of nearby churches at Mapledurwell (1850–4) and Newnham (1846–7) describing himself for one as architect and for the other as surveyor.[162] His directory entries between 1844 and 1875 describe him variously as builder, carpenter, joiner, upholsterer and cabinet-maker.[163] Several deeds of the 1860s relating to land in the town describe him as a builder, suggesting involvement in the early growth of the town.[164] He employed 28 men in 1851.[165]

The rapid expansion of Basingstoke later in the century gave more employment to the building and allied trades. Builders included William Mussellwhite, who employed 32 men and two apprentices in 1881[166] and Joseph Tigwell, and later, his son, William Henry (fl.1880–1935+).[167] There were also William Powell (fl. 1880–

157 HCT, Thornycroft Archive, 208/1/1 and 2.
158 HCT, Thornycroft Archive, 3/12.
159 *Census*, 1921: the figures are for those living in the municipal borough and represent a slight underestimate of the work force and the unemployed.
160 HCT, Thornycroft Archive, 11/2.
161 *The Times*, 23 Dec. 1924, 10 Dec. 1925. Thornycroft ceased production in Basingstoke in 1969.
162 *Mapledurwell*, 78–9; LPL, ICBS/04289/15, ICBS Vol. 13, 84.
163 B. Meehan, 'Unfortunately Romanesque'. Two churches of the 1840s in Hampshire', *Proc. HFC* (2020), 125; *Pigot's Dir.* 1844, 10; *Mercers and Crockers Dir.* (1871), 119; *P.O. Dir.* (1875), 32.
164 HRO, 8M62/C5 /1/15; 10M57/ T110; 12M49/A21/12; 12M93/9.
165 Meehan, 'Unfortunately Romanesque', 125.
166 *Census*, 1881.
167 *Kelly's Dir.* (1885), 597, (1935), 61.

1903),[168] George Jennings, who employed five men and four boys in 1881 and Henry James Goodall, who started his business in 1875 and later won the contract to build Fairfields schools (opened 1888).[169] Glover and Milsom, plumbers and decorators, later Milsom and Son, employed 25 men and two boys in 1881; and William Ayliffe, plumber and decorator, employed eight men and one boy in 1881.[170] In 1901 there were 559 males in the town (17.7 per cent of the employed male workforce) categorised as being employed on building and works of construction.[171]

Coachbuilding

In 1800 Basingstoke's position at an important junction on the Great Western Road meant there was a demand for the building and repair of horse-drawn vehicles. In 1844, for example, William Draper was a coachbuilder, making vehicles for the tradesmen of the town and the neighbourhood gentry.[172] Some coachmakers survived the arrival of the railways. John Follett and his son, William (fl. 1865–1899) were

Fig. 22. Joice's yard and workforce early 20th century. Hampshire County Council. Provided by Hampshire Cultural Trust, 2025.

168   *Kelly's Dir.* (1885), 596, (1903), 53.
169   HRO, H/CL5/1f/5.
170   *Census*, 1881.
171   *Census Report Hants* 1901, 94.
172   *Pigot's Dir.* (1844), 11.

coachbuilders in Sarum Hill.[173] In 1881 John Follett employed six men and two boys, and in the same year John Fencott was employing eight men and six boys in his workshop in Old Crown Yard.[174] When he retired in the 1880s he sold the business to John Joice.

Joice undertook the manufacture and repair of high-class town carriages, and horse-drawn vans for local firms, sold second-hand carriages on commission and bought and sold carriage horses. The business prospered to the extent that, by 1888, he was able to buy H. Carpenter's carriage works in Staines and he employed an average of 18 craftsmen in his Basingstoke works in the late 1890s (Fig. 22).[175]

During the first years of the 20th century the firm began making motor-car bodies.[176] In 1915 Joice was described as a 'coach & motor body builder'.[177] But this proved transient as car bodies became less like coach bodies and motor manufacturers began to make complete cars in their factories. The business expanded briefly during the First World War as the result of contracts to repair horse-drawn vehicles for the army but declined thereafter and the firm closed in 1959.[178]

Other businesses

Percy Fisher, leather manufacturer employed 45 people by 1921.[179] Two timber yards, E.C. White at the Wharf and Tagart, Morgan and Cole, Kingsclere Road had sawmills, boiler houses, offices and stables in 1901.[180]

Trade Unions

Trade unions developed in Basingstoke in the latter part of the 19th century. A branch of the Carpenters' society was established in 1864 (later called the Amalgamated Society of Carpenters and Joiners).[181] They were joined by the House Decorators' and Painters' society and the Operative Bricklayers' society in 1894,[182] which had a membership of 26.[183] In the same year the Carpenters' union called a strike demanding a pay rise.[184] The unions enabled workers to claim sick pay among

173 *Harrod's Dir. Hants* (1865), 607; *Kelly's Dir.* (1899), 54.
174 *Census*, 1881.
175 HRO, 32M65/8.
176 M.D. Freeman, 'John Joice & Son – a Note', in *Transport History* (Nov. 1972).
177 *Kelly's Dir.* (1915), 60.
178 Freeman, John Joice; HRO, 32M65.
179 *Census*, 1921.
180 HRO, 58M74/BP162, 148.
181 *HBG*, 28 July 1894.
182 *HBG*, 28 July 1894.
183 Univ. of Warwick, MRC, MSS.78/OB/4/2/19.
184 *HBG*, 25 Aug. 1894.

other benefits.[185] A representative from Basingstoke attended the annual meeting of the National Union of Teachers at Aberystwyth in 1911.[186] The Journeymen Butchers' Federation of GB,[187] the National Union of Agricultural Workers[188] and the Amalgamated Engineering Union,[189] all had branches in Basingstoke.

An outstanding trade unionist was Russell Henry Howard, born 1890. Howard worked as a boiler washer with the LSWR, and joined the National Union of Railwaymen in 1913.[190] He established a branch of The Workers' Union in 1919 with the assistance of the local Trades Council.[191] Immediately he secured pay rises for the Basingstoke gas company workers and negotiated with the borough council to gain benefits for their staff.[192] He worked with trade unions, and for workers who did not have a union, as an advocate for better pay and conditions for all. He was elected to the council for the first time in 1919[193] and was one of the first Labour councillors.

Markets and Other Services

A S A MARKET town, Basingstoke offered services to the surrounding agricultural area, such as selling agricultural produce, retailing, hospitality, legal services and entertainment.

Fairs

Fairs were held in Basingstoke from the Middle Ages.[194] In 1787 following the enclosure of Basingstoke Down the 'Basingstoke Down Fair for Sheep and other Cattle, Cheese, and all other Kinds of Merchandise', was moved near to the Market Place.[195] However, as the space proved inadequate this was moved to the Common in 1840.[196] The fair moved to Fairfields in 1870 and the date changed to July. At the fair on 13 July 1870, some 10,000 sheep were penned, and dealers came from

---

185 Univ. of Warwick, MRC, MSS.78/OB/4/2/18.

186 *HBG*, 22 Apr. 1911.

187 Univ. of Warwick, MRC, MSS.292C/230.2/8/31.

188 *HBG*, 27 Dec. 1919.

189 *HBG*, 7 Mar. 1925.

190 Univ. of Warwick, MRC, MSS.127/NU/OR/2/28, folio no. 62.

191 Univ. of Warwick, MRC, *The Workers' Union Jnl, Record*, Mar. 1918, 14; MSS.126/ WU/4/2/1.

192 Univ. of Warwick, MRC, *The Workers' Union Jnl, Record*, Apr. 1918, 3; MSS.126/ WU/4/2/1.

193 *HBG*, 20 Feb. 1970; below, Municipal Government and Politics, 1872–1925.

194 Hare, *Medieval Basingstoke*, 2–3.

195 *HC*, 17 Sept. 1787.

196 *RM*, 16 Sept. 1840.

Hertfordshire, Buckinghamshire, Cambridgeshire, Essex, Sussex and Surrey.[197] However, numbers declined rapidly and only 990 sheep were penned at the July 1888 fair.[198] There was a reluctant acceptance at the Sheep Fair Dinner that the 1888 fair would be the last, and there is no reference to a fair in 1889.[199] The first of a series of half-yearly cheese fairs was held at the canal wharf on 28 May 1840. Initially successful,[200] it moved to the Railway Station Yard in 1842.[201] However, it was in difficulties by November 1850,[202] and it is possible that this was the last.

The Michaelmas Hiring and Pleasure Fair attracted a large influx of country visitors and showmen. It comprised, 'a great number of shows, booths, and stalls in the Market Place and streets adjacent'.[203] By the 1880s, most hiring was done by advertising in the local newspaper, and the fair was essentially a pleasure fair. The Market Place and Wheatsheaf meadow south of the town were used for Michaelmas pleasure fairs which had succeeded the cattle fairs. The 1898 fair had a switchback railway, roundabouts, shooting ranges and coconut shies.[204]

Markets

From the Middle Ages Basingstoke had a market for the produce of farmers on the chalk downland and clay lowland. The importance of this market throughout the 18th century is evidenced by the number of London newspapers that quoted the prices of wheat, barley, oats, beans and peas at Basingstoke market.[205] This continued into the 19th century when the market was transformed. The 1829 Act for enlarging the Market Place in Basingstoke authorised the compulsory purchase of 13 houses, inns and shops in Church Street and Wote Street. This was to increase the area for the sale of corn, grain and other agricultural produce, malt, meal and flour. In 1837 the market was said to be 'well attended, being resorted to by persons from Andover, Winchester, Newbury and Reading'.[206]

Under the 1829 Act a separate market for cattle and swine was established near, but south of, the corn market on the Fair Close.[207] This market was challenged when Hugh Raynbird and his two sons set up an auction mart at the top of Station Hill in

197 *RM*, 16 July 1870.
198 *RM*, 14 July 1888.
199 *RM*, 21 July 1888.
200 *RM*, 30 May 1840.
201 *RM*, 26 Nov. 1842.
202 *BC*, 30 Nov. 1850.
203 *HC*, 12 Oct. 1818; *RM*, 15 Oct. 1864.
204 *HBG,* 15 Oct. 1898.
205 *Grub-street Jnl* and *London Evening-Post* in the 1730s, *Lloyd's Evening Post* and *Owen's Weekly Chronicle* in the 1750s and *Whitehall Evening Post* in the 1780s.
206 Parl. Papers, 1837 (238).
207 10 Geo. IV. 14.5.1829; Notice dated 21 Aug. 1829 in *RM*, 14 Sept. 1829. Between Council Road and the cricket field and behind the Bounty public house (2024).

1873.[208] This took the trade away from the Fairfields cattle market, which ceased in the late 1870s.[209] In the 1880s the board schools were built on part of the site.[210]

The Act also provided for the lesser market just north of the town hall, for the sale of meat, poultry and eggs on Wednesdays and Saturdays, and fish, fruit and vegetables daily, except Sundays. The cattle market and the lesser market were opened for business in October 1829. The lesser market proved to be popular with traders and customers alike as its first Christmas reports indicated.[211] It was well supplied and enjoyed high sales.[212] In 1884 work began to convert the front of the lesser market to five shops at an estimated cost of £200.[213] Tenancy agreements in August 1885 show that the shops were occupied by greengrocers and fishmongers.[214]

In 1851, the corporation tried to levy tolls on the corn market in accordance with the 1829 Act on the grounds that the facilities provided for the farmers were paid for by the town's ratepayers. The farmers threatened to boycott the market and set up an alternative market in Old Basing.[215] Following representation from the town's tradesmen, the corporation decided not to levy tolls as it was estimated that Basingstoke gained directly and indirectly from the market some £2,500 a year.[216] There were five corn dealers listed in 1844, six in 1852, and seven in 1859.[217] In 1881, Smith Bros, corn merchants, employed 31 men and four boys in Wote Street and Eastrop Mill.[218]

In 1886, 20,153 quarters of wheat, 2,554 quarters of barley, and 8,055 quarters of oats were sold at Basingstoke, largely produced in the surrounding rural areas. This compared with 17,821 quarters of wheat, 10,207 quarters of barley and 968 quarters of oats sold at Reading in the same year.[219] Because Basingstoke was close to a large area of corn production, but generated low consumption, many dealers who bought corn at Basingstoke paid for it to be carried to Reading, where it was turned into Huntley and Palmer's biscuits.[220] In 1900, 32,203 quarters of wheat, 9,236 quarters of barley, and 16,742 quarters of oats were sold at Basingstoke.[221] These fell in 1910 to 20,106, 6,446, and 12,288 respectively.[222] In both years, Basingstoke was the biggest market in Hampshire.

208 *BG*, 27 Apr. 2006.

209 S. Pugh, *Fairs and Markets of Basingstoke* (2001), 12. The book was self-published.

210 Below, Social Hist., Education.

211 *BC*, 2 Jan. 1830.

212 *BC*, 13 Mar. 1830 and 11 June 1831.

213 *RM*, 11 Oct. and 8 Nov. 1884.

214 HRO, 148M71/4/21/11–15.

215 *HC*, 15 Feb. to 12 Apr. 1851.

216 *HC*, 22 Mar. 1851.

217 *Pigot's Dir.* (1844), 11; *Slater's Dir. Hants* (1852–3), 13; *White's Dir.* (1859), 493.

218 *Census*, 1881.

219 Parl. Papers, 1888 (312), *Select Committee on Corn Averages*, 176–90.

220 Parl. Papers, 1888 (312), 76–7.

221 Parl. Papers, 1901 (Cd.576), *Agricultural Returns for Great Britain,* 1900, 108.

222 Parl. Papers, 1911 (Cd.5585), *Agricultural Statistics, 1910*, 229.

A wool market was held on 20 June 1851, at which 30,080 fleeces were offered.[223] Thereafter wool markets were held at the town hall until at least 1858.[224]

Retailing

The main shopping streets from 1800 to 1925 were in the upper town around the Market Place. These streets survive in 2024 although the main shopping area in 2024 was to the north of the traditional area, in Festival Place and the Malls built since town redevelopment. From the 1890s a few shops opened in the lower town in Brook Street and Essex Road while corner shops developed in the new residential areas.

1800 to 1860

The main shopping area was centred on Market Place and the four roads that met there: London Street, Winchester Street, Church Street and Wote Street. In 1792 the shopkeepers included six bakers, four butchers, four drapers, three peruke makers, two grocers, two hatters and an ironmonger.[225]

The importance of Basingstoke for affluent people in the town and surrounding area can be seen from John Ring's accounts from 1785 to 1792 which listed all customers and their purchases.[226] He supplied furniture and furnishings to the Prince of Wales at Kempshott and local county grandees. These included the duke of Bolton at Hackwood, William Chute of the Vyne, Bigg-Withers of Manydown and Jervoise of Herriard, as well as to the publicans and tradesmen of Basingstoke and district. His clients included many local clergy, such as Jane Austen's father, who purchased Jane's little writing desk.[227] As well as supplying everything that was needed to furnish a house, down to the wallpaper, nails and glue, he also supplied coffins, both to Basingstoke corporation for paupers' funerals and more expensively to private families.[228] The accounts ceased when Ring died intestate and childless in 1796 and the business was sold to grocers.[229] 19th century customer accounts survive for Robert Mansbridge, tailor, whose customers included the earl of Dorchester.[230]

Drapers stocked a wide range of products. John Chambers was a woollen and linen draper who also sold pocket books, atlases, books and almanacs, likewise millinery, perfumery, and a variety of patent medicines.[231] He kept two men constantly employed making hats.[232] The stock of the draper Nathaniel Jackson in 1801 included

223 *RM*, 28 June 1851.
224 *BC*, 28 June 1856, 26 June 1858.
225 *Universal British Dir.* (1792), 317–8.
226 HRO, 8M62/14 and 15.
227 HRO, 8M62/15.
228 HRO, 8M62/14.
229 HRO, 149A10/B16/2/4.
230 HRO, 8M62/8.
231 *RM*, 26 Nov. 1792.
232 *RM, 27* Apr. 1789.

'Gentlemen's Liveries' and 'a large and elegant assortment of Hats of the finest manufactures'.[233] Basingstoke customers therefore had a choice between locally-made articles and imported goods. Jackson's Winchester Street shop was successively taken over by William Castleman (fl.1830–44), John Loader (fl. 1852–56) and by Thomas Burberry in 1856.[234]

Advertisements emphasise the links with the wider fashionable world. In 1799 the 'Ladies of Basingstoke, and its Neighbourhood' were advised that every branch of mantua-making and fancy-dress making was executed by Maria Somers at Mrs Cooper's in Winchester Street, where there was a constant supply of every new fashion from London and Bath.[235] The same year Miss Bishop of London Street announced that she had just returned from London with 'a new and elegant assortment of millinery, flowers, rich alamode for cloaks, gloves, etc'.[236] Jane Austen, however, had severe reservations about the quality of tailoring in Basingstoke: 'I do not believe', she wrote, 'that Southampton is famous for its tailoring, but I hope it will prove itself better than Basingstoke'.[237]

By the 1850s specialist shops included saddlers, watch and clock makers, milliners, cabinet makers, wine and spirit merchants, straw bonnet makers, a hatter and a breeches maker.[238] Five hairdressers advertised their services in 1859.[239]

Retailers also provided for the poor in the Union workhouse in Basing Road which from 1836[240] required bulk suppliers of food and other goods.[241] In 1838, for example, William Miles, a London Street grocer, supplied bacon, cheese, butter, soap, starch, sugar, teas, candles, oatmeal, brooms and mops.[242] More specialist traders included John Gilkes, a Wote Street baker, who provided bread and flour at various dates between 1838 and 1870.[243] John Barton, a London Street butcher, provided meat and milk between 1838 and 1850 and William Tredgold, boot and shoe maker, of London Street, supplied footwear from 1838 to 1850.[244] By 1858 Burberry was supplying drapery items to the workhouse.[245]

1860 to 1925

The coming of the railways enabled goods manufactured elsewhere to be brought

233 *Universal British Dir.* (1792), 317; *RM*, 11 May 1801.
234 *Pigot's Dir.* (1831–2), 409; (1844), 11; *White's Dir.* (1859), 493; HRO, 42M66/128.
235 *RM*, 12 Aug. 1799.
236 *RM*, 13 May 1799.
237 D. Le Faye (ed.), *Jane Austen's Letters*, 3rd edn (Oxford 1995), 150.
238 *Census*, 1851; *Slater's Dir. Hants* (1852), 12–14.
239 *White's Dir.* (1859), 493.
240 *White's Dir.* (1859), 485–6; below, Social Welfare and Administration of Poor Law.
241 HRO, PL3/5/2 to 13.
242 *Pigot's Dir.* (1844), 11; HRO, PL3/5/2 and 4.
243 *White's Dir.* (1859) 493; HRO, PL3/5/2 to 13.
244 *Pigot's Dir.* (1844), 10; HRO, PL3/5/2 to 8.
245 HRO, Pl/3/5/10.

to the town relatively cheaply. This helped the emergence of larger retail units or department stores. Towards the end of the period national chain stores opened in the town.

Thomas Burberry

Although Burberry was best known as a manufacturer, he had started as a shopkeeper in 1856 and was well-established as a draper on the north side of Winchester Street before he turned to mass manufacture.[246] He had purchased the premises by 1872.[247] In 1861 he bought premises on the south side of London Street[248] by which time he was employing seven men, seven women and three boys.[249] In addition, he was the local agent for Epps's Homeopathic Cocoa, and the Y and N Patent Diagonal Seam Corset.[250] He turned his shop on the north side of Winchester Street into a department store, renaming it 'The Emporium'. Further expansion occurred in 1898 when Burberry took over a large shop on the south side of Winchester Street.[251] In 1904 he opened a showroom in Winchester Street, near the Market Place and next to the Old Angel Café (Fig. 12), for the sale of antique furniture, curios, bric-a-brac, pianos, dinner services, glassware, etc.[252] He also had a shop in Church Street for the sale of furniture, carpets, floor cloths and linoleum.[253] On 7 April 1905 the Emporium burnt down. Burberry quickly purchased new stock, which he sold from his other shops.[254] He rebuilt the Emporium, which opened for business on 29 August 1906. The building was still in existence in 2024.[255]

In 1911 he advertised that Burberry were the leading 'Drapers, Clothiers and Home Furnishers in Basingstoke', and that the Emporium was 'spacious, conveniently arranged, well ventilated, and during the cold weather heated throughout with hot water'.[256] Edgar Lanham another draper, leased the Winchester Street Emporium from Burberry in 1913 and bought the property in 1922.[257] In 1915 Burberry had also sold the shop on the south side of Winchester Street to Lanham.[258]

246 Above, Clothing Industry.
247 HRO, 42M66/128, 129.
248 HRO, 42M66/131 and 132 read with 42M66/122.
249 *Census*, 1861.
250 *HA*, Aug. 11, 1860; *HC*, 28 Oct. 1865; *HBG*, 22 Mar. 1884.
251 HRO, 42M66/162, previously owned by Thomas Edney, see above, Market Gardening and Plant Nurseries.
252 *HBG*, 20 Aug. 1904.
253 M. Felgate and B. Applin, *Going Down Church Street to the Felgate Bookshop* (BAHS, 1998).
254 *HBG*, 29 Apr. 1905, 6 May 1905.
255 *HBG*, 1 Sept. 1906.
256 *Kelly's Dir.* (1911), 61; *Basingstoke, the Official Publication*, 1911–12.
257 HRO, 42M66/177, 187.
258 HRO, 42M66/180.

Alfred Milward

Another large-scale business that developed in the later 19th century was that of Alfred Milward who came from Henley-on-Thames (Oxon.). He started his boot and shoe business in Basingstoke in 1857 by selling boots obtained from wholesalers from a handcart.[259] He opened a shoe shop in Winchester Street, and by 1881 was employing 12 men and two boys in his retail and manufacturing business.[260] He opened a warehouse in Cross Street in 1896 and two years later, Milwards became a limited company.[261] Milward and Sons advertised that in their Bespoke Department, hand-sewn work was a speciality, and they gave prompt attention to all repairs.[262] Milwards opened a branch in Reading in 1890 and later established a chain of shoe shops across the United Kingdom.[263]

Other Traders 1860 to 1925

The Basingstoke Co-operative Society started in 1892 with a shop in Brook Street.[264] In 1899 it moved into a purpose-built store in Essex Road (Map 3), which was extended in 1905 and again in 1912. By 1920, the Basingstoke Co-operative Society had a turnover of £125,000 and 2,600 members.[265]

John Lodwidge, for a short period in the early 1850s, was in partnership with Arthur Wallis in an ironmonger's shop in the Market Place.[266] By 1855 Lodwidge had taken over the shop after Wallis left to start what later became the manufacturing firm of Wallis and Steevens.[267] From around 1865 Lodwidge was in partnership with Thomas Maton Kingdon.[268] In 1881 Lodwidge and Kingdon were employing eight men and six boys.[269] When Lodwidge retired in the 1880s, Kingdon took sole control of the shop.[270] By 1915 T.M. Kingdon & Co had opened branches in Winchester and Alton. Frederick Temple (fl. 1865–1881+), an ironmonger in Church Street, employed ten men and two boys in 1881. This business was later taken over by Henry Julian who in 1892 advertised that he was a wholesale furnishing and general ironmonger, a gas and cold-water engineer, dealer in oils, paints, breech loading guns and ammunition and was a maker of kitchen ranges, stable fittings, entrance gates.[271] In the 20th century Julian and Sons described

259   Anon., *The Milward Story* (*c*.1957).

260   *Census*, 1881.

261   HRO, 46M97/11; *Kelly's Dir.* (1899), 55.

262   *Basingstoke, the Official Publication, 1911–12.*

263   *The Milward Story.*

264   B. Applin (ed.), *The Co-op and Basingstoke* (BAHS, 2012), 8, 10–11.

265   B. Applin (2012), *Co-op*, 15, 17, 23–4.

266   *Slater's Dir. Hants* (1852), 14.

267   Above, Industry.

268   *White's Dir.* (1878) 136; *Harrod's Dir.* (1865), 607.

269   *Census*, 1881.

270   *Kelly's Dir.* (1889), 46.

271   HRO, 46M74/PZ41.

themselves as ironmongers and motor engineers.[272]

In 1903, when the town's population was approaching 10,000, the main shopping area included 15 drapers, 13 grocers, 11 butchers, and five boot and shoe shops. Other businesses included ironmongers, saddlers, watchmakers, cabinet makers/furniture shops and wine and spirit merchants. New shops included bicycle dealers. A significant change was the growth of some 30 shops outside the main shopping area, mainly general shopkeepers and grocers, serving the new residential areas.[273]

By 1911 a number of national chains had opened branches in the Market Place: Home and Colonial, International Stores, Liptons and Timothy Whites.[274] The inter-war years saw the further growth of nationally based department stores. Woolworths opened its 'Bazaar' in London Street in 1921.[275]

Inns and Public Houses

Inns

At the start of this period, Basingstoke's position as an important staging and refreshment point for coaches was vital to the wealth of the town. The Red Lion in London Street, the George and the Angel in the Market Place, the Crown and the Bolton Arms (formerly the Maidenhead), the Wheatsheaf in Winchester Street and the Feathers in Wote Street competed for contracts to provide this service. The coaching business gave employment to a large number of support workers (innkeepers, tapsters, domestic staff, ostlers, grooms, porters and postboys), and employed the local services of wheelwrights, farriers, saddlers and harness makers. The agricultural sector provided support for at least 148 horses for the stagecoach services alone, not counting the reserves and the carriers' and tradesmen's horses.[276]

In 1782, the Feathers had stabling for about 60 horses.[277] The Maidenhead had stabling for about 100 horses in 1788[278] while the Angel had stabling for 80 horses in 1850.[279] In 1830 innkeepers and horse keepers rented 13 per cent of the land in the parish.[280] At this period most of the land was rented by maltsters and brewers to grow barley, or by tradespeople, particularly inn keepers, to graze and keep horses for the coaching trade. Forty-nine per cent of the agricultural land was either owned (5 per cent) or rented (44 per cent) by trades people. Particularly prominent were the

272 *Kelly's Dir.* (1915), 60.

273 *Kelly's Dir.* (1903), 51–4.

274 *Kelly's Dir.* (1911), 62–4.

275 *BG*, 10 July 2008; *Kelly's Dir.* (1923), 67.

276 Stokes, *Basingstoke*, 62.

277 *HC*, 9 Sept. 1782.

278 *Salisbury and Winchester Jnl*, 19 May 1788.

279 *RM*, 8 June 1850.

280 D. Spruce, 'Basingstoke 1780–1860: Aspects of the Development of a North Hampshire Market Town'. (MSc. Dissertation, Univ. London (1977), 37. Copy in Basingstoke Discovery Centre.

Curtis brothers, brewers, maltsters and post horse keepers of the Angel, who rented 563 a. including the Merton College farm but only owned 22 a.[281] They were to go out of business after the coming of the railway in 1839. Richard Curtis, landlord of the Angel, was said to have been worth upwards of £45,000 in 1830, and at one time kept some 500 horses for his coaching business.[282] When the Crown was put up for auction in 1840, the items for sale included 21 post horses and other livestock, various types of carriages, as well as wines and the contents of its 30 rooms.[283] The other inns and the larger public houses also had ample accommodation for travellers and visitors.

The coming of the railway in 1839 devastated the innkeeping and coaching trades.[284] The loss of employment following the collapse of the coaching trade was not immediately offset by the benefits of being a railway hub. One observer noted in 1841 that, because the coaches had ceased to run through Basingstoke, 'not only is the appearance of the town much less cheerful ... but many local interests are suffering from the transition'.[285]

In 1839 James Biggs, a Basingstoke coach master, was made bankrupt.[286] In 1840, Charles Tubb, a Basingstoke innkeeper was imprisoned for debt.[287] Eliza King, the landlady of the Crown, was made bankrupt.[288] One of her ostlers committed suicide for fear of being sent to the workhouse. The Crown ceased to be an inn,[289] although part of the building was later used as an ordinary public house, which retained its name.[290] The George with its seven bedrooms was put up for auction in 1843, 'the Business of the Inn being relinquished'.[291] Even the hitherto rich Richard Curtis, the owner of the Angel, was unable to pay his debts and in 1850 his assigns put his property up for auction.[292]

Despite the loss of the coaching trade, there was still a demand for overnight accommodation for visitors and others who had business in the town. The proximity of Basingstoke to the military camp at Aldershot meant that billeting was frequently used. During the autumn manoeuvres in 1871 some 1,400 mounted troops were billeted in the inns and public houses in the town for eight days.[293]

The coming of the railways led to the opening of new premises in front of the two stations, but significantly away from the concentration of former inns on London

281 For background to Merton Farm, Baigent and Millard, *Basingstoke*, 40–52.
282 *HC,* 10 Mar. 1855.
283 *RM*, 16 May, 13 June, 19 Sept. 1840.
284 Above, Introduction, Roads.
285 C. Knight, *The Journey Book of England – Hampshire* (1841).
286 *London Gaz.,* 14 June 1839.
287 *London Gaz.,* 20 Mar. 1840.
288 *London Gaz.,* 22 May 1840.
289 *HA,* 16 May 1840; *Census,* 1841; *Pigot's Dir.* (1844), 11.
290 *Census,* 1851.
291 *RM*, 4 Mar. 1843.
292 *RM*, 19 Jan., 8 June 1850.
293 HRO, 10M57/O2/4.

Street and Winchester Street. The LSWR station was served by the Railway Arms at the corner of Brook Street and Station Hill which opened in 1839 and the Trial Inn (later the Junction Inn) which opened in Station Hill some time before 1857.[294] The Junction Inn was rebuilt and opened in 1906 as the Station Hotel.[295] The GWR station was served by the Great Western Hotel which opened in 1887 and had six public bedrooms.[296]

The Wheatsheaf was the official hotel in Basingstoke of the Cyclists' Touring Club.[297] In 1898 the Red Lion advertised itself as a 'Family and Commercial Hotel' with 'Every Accommodation for Hunting and Shooting Gentlemen'.[298] It later became the Royal Automobile Club's approved hotel in Basingstoke.[299]

Public Houses

At the start of the 20th century Basingstoke had 54 public houses (38 with full licences and 16 beerhouses).[300] In 1902 as part of a nationwide campaign, the Hampshire quarter sessions resolved that magistrates should refuse to renew licences where they were excessive in relation to the population.[301] Basingstoke was particularly vulnerable. It possessed a large number of public houses with a ratio of 49 adult males for each. As a result of these pressures, the town lost 11 between 1903 and 1912.[302] This represented a drop of just under 21 per cent, compared with a reduction of ten per cent nationally during the same period.[303]

Banking

For the first half of the 19th century Basingstoke was served by two banks. The Basingstoke and Odiham Bank, otherwise known as Seymour, Lamb, Brooks and Hillier, opened in 1806 in Winchester Street.[304] The Basingstoke Savings Bank opened in 1817 in the town hall.[305] Sometime before 1859 they were joined by the London and County Bank which opened a branch in Winchester Street.[306] In 1864 J. & C. Simonds & Co, otherwise known as the Reading Bank, opened a branch in

---

294 HRO, 10M57/SP95; *HA*, 18 Apr. 1857; *HBG*, 5 Oct. 1901.

295 *HBG*, 10 Nov. 1906.

296 *RM*, 29 Oct. 1887; *HBG*, 6 Mar. 1909.

297 *The Cyclist and Wheel World Annual*, 1883.

298 *HBG*, 12 Mar. 1898.

299 R.A.C. Yearbook 1911.

300 HRO, 29M98/2/1.

301 *Portsmouth Evening News*, 8 Apr. 1902.

302 HRO, 29M98/2/1.

303 P. Jennings, *The Local: A History of the English Pub* (2011), 173.

304 *HC*, 26 May 1806.

305 *HC*, 17 Nov. 1817.

306 *White's Dir.* (1859), 492.

Winchester Street.[307] This branch moved to Wote Street shortly after it opened, and later moved to the Market Place.[308] In 1913 it became part of Barclays Bank.[309] In 1864 the Basingstoke and Odiham Bank transferred its business to the Hampshire Banking Company,[310] which changed its name to the Capital and Counties Bank in 1878.[311] This was taken over by Lloyds Bank in 1918 and moved to the Market Place by 1927.[312] The Basingstoke Savings Bank continued until November 1890 when depositors were advised they could either withdraw their money or have it transferred to the Post Office Savings Bank.[313] The London and County Bank moved its branch to its new building in London Street in 1866.[314] It later became the London, County and Westminster Bank and shortened its name to the Westminster Bank in 1923.[315]

307 *BC*, 16 July 1864; *Kelly's Dir.* (1889), 47.
308 *P.O. Dir.* (1867), 484; *White's Dir.* (1878), 137; *Kelly's Dir.* (1889), 47.
309 *Westminster Gaz.*, 9 Oct. 1913.
310 *RM*, 16 July 1864.
311 *BC*, 11 May 1878.
312 *Westminster Gaz.*, 8 Aug. 1918; *Kelly's Dir.* (1927), 63.
313 *HC*, 8 Nov. 1890.
314 *BC*, 26 May 1866.
315 *The Times*, 1 Mar. 1923.

SOCIAL HISTORY

T HE TRANSFORMATION OF Basingstoke from a small rural market and agricultural town to a substantial manufacturing and industrial centre led to changes in its character. This chapter considers the structure of society, how people spent their leisure time, the growth of education, care of the poor and the impact of the First World War on the townspeople.

Social Structure

F ROM 1256 THE mayor, aldermen and burgesses of Basingstoke were the lords of the manor.[1] In 1800, the largest landowner, Thomas Orde Powlett, created first Baron Bolton in 1797 and Lord Lieutenant of Hampshire 1800–07, lived just to the east of Basingstoke at Hackwood House in Old Basing parish.[2] Thomas died in 1807 and his son, William, inherited the Hackwood House estate. William supported Basingstoke people, businesses and events. For example, he was patron of the Savings Bank in 1842 and a life member of the Mechanics' Institute from 1844. He donated to Basingstoke schools, charities and the poor and was much mourned after his death in 1850.[3] From 1850 his heirs lived at Bolton Castle (Yorks. N.R.), and Hackwood was leased to tenants.[4] While most professionals, especially lawyers and doctors, were concentrated in the county town of Winchester, 18 miles to the south, Basingstoke had a small but significant group of such people.

Wills of 15 Basingstoke gentlemen, dating from 1800 to 1840, which were proved in the Prerogative Court of Canterbury[5] reveal that their social world extended well beyond Basingstoke, with executors and legatees living in London, Berkshire, Wiltshire, Dorset, Somerset, Penzance and the Isles of Scilly in Cornwall, and Bayonne in France.[6] As well as freehold and/or leasehold property many had money invested in government stocks. John Mulford (d. 1814), aged 92, left over £17,000 and five houses in Basingstoke and Overton, together with bequests to chapels and

---

1 Hare, *Medieval Basingstoke*, 18.
2 HRO, DS/UK/333. Created Baron Bolton of Bolton Castle, Yorks. N.R. in 1797.
3 Above, Banking; *RM*, 29 Dec. 1842, 11 May 1844, 20 July 1850.
4 *Complete Peerage*, (2nd edn, 1912), II, 217.
5 These were proved in the Prerogative Court of Canterbury as they had possessions in more than one diocese or chose to prove them in Canterbury for reasons of status. They are held in The National Archives.
6 See for example, TNA, PROB 11/1659/230, 1643/239.

religious societies such as the Missionary Society and Lady Huntingdon's Connexion. David Graham (d. 1820) left bequests of £6,000, including a horse and chaise to his wife, Sarah, as well as land. John Hasker (d. 1822) who had purchased West Ham farm from the earl of Dartmouth had goods valued at £3,000.[7] John Lyford (d. 1830) describing himself as a gentleman and surgeon, left his business to his son, Charles, who worked with him. He left a freehold house in Basingstoke with a carriage house and substantial outbuildings together with business premises at Flaxpool. He held shares in the Basingstoke Canal Navigation and £3,500 in Bank of England 3 per cent stock.[8] Roger Attwood (d. 1811) described himself as a banker and wine merchant, but he also owned the Black Boy public house and other property. He prospered leaving £10,000 in cash bequests mainly to his wife and children as well as his business and property.[9] George Glover (d. 1833) lived in Winchester Street but also owned land and four-fifths of the advowson and rectory of Eastrop.[10]

The majority of other testators only had possessions within Winchester diocese and their wills were proved in the consistory court in Winchester. From 1800 to 1840, most were craftsmen and shopkeepers: rural (millers, blacksmiths) and urban (bakers, maltsters, tailors). The urban craftsmen included a few specialists catering for increasing consumerism including watch and clock makers, jewellers and cabinet makers,[11] a coachmaker, a paper maker, a boat builder, an umbrella maker, a hatter and a habit maker.[12] Wine merchants and a brandy merchant served affluent customers.[13] In the 1830s a veterinary surgeon was working in Basingstoke.[14] To ensure greater peace of mind for home and business owners, there was also a rat catcher in 1826.[15] Sixty-five of these wills included probate values, ranging from £50 to £4,000 with an average of £550. The wealthiest was Samuel Jesse, an innkeeper, who died in 1837, just before the railway arrived.[16] The others whose goods were worth over £1,000 were a draper, a brewer, a landowner, a grocer, a baker and another innkeeper.[17]

Most testators owned property in the historic core of the town in Church Street, Market Place, New Street, Church Lane, Winchester Street, London Road, Wote Street and Flaxpool Street: the 'good streets lined with neat houses, shops, inns and taverns', described in 1859.[18] Others had property built in the fields after the enclosure of 1786.

7   HRO, 1822A/36.
8   TNA, PROB 11/1767/10.
9   TNA, PROB 11/1527/276.
10   TNA, PROB 11/1810/209.
11   HRO, Basingstoke probate, 1800 to 1840.
12   HRO, 1803A/050.
13   HRO, 1820B/04.
14   HRO, 1833B/049.
15   HRO, 46M74/PR10.
16   HRO, 1837A/066.
17   HRO, Basingstoke probate, 1800 to 1840.
18   *White's Dir.* (1859), 486.

Farmers and yeomen lived in the town and farmed 3,500 a. of the parish.[19] No full list of possessions owned by any of these testators survives but there are indications of comfort and luxury with references to china, silver spoons and tongs, furniture and to beer and liquor within the house. Where outbuildings were listed a chaise house was frequently recorded.[20]

The number of professional men recorded as fathers in the baptismal records from 1813 was also increasing slowly. These included auctioneers, bankers, land agents, wine merchants and lawyers, together with a land surveyor and a supervisor of excise. Three companies of lawyers existed in 1831–2 of which the most prominent was Cole, Lamb and Brooks in Winchester Street,[21] who dealt with a wide range of legal matters including estate and property management and executorship for the surrounding gentry and townspeople.[22]

In 1851 some of the main landowners in Basingstoke lived outside the parish. Those who played a part in town affairs included Spencer Wyndham Portal at Malshanger and Sir Richard Rycroft at Manydown. However, there were 'gentry' living in the town: Lefroy at West Ham and William Apletree, an annuitant, at Goldings who donated land to extend Eastrop church and cemetery.[23] The mayor, aldermen, councillors or magistrates were tradesmen and in the second half of the 19th century were often Nonconformists.[24] Among those of higher social status were 76 people supported by private or rentier incomes. 143 (16 per cent) households had live-in servants, usually young unmarried women; male live-in servants were rare. Of the 315 servants recorded 28 were male. Only a small number of households had more than two live-in servants. There were a few professionals: an architect, an engineer, three lawyers, one surgeon apothecary, three general practitioners – one also acting as a banker, the company secretary of the canal company, six ministers of religion,[25] five surveyors, 20 teachers and one veterinary surgeon. [26]

By 1881, the town had new industries, particularly clothing and engineering, and a rapidly growing urban area.[27] Forty-five people were living on their own means. Professionals still included an architect, three lawyers, but general practitioners had increased to five with 12 nurses, two midwives and one chemist. Ministers of religion, reflecting particularly the expansion of Nonconformity, had increased over twofold to 15 with four organists; similarly teachers had increased to 36 with eight governesses. Vets had doubled to two and surveyors increased to nine. There was greater diversification of roles with seven builders, three bank managers, two

19   Above, Economic Hist., Agriculture.
20   TNA, PROB 11/1633/295.
21   *Pigot's Dir.* (1831–2), 408.
22   See for example, HRO, 88M72/F1; 11M49/E/B4/3; 63M83/A5/1.
23   *RM*, 8 June 1835.
24   *Census*, 1851; *White's Dir.* (1859), 487.
25   Below, Religious Hist.
26   *Census*, 1851.
27   Above, Economic Hist., Industry.

civil engineers, three auctioneers, two magistrates and a reporter. There were 239 households with between them 378 servants. Only 28 servants were male, but two of these were butlers, a high-status role (at Goldings, owned by Samuel Field, a retired solicitor and The Shrubbery, where Ambrose Baker's income came from house property). Goldings also had the largest number of traditional servants – six. Only 86 houses had more than one servant, but one household recorded eight. However, in this household, most were indoor farm workers – possibly in the dairy. Across the town there were ten of these servants in husbandry, a role once considered to have ceased before 1881.[28]

Fig. 23. Lt Col John May, brewer, and six times mayor of Basingstoke.

Towards the end of the 19th century town society became increasingly dominated by some leading industrialists. The best example was John May, co-owner of the biggest brewery, who was mayor of Basingstoke six times between 1883 and 1902[29] and major benefactor to the people of Basingstoke. He built the Drill Hall in Sarum Hill and gave it to the town.[30] He erected a clock on the town hall in 1887 at a cost of £1,200 and donated the cricket ground to the club (Figs 23, 25).[31] John Mares, clothing manufacturer, entrepreneur and property dealer, owned the splendid Manor House (Fig. 24) from 1897 and many other residential and business properties in Basingstoke. He was a benefactor of the Cottage Hospital.[32] When he died in 1930 his estate was valued at £67,126 (£3.7m. in 2024).[33]

28   A. Kussmaul, *Servants in Husbandry in Early Modern England* (Cambridge, 1981); A. Howkins and N. Verdon, 'Adaptable and sustainable? Male farm service and agricultural labour in Midland and Southern England, *c*.1850–1925', *EcHR*, 61, 2 (2008), 467–495.

29   F. Ray, *The Mays of Basingstoke* (London and Basingstoke, 1904), 40. John May was a Lt Col in the Hampshire Volunteers (K Company, Basingstoke) and was often described as Lt Col John May or Col John May.

30   Below, Communal Life.

31   *Kelly's Dir.* (1923), 58; A. Attwood, *The Illustrated History of Basingstoke* (2001), 105–8; W. Fergie, 'Basingstoke's New Town Hall – Architect Lewis William Wyatt', *HFC Newsletter*, 68 (2017), 27.

32   *HBG*, 19 Apr. 2024.

33   HRO, 149A10/B10/10. https://www.bankofengland.co.uk/monetary-policy/inflation/inflation-calculator (accessed 7 Aug. 2024).

At the lower end of the social scale in the early 19th century the unskilled included up to 40 fathers a year who were labourers.[34] Some worked on farms while others were employed on construction and other sites. Below them were those who depended on poor rates. In 1851 there were 58 paupers and ten occupants of almshouses.[35] Many of these poor lived in the Totterdown area of the lower town south of the railway. In 1881 the disadvantaged included six paupers and 14 people living in almshouses. [36]

Fig. 24. John Mares' Manor House in 1930. HRO, 149A10/B10/10.

The next decades saw a considerable expansion of streets and population.[37] The population increase was mainly but not solely in the working classes.[38] Organisations representing their interests, such as trade unions and the Labour Party, began to play a more prominent part in the town's affairs during the early years of the 20th century.[39] The urban area developed dramatically to house the industrial workforce and some of the middle classes.[40] By the early years of the 20th century while some members of Basingstoke's wealthy industrial families had moved out into the surrounding villages, others remained in the town. In 1901 Thomas Burberry was living at the Elms in Hook[41] but two of Arthur Wallis' three older sons, all of whom were directors of Wallis and Steevens Ltd, were living in Basingstoke. John Ernest's home was at Erdesley[42]

34   HRO, 46M74/PR10, baptism registers.
35   *Census*, 1851.
36   *Census*, 1881.
37   HRO, 46M74/PZ49, 57.
38   TNA, ED109/1782.
39   Above, Economic Hist., Trade Unions; below, Local Government.
40   Above, Introduction, Settlement.
41   *Census*, 1901.
42   *Census*, 1911.

and Francis Ashby's at Sherborne House.[43] Both had 17 rooms and four servants. The remaining brother, William Alfred, had moved to Lawnswood in Mortimer West End, which had 16 rooms with three live-in servants.[44] In 1921 there were a few professional households including Dr James McPherson from Caithness whose visitor was a chartered accountant from London and who had two servants: a cook and a parlour maid.[45] Charles William Noakes of Ashley Lodge was managing director of John Mares with three domestic servants: a nurse, a parlour maid and a cook, together with a gardener. Hackwood House and its holdings in Basingstoke were leased by Lord Bolton to Lord Curzon of Kedleston Manor.[46]

One feature of Basingstoke society remained constant from 1800 to 1925. In 1921 Basingstoke, despite its industrialisation and national and world markets for its goods, still had fewer men in commercial and financial occupations than other Hampshire urban areas such as Bournemouth, Alton, Havant and Petersfield. Similarly, there were fewer professional men such as lawyers and doctors than in other towns including Bournemouth, Winchester, Fareham and Petersfield.[47] The number of female indoor servants was also lower in Basingstoke (26 per 1,000 of the total borough population) than other towns such as Winchester (63 per 1,000), Andover (36 per 1,000) or Fleet (80 per 1,000). This may be partly explained by Basingstoke having the highest number in the county (333 per 1,000 employed females) producing textiles and clothing.[48]

Communal Life

BASINGSTOKE'S GROWTH IN the 19th century provided new opportunities for the development of social, sporting and cultural activities but the town did not have a public library by 1925. Newly developed Bournemouth, in contrast, had public libraries from the 1890s.[49]

Friendly Societies

By 1837 the Oddfellows and other local benefit societies organised annual processions and country dances.[50] Later in Victoria's reign, similar programmes were hosted at the

---

43 *Census*, 1911.
44 *Census*, 1911.
45 *Census*, 1921.
46 *Kelly's Dir.* (1923), 61; HRO, 54M98/E/B4/45.
47 *Census Report Hants*, 1921, xxxiii.
48 *Census Report Hants*, 1921, xxxiv, xxxvi.
49 Following the Public Libraries Act of 1892; D.S. Young, *The Story of Bournemouth* (Wakefield, 1970), 144–5.
50 *HA*, 6 May 1837; *RM*, 29 June 1839; *BC*, 30 June 1849.

annual flower shows of the Horticultural Society.[51]

Freemasons

W.W.B. Beach MP of Oakley Hall founded Oakley Lodge in Basingstoke in August 1857 with 16 members. Meetings were originally held in a room at the Black Boy in Church Street. In 1885 a Masonic Hall was built as an annexe to the Drill Hall in Sarum Hill. Early members included John May, John Burgess Soper, John Lodwidge and John Lamb. In 1907 the Lodge had 55 members.[52]

Social Activities of Religious Organisations

A lot of social life in the Victorian period revolved around local churches. They entertained their congregations and the wider community at, for example 'Pleasant Saturday Evenings' with music and refreshments, arranged by London Street Congregational Church during the late 19th and early 20th centuries.[53] Bazaars and sales of work offered amusements, such as nail driving competitions for ladies and hat trimming competitions for gentlemen.[54] St Michael's offered Church of England Temperance Society meetings, Men's Society meetings, Church Lads' Brigade meetings, the choir, Sunday schools and occasional social events.[55] Primitive Methodists evangelised through anniversary celebrations, missions, camp meetings, concerts and entertainments.[56]

Temperance

The temperance movement in Basingstoke as elsewhere gained increasing prominence from the mid 19th century. Supporters of a war against drink included Thomas Burberry, the clothing manufacturer, who was President of the Basingstoke Total Abstinence Society; Revd Henry Barron, Minister of the London Street Congregational Church; Richard Wallis, a senior magistrate; Alderman Arthur Wallis of Wallis and Steevens and Councillors John Burgess Soper, Thomas Maton Kingdon who was president of the local branch of the teetotal Blue Ribbon Army,

51   *RM*, 24 Aug. 1878; *HBG,* 6 Aug. 1904.
52   *HBG,* 26 Oct. 1907. In 2024 the Masonic Hall was in Victoria Street.
53   R. Ottewill, 'Faith and Fun: Congregational Sponsored Social Activities in late Victorian and Edwardian Basingstoke – c.1880–1914', *Congregational Hist. Soc. Magazine,* 6, (Autumn, 2021), 297–309.
54   Below, Religious History.
55   HRO, 46M74/PZ57.
56   R. Ottewill, 'From Flaxfield Road to Sarum Hill: The Consolidation of Primitive Methodism in Basingstoke, c.1833 to 1923', *Proceedings of the Wesley Historical Society,* 62 (6), Autumn 2020, 247–55.

and Arkas Sapp, who was a deacon at the London Street Congregational Church.[57] The Basingstoke branch of the Church of England Temperance Society was founded in 1878.[58] The Angel Temperance café opened in 1881 (Fig. 12).[59] During the 1890s, the Basingstoke school board was commended by temperance organisations, such as the Good Templars and Band of Hope Union, for permitting lecturers to speak to the pupils about the adverse impact of alcohol on the human body and for allowing the school to be used for temperance examinations.[60] Some of those who opposed temperance joined the anti-Salvation Army riots in 1880–81.[61] Temperance continued to be important into the 20th century.

Institutes and Reading Rooms: the Mechanics' Institute

Founded in 1841, the Mechanics' Institute offered scientific and philosophical lectures and discussions. A library was established at Sarum House and public lectures were held at the town hall.[62] It was intended for boys and men but ladies and children under 14 could attend occasional lectures and social functions. In 1852 there were 190 members. Lord Portsmouth, its patron, believed that the Institute was the 'best means of keeping working classes from the dangers of the beer house and the allurement of the tempting doctrines of Socialism and Chartism'.[63]

A replacement building, including a concert hall, was opened in New Street in 1870 by Canon Charles Kingsley, rector of Eversley and author of *The Water Babies*.[64] The Institute with a membership of 300 became affiliated to the London Working Men's Club and Union.[65] The library contained 2,000 volumes in 1878 and 5,000 by 1927. There were calls by the 1890s for the Mechanics' Institute library to be transferred to the council and opened to the public,[66] although this eventually occurred only in 1928.[67] Ladies were admitted as full members in 1890. Chess and billiard tournaments were held as well as dinners, dances and concerts.[68] The Institute band played at special events in the town.[69]

---

57   B. Clarke, *The Basingstoke Riots: Massagainians v. the Salvation Army 1880–1883* (BAHS, 2010), 6.
58   HRO, 46M74/PZ26.
59   *HBG*, 16 Apr. 1881.
60   For example, *HBG*, 11 Jan. 1890, 10 Oct. 1894, 10 Dec. 1898.
61   Below, Riots and Disorder, Salvation Army Riots.
62   HRO, 148M71/13/1, 26 Feb. 1841, 2 Mar. 1841; *White's Dir.* (1859), 490.
63   HRO, 180M88/2.
64   Baigent and Millard, *Basingstoke*, 570. Building rebuilt as commercial offices in the 21st century.
65   *P.O. Dir.* (1875), 28.
66   *HBG*, 26 Nov. 1898.
67   Below.
68   *BG*, 16 Nov. 1990; *RM*, 9 July 1856, 11 Aug. 1883.
69   *HC*, and *RM*, both 23 Mar. 1867; Stokes, *Basingstoke*, 182.

By 1904–5 lectures were poorly attended as adult education classes developed in board schools and, after 1903, in council schools.[70] The military occupied the building for several months in 1915 and caused considerable damage. On re-opening there were only 56 members.[71] By 1928 despite an increase in numbers to 189 the Institute was insolvent and its library faced competition from libraries established in stationers' and chemists' shops in the town.[72] In 1911 three stationery shops had lending libraries, Bartlett's and Buckland's in Wote Street, and Knowles' in Winton Square.[73] A majority of Institute members decided the Institute was no longer viable and voted in 1928 to hand the building to the borough council who ran it as a free public library and museum.[74]

Entertainment Venues

Town Hall

Dances were held in the town hall in 1800 and these continued into the 20th century. Jane Austen attended these assembly balls.[75] The venue also staged June assemblies held in honour of the Monarch's birthday,[76] balls for the races, the Vyne Hunt and balls sponsored by Lady Patronesses led by Lady Bolton.[77] It was also a concert hall for the Choral Society and Philharmonic Society both founded in 1880.[78] In 1883 the two societies merged to form the Basingstoke Harmonic Society.[79] A new Basingstoke Choral Society was started in 1887.[80] It moved its concerts from the town hall to the Drill Hall in 1890 and disbanded in 1906 owing to a lack of male singers.[81]

The Corn Exchange

The Exchange, built in 1865,[82] also hosted travelling theatrical companies and minstrel

---

70   Below, Adult Education.
71   *HBG,* 23 Oct. 1915.
72   *HBG,* 25 Feb. 1928; HRO, 180M88/15.
73   *Basingstoke and District Dir.* (1911), 72.
74   HRO, 180M88/15.
75   Austen *Letters,* 25 Nov. 1798, 23 Jan. 1799, 1 Nov. 1800, 20 Nov. 1800; *RM,* 11 Sept. 1780, 14 Mar. 1796, 27 Oct. 1800, 16 Nov. 1801.
76   *RM,* 28 May 1798, 2 June 1800.
77   *RM,* 4 Sept. 1786, 16 Sept. 1800; *HC,* 24 Sept. 1792, 10 Oct. 1842; *London Evening-Post,* 10 June 1736, 28 Aug. 1746; *RM,* 20 Apr. 1772, 22 June 1778; *HC,* 9 Sept. 1811, 3 Sept. 1827, 13 Nov. 1841, 29 Sept. 1849; *RM,* 13 Nov. 1841; *HC,* 17 Feb. 1883, 21 Dec. 1907.
78   *BC,* 10 Apr. 1880, 23 Apr. 1881, 31 Dec. 1881, 15 Apr. 1882; *HC,* 1 July 1882; *RM,* 18 Dec. 1880, 25 Feb. 1882.
79   *BC,* 3 Feb. 1883, 5 Jan. 1884; *RM,* 24 Mar. 1884, 5 Mar. 1892; *HBG,* 2 Dec. 1893, 2 Feb. 1895, 8 Jan. 1898, 13 Oct. 1900.
80   *HBG,* 10 Sept. 1887.
81   *HBG,* 19 Apr. 1890, 28 Apr. 1906. There is a choral society in Basingstoke in 2024 but tracing a continuous history is difficult.
82   *BC,* 25 Feb. 1865.

shows.[83] The Amateur Dramatic Society performed in aid of the Royal Hampshire County Hospital[84] and the Cottage Hospital.[85] Madame Selby's Court Choir show in 1898 featured a cinematograph showing 'moving pictures'.[86] In 1913 Edwin Casey opened the Grand Exchange Cinema and Vaudeville Theatre showing films and live entertainment.[87] It was badly damaged by fire in 1925 and later rebuilt, becoming the Haymarket Theatre in 1951.[88]

Cinema

The first purpose-built cinema in Basingstoke was the Electric Theatre on Wote Street which opened in 1910 with seating for over 500.[89]

Drill Hall

John May of May's Brewery built the Drill Hall in 1884 on Sarum Hill for the K (Basingstoke) Company of the Hants Rifle Volunteers, of which he was the commander. It was the largest hall in the town measuring 100ft by 50ft[90] and hosted theatrical performances, concerts and dances. Mr D'Oyly Carte's company performed there in 1888 and 1890.[91] Amateur dramatic performances raised funds for the Cottage Hospital.[92]

Inns and Alehouses

Public houses continued to provide lively centres for leisure activity, endorsed by many but frowned on by some.[93] Two public houses, the Grapes and the Victoria, had bowling clubs. Each had their own green for home matches until the early 20th century. Some pubs, including The Rose [Inn], Anchor, Red Lion and The Barge, had their own benefit societies. They usually marked their anniversaries by parading through the town and holding a dance in the evening. The dances were held either in a hall above the pub or in a nearby meadow.[94]

83   *HBG,* 12 Aug. 1893, 15 May 1897, 7 Sept. 1901, 30 Nov. 1901.
84   *HC,* 16 Jan. 1869, 7 Oct. 1882; *BC,* 18 Apr. 1874, 2 Dec. 1876; *RM,* 9 Feb. 1878.
85   *RM,* 6 Jan. 1883, 19 Nov. 1887.
86   *HBG,* 23 Apr. 1898.
87   *HBG,* 14 June 1913.
88   *HBG,* 23 May 1925; https://www.anvilarts.org.uk/about-us/history/history-of-the-haymarket (accessed 10 Nov. 2024).
89   *HBG,* 15 Oct. 1910.
90   *HC,* 2 Feb. 1884.
91   *The Stage,* 8 June 1888, 11 July 1890.
92   *HBG,* 13 Jan. 1894, 20 Apr. 1901.
93   Above, Economic Hist., Public Houses; above, Temperance.
94   *HBG,* 3 Sept. 1892, 25 Sept. 1897, 17 Oct. 1903, 15 Sept. 1906; *HA,* 6 May 1837; *BC,* 30 June 1849; *HC,* 2 July 1859; *RM,* 31 May 1856.

Amateur sport

Athletics

In 1884 the football, cricket and cycling clubs amalgamated as the Basingstoke Athletic Club[95] whose sports day in 1892 attracted 2,000 visitors.[96] In 1893 the Athletic Club had 250 members practising many sports and was the second largest athletics club in Hampshire[97] but the amalgamation ceased in 1894 when the committee concluded that it was unworkable and, if continued, would probably result in bankruptcy.[98]

Cricket

In 1824 Basingstoke Cricket Club [99] played home matches on Basingstoke Common[100] and from 1853 at Paice's Folly, also known as the Folly.[101] In 1880 John May, then President of the Cricket Club, purchased the Folly and in 1905 he donated it to

Fig. 25. John May handing over the cricket ground 23 May 1905.

95   *RM*, 20 Dec. 1884.
96   *HBG*, 11 June 1892.
97   *HBG*, 24 June 1893.
98   *HBG*, 12 May 1894.
99   *Star*, 23 Aug. 1824.
100 HRO, 8M62/27 (1830 entry); *Windsor and Eton Express*, 2 Aug. 1828; *Salisbury and Winchester Jnl*, 9 Sept. 1833; *BC*, 17 Sept. 1842.
101 *HC*, 13 Aug. 1853.

trustees for the club (Fig. 25).[102] The ground was renamed May's Bounty in 1881.[103] In 1901 a new pavilion was built and the club became the Basingstoke and North Hants Cricket Club.[104] Hampshire played Warwickshire at May's Bounty in 1906[105] and Derbyshire in 1914, after which county matches were not played there until 1938.[106] In 2024 the thriving club was still playing at the Bounty.[107]

Cycling

The Basingstoke Cycling Club was started in 1892.[108] At their first annual dinner held at the Wheatsheaf in February 1893, a speaker remarked that 'persons of both sexes who went in for cycling derived great benefit from it'.[109] Occasionally both men's and ladies' cycle races were held on the cycle track at May's Bounty.[110]

Football

Basingstoke Football Club was founded in 1870[111] based at the Folly.[112] For a decade from 1884 it was part of the Athletic Club (above). In 1894 it restarted based[113] at Cannon's meadow, adjoining May's Bounty.[114] In 1895 there were three football clubs: Basingstoke, Basingstoke Albion and North Hants Iron Works.[115] Basingstoke joined the Hampshire Football League in 1901, in combination with the North Hants Iron Works' team from 1910.[116] Thornycroft Athletic Club was admitted to the North Division of the Hampshire Football League in 1912.[117]

Golf

Basingstoke and District Golf Club opened in 1907, with a nine-hole course on a 60 a. field west of Reading Road.[118] The course was extended to 12 holes in 1909 when the club had 150 members.[119] During the First World War the golf course was used as

102 *HBG*, 8 July 1905.
103 *HBG*, 21 May 1881; HRO, 50A07/E68.
104 *HBG*, 25 May 1901.
105 *HBG*, 26 May 1906.
106 *Westminster Gaz.*, 27 May 1914; HRO, 50A07/E68.
107 https://alloutcricket.com/clubs/basingstoke-north-hants-cricket-club/ (accessed 22 June 2024).
108 *HBG*, 27 Feb. 1892.
109 *HBG*, 11 Feb. 1893.
110 For example, *HBG*, 29 May 1897, 6 May 1899.
111 *BC*, 25 Nov. 1871.
112 *Newbury Weekly News*, 7 Nov. 1878.
113 *HBG*, 13 Oct. 1894.
114 *HBG*, 8 Dec. 1894.
115 *HBG*, 28 Sept. 1895.
116 *HBG*, 5 Oct. 1901, 27 Aug. 1910, 10 Sept. 1910.
117 *HBG*, 7 Sept. 1912.
118 *HBG*, 14 Dec. 1907.
119 *HBG*, 30 Apr. 1910.

an airfield to train pilots. It never reverted to a golf course and games were played elsewhere until 1928 when a replacement course was opened at Kempshott Park.[120]

Horse Racing

The Basingstoke races[121] featured on the national racing calendar, taking place until 1786 on a course on Basingstoke Down.[122] They restarted in 1811 but the location is unknown.[123] The duke of Wellington officiated as steward at the 1823 races, with an audience reputedly of 'many thousands'.[124] There were no races from 1830 to 1845,[125] but one last race took place in 1850 on the common.[126]

Swimming

The Basingstoke Swimming Club began in 1892,[127] meeting at Wote Street baths. It organised sports competitions including water polo[128] until 1900 when the baths closed.[129] In 1906 the corporation open-air swimming baths at West Ham opened[130] and a new swimming club was formed.[131]

Tennis Clubs

The London Street Mutual Improvement Society had a tennis club.[132]

Civic Celebrations

The streets of Basingstoke staged civic celebrations. In 1856 a procession half a mile long, led by the mayor and accompanied by a band, celebrated the end of the Crimean War. Some 2,200 poor parishioners from Basingstoke and Eastrop dined out along London and Winchester Streets, followed by dancing, wheelbarrow races, greasy pole climbing and fireworks.[133] Processions celebrated Queen Victoria's Golden and Diamond Jubilees.[134] Following the armistice in 1918 a mile long Grand Armistice Carnival Procession with 60 floats, mainly organised by Thornycroft staff,

---

120 B.E. Knight, *The History of Basingstoke Golf Club 1907–2007* (2007), 7; See also *Dummer and Kempshott,* 79.
121 *VCH Hants,* V, 543–4.
122 *London Gaz.,* 29 Aug. 1689; *RM,* 19 June 1786.
123 *Salisbury and Winchester Jnl,* 26 Aug. 1811.
124 *Morning Chron.,* 10 Sept. 1823.
125 *BC,* 2 Oct. 1830, 19 July 1845; *RM,* 6 Sept. 1845.
126 *Bell's Life in London,* 29 Sept. 1850.
127 *HBG,* 12 Mar. 1892.
128 *HBG,* 1 Oct. 1892 and 22 Sept. 1894.
129 *HBG,* 28 July 1900.
130 *HBG,* 14 July 1906.
131 *HBG,* 21 July 1906.
132 *HBG,* 16 July 1892. Below, Parks, for public courts.
133 *BC, HC* and *RM,* 31 May 1856.
134 *RM,* 25 June 1887; *HBG,* 26 June 1897.

paraded the town centre.[135] Circuses visited Basingstoke from the mid 19th century. They paraded the streets with elephants and camels before setting up in a field.[136] Their acts included wire walkers, acrobats, performing lions, freak shows and the flying trapeze.[137]

Parks

The Castle or Fairfields Recreation Ground opened on 19 May 1892 with a bandstand, a children's play area with swings, a seesaw and a sand pit for infants.[138] In 1904 two tennis courts and a bowling green opened.[139] The council decided in 1909 to buy Deep Lane Meadow for £600 to become a public park which was named King George's Playing Fields in 1911.[140] A third public park, the War Memorial Park (18 a.) opened in 1923 with nine tennis courts and a bandstand.[141]

Education

I N 1800 THE Holy Ghost grammar school provided classical education to fee-paying pupils. During the 19th century some small private schools, often short-lived, attracted better-off families. The Blue Coat school and churches, in Sunday and charity schools, offered some education for the poor.

The 19th century saw the implementation of a national system of elementary education for poor children.[142] From 1811 Church of England National schools and from 1838 Nonconformist British schools educated the poor of Basingstoke.[143] In 1818 the poor were reported by a government commission to have ample means of education in Basingstoke.[144] There was a small Roman Catholic school by 1881.[145] The introduction of non-denominational board schools after 1870 was at first resisted but in 1885 a school board was established made up of Anglicans and Nonconformists. The board schools opened in 1888 and transferred to Hampshire County Council in 1903, which in 1908 founded the Girls' High School. Adult education in the 19th

135 https://collections.hampshireculture.org.uk/object/thornycroft-float-armistice-procession-1918–1, (accessed 23 June 2024).
136 *RM*, 21 June 1845, 23 Aug. 1862; *HBG*, 10 June 1899, 19 Sept. 1910.
137 *HBG*, 23 July 1892, 10 June 1899.
138 *HBG*, 21 May 1892.
139 *HBG*, 30 Apr. 1904.
140 *HBG*, 25 Dec. 1909; *HO*, 10 May 1911.
141 Below, First World War and its Aftermath; *Kelly's Dir.* (1923), 58.
142 Elementary schools taught pupils up to the age of 14.
143 HRO, 128M84/16; 8M62/C2/21.
144 Parl. Papers, 1818 (224). *Select Committee on Education of the Poor*.
145 *Census*, 1881; TNA, ED 2/191.

century was provided by the Mechanics' Institute and churches but from 1890 more formal classes, offered at the board schools, superseded these.

Private Schools

Holy Ghost/Queen Mary's Grammar School

The Holy Ghost (later Queen Mary's) grammar school was founded in 1555, next to the Holy Ghost chapel in the Liten (Fig. 26).[146] The school received bequests and endowments of money and land before 1800. By 1800 the Crown appointed the headmaster.[147] Classics was taught free of charge,[148] but fees were charged for history, geography, writing and arithmetic. There were 12 scholars in 1825 but only

Fig. 26. Liten (Holy Ghost) chapel and school in the 18th century.

eight in 1849 when the school closed temporarily.[149] In 1852 the Court of Chancery established a new management scheme with eight trustees: the vicar and mayor; with three chosen by the town council and three by the Borough Charity Trustees.[150] All had to be Anglican (except the mayor). The headmaster, a graduate of Oxford or Cambridge, was assisted by an usher appointed by the corporation. Pupils were aged

146 Hare, *Medieval Basingstoke,* 83–88; *VCH Hants,* II, 372.

147 *VCH Hants,* II, 383–4.

148 *HA,* 29 Mar. 1845.

149 HRO, TOP19/1/37.

150 *VCH Hants,* II, 383; HRO, 8M62/C5/1/7.

seven to 18 years; 30 boarders were permitted. A new school building was opened on Worting Road in 1855.[151] In 1866 the school was renamed the Queen's Free school and soon became known as Queen Mary's school.[152] Robert Cottle (d. 1862), mayor and bookseller, bequeathed £220 for three prizes of 'good and useful books'.[153] A brass inscription commemorating the Cottle Prize was in the Vyne Community school in 2024.[154]

From 1861–6 five boys went to Oxford, Cambridge and Dublin Universities; others passed examinations for the civil, military and East India services.[155] Concerns about educational standards, particularly of the younger boys, and whether more commercial subjects should be taught, were expressed at times, especially in 1869–70.[156] When Revd Arthur Forster Rutty (1873–1883) became headmaster he brought 60 boarders from his old school in Kent creating much needed revenue for paying the masters.[157] A new school room was completed in 1875 funded by a sale of some Liten land and voluntary subscriptions.[158] Some less affluent boys received scholarships from the Richard Aldworth Foundation.[159] When Rutty resigned in 1883 there were 85 boys on the register, 55 of them day boys, the highest number ever achieved. In 1885 governors replaced trustees.[160]

In 1893 the school offered science, shorthand, bookkeeping, commercial arithmetic, mathematics, English, French and classics.[161] Results were good especially in Latin and mathematics.[162] In 1898 a physics laboratory was constructed, financed by the town council and the Science and Art Department of the Board of Trade in London. This was in accordance with government policy from 1890, of promoting secondary advanced science and technical education, to give pupils skills for industrial employment.[163]

Following the 1902 Education Act, the school received grants from Hampshire County Council and the Board of Education which, with real estate, provided most of its income.[164] Free places were offered to elementary students resulting in an increased roll from 56 in 1906 to 73 in 1907. By 1912, the numbers stabilised as wealthier

151 HRO, 28M68/15/4; the land belonged to Thomas Workman, surgeon.
152 HRO, 8M62/C5/1/7; TNA, ED 27/1491.
153 HRO, 28M68/1.
154 TNA, ED 27/1494.
155 Parl. Papers (1867–8), (3966-X), *School enquiry commission, S.E. division*, 315–9.
156 HRO, 22M68/1.
157 HRO, 28M68/1.
158 HRO, 28M68/1.
159 Below, Blue Coat school.
160 HRO, 28M68/1.
161 *BG,* 25 Mar. 1893.
162 TNA, ED 27/1504.
163 E.G. Stokes and R.C. Crossman, *Queen Mary's School 1556–1972* (1972), 26–7; G.R. Searle, *A New England? Peace and War 1886–1918* (Oxford, 2004), 628; TNA, ED 109/1781.
164 TNA, ED 109/1782.

parents opted for children to board at public schools and the population increase was largely in the working classes who attended the council schools.[165] Queen Mary's school was the boys' school for post 14 education with 146 pupils in 1922 but only 11 of them were over 14 and the inspector lamented that many boys treated it like a public elementary school.[166]

Blue Coat School 1646–1879
Sir Richard Aldworth (d. 1646) bequeathed £2,000 to Basingstoke corporation to provide education, food and clothing to ten poor boys of the town, aged seven to 14 to learn reading, writing and arithmetic at the school in Cross Street and to attend church.[167] The school was a symmetrical, five-bay, two-storey, gothic revival building, with cross bays and exposed red-brick with strip courses in contrasting coloured brick.[168] After schooling they were apprenticed.[169] The boys' uniform included two blue jackets, hence the name.[170]

From 1811 the boys shared their teacher and the Cross Street premises with pupils of the newly created National school.[171] The Blue Coat boys lived on the premises and the cost of feeding and clothing them was frequently subsidized by the corporation.[172] The school closed in 1879 but the trust offered scholarships to support education for boys mainly at Queen Mary's and after 1907 for girls at the High school.[173]

19th Century Private Schools
Flaxfield College (c.1818–c.1899) was a boys' school, where in 1859 Thomas Browne was head.[174] By 1881 Dr Arthur Greenwood was headmaster and the school housed 16 boarders aged 11 to 16.[175] Some pupils left Queen Mary's in the 1870s to join this school,[176] as boys were trained for business pursuits. There were some 60 day boys

165 TNA, ED 35/928; ED 109/1781; 109/1782; HRO, 8M62/C5/1/23. It was renamed Queen Mary's School in 1941.
166 TNA, ED 109/1781. In 1971 Queen Mary's became part of Charles Chute secondary school (the Vyne School in 2024) for 11 to 16 year olds. Sixth formers transferred to a college which became Queen Mary's College.
167 HRO, 10M57/L149.
168 Stokes, *Basingstoke*, illustration page 169.
169 Aldworth's mother was born in Basingstoke; at the time of his death he lived in Milk Street, London. HRO, 10M57/L149; Parl. Papers 1826 (382) *Report of charities for the education of the poor*, 14, 393.
170 Parl. Papers 1826 (382) 14, 391; HRO, 10M57/L149.
171 Willis Museum, BWM, 2011,184.
172 Parl. Papers 1826 (382) 14, 394.
173 HRO, 49M97/17.
174 *White's Dir.* (1859), 492; R. Ottewill, 'Flaxfield House/College: A Brief History, *c.*1830 to *c.*1900', *BAHS Newsletter*, No 244, Aug. 2023, 16–23.
175 *Census*, 1881.
176 HRO, 22M68/1.

who studied an academic or commercial curriculum with good results.[177] By 1891 there were only two boarders and the school closed in 1899 and became a workshop owned by John Mares.[178]

National Schools 1811–1888

Basingstoke's National schools from 1811 promoted Anglican education in rented premises for boys (Cross Street), girls (Church Cottage, Church Square) and infants (part of the vicarage). The vicar of Basingstoke, Thomas Sheppard (d. 1814) left c.£1,000 in trust for boys and girls to be taught under the National Scheme.[179] By 1819 there were 170 pupils.[180] The National Society acknowledged that some opposed educating the poor as it could increase their power in society but it believed that a Christian education had a great moral and civilising impact.[181] Pupil numbers increased steadily: there were 370 pupils by 1870 when the Church Square premises were enlarged. The school relied on voluntary subscriptions and children's pence, which by the 1870s were inadequate and, from at least 1868 government grants were paid, providing about one third of its income.[182] Additionally from 1873 the Anglican mission at Totterdown, Reading Road, ran a ragged school for nearly 50 very poor children. The Education Department in London acknowledged that the school was doing good work but stated its methods could not be recognised by the Department.[183] By 1878 the National schools lacked the capacity to take all children who applied for admission so the National Society decided to convert the mission school in Totterdown into a public elementary school with a certificated mistress. The school was financed by parishioners.[184] Totterdown elementary school for boys and girls opened in September 1878 and in 1881 it had 79 pupils.[185] It received funding from the National schools but was only used as a school for ten years until Fairfields schools opened.[186] The mission hall continued to hold services.[187] The National schools resisted the establishment of a school board as they thought religious teaching would be neglected.[188]

By the 1880s, the poor state of the premises led to the creation of a school board.

---

177 *HBG*, 25 Dec. 1880.
178 HRO, 58M74/BP102.
179 *White's Dir.* (1859), 489.
180 Parl. Papers, 1819 (224), *Digest of parochial returns on schools,* 827.
181 HRO, 128M84/18 (1829 and 1830).
182 HRO, 128M84/16.
183 Below, Religious Hist., Anglican Mission Halls; TNA, ED 2/191; HRO, 46M74/PZ23.
184 HRO, 46M74/PZ23, 26.
185 HRO, 46M74/PZ32.
186 TNA, ED 2/191.
187 Below, Religious Hist., Anglican Mission Halls.
188 HRO, 8M62/C3/4; J. Butler and R. Ottewill, 'Resisting a School Board in Basingstoke: 1870–1885', *History of Education Researcher*, No 111, May 2023, 12–22.

When the Fairfields board schools opened in 1888 the National schools closed, and all pupils transferred.

British Schools

The British schools taught mainly Nonconformist pupils in purpose-built premises. The infants' school opened in 1838 in the Congregational church, followed in 1841 by the co-educational school for older boys and girls built on Sarum Hill with three rooms. It was a classical, four-bay, single-storey building, with sash windows separated by Tuscan pilasters. To the left of the main building was a covered open space. Following the 1870 Education Act, a new infants' school was built in 1875, partly funded by the Education Department in London.[189] The balance of the money was raised by grants from the corporation, the British and Foreign School Society and local subscriptions.[190] The cost of the school management was met by the children's pence, subscriptions from friends of the school and from 1862 by a government capitation grant.[191] It was not until 1877 that voluntary contributions were superseded by an annual grant from the corporation.[192] The trustees in 1867 included leading Nonconformists: John Burgess Soper, Charles James Steevens and Arthur Wallis.[193] In 1875 the British schools opposed setting up a school board.[194] In 1875–6 the school of 142 boys and 64 girls was rated satisfactory.[195] By 1884 the total roll was 378 comprising 134 boys, 96 girls and 148 infants.[196] When Fairfields board schools opened in 1888, all pupils transferred.[197]

Board Schools, later Hampshire County Council Schools

Revd Canon Millard in 1884 asserted that 1,500 pupils in the town needed proper education.[198] In 1885 a school board was established[199] because the National school buildings were unfit for use.[200]

---

189 HRO, 8M62/C2/21; TNA, ED 103/117. The land was purchased for £189 on a 999 year lease from John May.
190 TNA, ED 103/117.
191 HRO, 8M62/C2/21.
192 HRO, 8M62/C2/21.
193 HRO, 8M62/C2/23.
194 HRO, 8M62/C2/14/2.
195 TNA, ED 2/191.
196 HRO, 8M62/C2/21.
197 The building later became a Baptist church; below, Religious Hist., Open Baptists.
198 *HBG*, 3 Jan. 1885, 25 Mar. 1885.
199 HRO, 22M88/1, 1–2.
200 HRO, 22M88/1, 14.

Hants & Berks Gazette.

SPECIAL EDITION.   SATURDAY, FEBRUARY 18, 1888.   HALFPENNY.

BASINGSTOKE BOARD SCHOOLS.

SENIOR SCHOOL.

INFANTS' SCHOOL.

Fig. 27. Fairfields board schools, 1888.

Fairfields

The site for the Fairfields schools was chosen as a healthy location for children and the name reflected the fairs previously held there.[201] Three schools: infants, junior boys and junior girls opened on 16 February 1888 with 1,310 pupils (Fig. 27).[202] The head teachers included George Gage, former head of the British school.[203] Accommodation for 380 boys was on the ground floor with 430 girls on the first floor. The classrooms opened out from a central hall used for drill, assemblies and recreation and were fitted with dual desks, and galleries.[204] The girls' floor had a cookery area. The infants' single storey building was for 500 pupils (entering at age three or four and leaving at six years).[205]

From 1889–90 prizes and medals were awarded for good attendance but in 1892 a scarlet fever epidemic closed the schools for up to seven months.[206] No fees were charged for primary education following the 1891 Education Act.[207] Hampshire CC managed the schools following the 1902 Education Act. In 1909 the upper school was 'excellent' but by 1911 the lower school had difficulties owing to the number of 'very backward boys' admitted.[208] From 1909 no pupils under five were admitted to Fairfields or to Brook Street and St John's schools.[209] On leaving, the majority of boys did commercial or industrial work.[210] Cookery classes for girls were transferred to Sarum Hill.[211] Attendance in 1914 was 94 per cent for boys and 91 per cent for girls.[212]

The standard curriculum was expanded to include football, swimming and country walks outside school hours.[213] There were frequent closures for epidemic diseases such as whooping cough or mumps.[214] From December 1914 until March 1915 Fairfields, Brook Street and St John's schools were all taken over by the military.[215]

By 1916 the accommodation for boys was increased to 426.[216] In 1921 the girls' school was 'good', the boys achieved a lower standard and the infants suffered as some only started school at seven years.[217] In 1923 the mixed schools were reorganised to

201 TNA, ED 21/6272. The corporation of Basingstoke offered the land in 1886 on a 99 year lease.
202 TNA, ED 21/6272.
203 HRO, 22M88/1, 154.
204 J.R. John, *Fairfields Schools, Basingstoke 1888–1979* (1979), 15.
205 *HBG,* 18 Feb. 1888.
206 HRO, 22M88/1, 285, 416, 426.
207 HRO, 22M88/1, 383, 435.
208 TNA, ED 21/6272.
209 HRO, 309M97/A1, 75; below, Brook Street and St John's.
210 HRO, 309M87/A1.
211 HRO, 309M87/A1, 11.
212 HRO, 309M87/A1, 1.
213 HRO, 309M87/A1, 11.
214 HRO, 309M87/A1, 96, 118.
215 HRO, 309M87/A1.
216 TNA, ED 21/6272.
217 TNA, ED 21/29242.

become Fairfields senior boys and girls with 389 and 321 pupils. At the same time, the infants' department was renamed Fairfields junior mixed school.[218]

Brook Street (later Brookvale)

The growth of the town necessitated the provision of more school places and in 1909 a new council school opened in Brook Street for 280 mixed junior and 150 infant pupils mainly from the Brookvale area.[219] In 1914 an inspector noted that pupil attainments were low and that even allowing for the disadvantaged backgrounds of pupils more progress should have been made especially by the children aged 12 and 13.[220] Similar concerns about the older children were expressed in 1921.[221] In 1922 older children transferred to Fairfields school and by 1923 Brook Street became a junior school with 248 pupils. Pupils were received from the immediate area and St John's school.[222] The infant school achieved a good standard.[223] Concern was still being expressed about the low attainment of children and in 1925 an extra mistress was appointed to teach those certified as 'mentally deficient' by the county medical officer, but later reports suggested improvement.[224]

Girls' High School

In 1908 Hampshire County Council converted Brook House in Brook Street, opposite St John's, as a High school for girls.[225] It opened as the only state provided secondary school in Basingstoke with a pupil-teacher centre, training girls for teaching, which was financed by the Board of Education in London and 30 fee paying seniors.[226] The school received large grants from the London Board of Education and Hampshire CC.[227] During the first six months the roll increased to 60 of whom 15 were pupil-teachers.[228] Over half of the girls lived in Basingstoke, the remainder coming from further afield.[229] In 1912 the 80 pupils and six teachers moved to a new purpose built school in Crossborough Hill, off London Road, considered to be a healthy, elevated

218 TNA, ED 21/29242; since 1987 all the pupils have been accommodated in the old junior school building, to which more classrooms were added. The infants' school became an Arts Centre and then the venue for Proteus Theatre Company: https://www.fairfields.hants.sch.uk/, (accessed 23 June 2024).

219 TNA, ED 21/6270.

220 HRO, 309M87/A1; TNA, ED 21/6270.

221 TNA, ED 21/29240.

222 HRO, 309M87/A1; below, St John's Church of England schools.

223 TNA, ED 21/29240.

224 HRO, 309M87/A1. Brookvale school closed in 1985 and the buildings were converted into housing: HRO, 142M85.

225 HRO, 64A00/P7; TNA, ED 109/1778; ED 35/927; HRO, H/CX12/1, Vol. I.

226 HRO, 30M65/23; TNA, ED 109/1778.

227 TNA, ED 109/1781.

228 HRO, 44M99/4.

229 From Farnborough and Whitchurch, for example. HRO, 64A00–P7–1; TNA, ED 109/1778; HRO, H/CX12/1, Vol. I; TNA, ED 35/927.

location.[230] By 1922 there were 207 pupils but most left at 14 or 15 and academic results varied: botany was good, but history, geography, French and mathematics were less satisfactory. Only five pupils stayed for sixth form.[231]

St John's Church of England School

The vicar of Basingstoke, Revd H. Cooper Smith, launched an appeal fund in 1894 to build new Sunday schools to promote the Anglican faith.[232] The fund, aided by an anonymous donation of £1,500, purchased the old Merton farm on Church Street, where St John's Hospital had been. Commodious Sunday school buildings were opened on the site by the bishop of Winchester in November 1900.[233] The two-storey building was Arts and Crafts inspired with a tiled gabled roof, an exposed brick ground floor and a rendered first storey. In 1901 the Board of Education, recognising that educational provision in the town was insufficient, approved the use of St John's as day schools.[234] They opened in June of that year, with 150 infants and 151 mixed junior pupils, financed by government grants and donations but not by the school board. Enrolment prioritised children whose parents wanted an Anglican education in the tradition of the National schools, followed by children who lived near the school.[235] The school was frequently oversubscribed. Attendance was free but many parents made contributions to school funds.[236] Appeal funds helped to finance desks and other equipment. Gifts such as a doll's house with furniture from Burberry's for the infants and a typewriter for older girls enhanced the school's teaching. In 1904 a fund was launched to enlarge the schools.[237] Religious teaching in the schools was highly rated by Diocesan inspectors.[238] In most years HMI's reports were very positive but reservations about lack of effort by girls in 1908 and of indiscipline and lower attainments of the pupils were expressed by the inspector in 1910, after which reports improved again.[239] Reservations were frequently expressed about girls' absences to look after younger siblings.[240] In 1914 arithmetic teaching required improvement and the infants needed greater skills to enable independent work.[241] In 1909 there were 246 infants and 232 mixed pupils.[242] By 1922 there were 245 mixed pupils and 180 infants and the school

230 TNA, ED 35/927; ED 109/1778.
231 TNA, ED 109/1779. Renamed Harriet Costello school in 1971 and converted into a mixed comprehensive. From 2012 renamed The Costello school.
232 HRO, 46M74/PZ43; PZ45, 13–14.
233 HRO, TOP 19/3/25; 46M74/PZ44, 26; PZ49, 110.
234 HRO, 138A14/3.
235 HRO, 46M74/PZ46, 35; PZ50, 14, 43, 67; PZ51, 14–15, 27.
236 HRO, 46M74/PZ51, 110.
237 HRO, 46M74/53, 4, 131–2.
238 For example, HRO, 46M74/PZ52, 8; 46M74/56, 31.
239 HRO, 46M74/PZ52, 39.
240 HRO, 46M74/PZ52, 47.
241 HRO, 138A14/9.
242 HRO, 46M74/PZ57, 31.

received largely satisfactory reports from the Board of Education.[243]

Adult Education

The need for technical education to equip the workforce was recognised in the 20th century. Before that, the Mechanics' Institute, founded in 1841, educated adult members especially about science and technology.[244] Evening classes were offered during the winter for reading, writing and arithmetic.[245] Similarly, Nonconformists, believing that the institutional church should enhance people's lives, opened mutual improvement societies for adults.[246] From the mid-19th century London Street Congregational church offered lectures and stimulated debates to develop understanding and skills. St Michael's church also offered classes.[247]

However, before 1914 both the lectures of the Mechanics' Institute and the debates of the Congregationalists lost attendees. Adult learning transferred to more formal classes. From 1889 the school board organised evening classes for those over 13 years, financed by the sale of the British school buildings.[248] They ran evening classes in Fairfields and Sarum Hill in technical drawing, woodwork, technology, engineering, art, domestic science, shorthand, bookkeeping, typewriting and tailoring.[249] Evening classes were open to men and women, but the biggest group was boys under 16 studying mathematics and technical drawing. From 1924 metalwork and woodwork classes were held at Fairfields.[250]

By 1925 the Board of Education in London, noting that engineering to produce motor lorries and steam rollers were two of the staple industries of Basingstoke, advocated the building of a technical school which offered senior engineering, science and mathematics courses.[251]

Thornycroft Works School

To meet the need for technical education in 1920 Thornycroft opened a works school. At this, engineering pupils studied mathematics, mechanics, heat, physics, machine design and geometry, chemistry, magnetism and electricity two half days a week

---

243 HRO, 138A14/13; TNA, ED 21/29241. Building demolished 1960s. Rebuilt south of town centre. St John's still thrived in 2024. https://www.st-johnscofe.hants.sch.uk/ (accessed 23 June 2024).

244 HRO, 148M71/13/1 and above.

245 HRO, 148M71/13/1.

246 R. Ottewill, 'Churches and Adult Education in the Edwardian Era: Learning from the Experiences of Hampshire Congregationalists' in M. Ludlow, C. Methuen and A. Spicer (eds) *Studies in Church History 55: The Church and Education* (Cambridge, 2019), 494–510.

247 HRO, 46M74/PZ10.

248 HRO, 22M88/1, 272, 276, 363; 8M62/C2/24.

249 HRO, 22M88/1, 371, 431; TNA, ED 41/55; 114/240; *Kelly's Dir.* (1915), 57.

250 TNA, ED 21/29242.

251 TNA, ED 41/55; ED 114/240.

for three years.[252] Pupils aimed to become mechanical engineers and managers at Thornycroft works or in the wider world. Apprentices attended technical classes studying to be fitters and machinists in the workshops. Twelve different classes catered for ability and attainment with a maximum of 15 students in each. From 1922 a brochure advertised the school to potential recruits. They wanted recognition by the Board of Education but did not reach an agreement with Hampshire CC until 1929, when the school was inspected by the Board of Education and found to be efficient.[253]

Social Welfare

The Poor Law

In 1800 the town had a workhouse in Brook Street, where inmates were farmed out by the parish for 2*s*. 6*d*. to 4*s*. a week.[254] In 1803, 33 paupers were relieved in the workhouse and 124 outside (and 1,865 vagrants received casual relief).[255] This increased to 230 paupers in 1815,[256] causing more properties to be used. Between 1783 and 1827, the annual cost of poor relief in Basingstoke increased from £632 to £2,436.[257] This was in line with national trends, resulting from increased population, war, depression and poor harvests. The national cost led to the 1834 Poor Law Amendment Act which introduced the workhouse test to deter the poor from claiming relief.[258]

Basingstoke poor law union, comprising 37 parishes from Basingstoke, Bramley, Dummer and Old Basing districts, built a workhouse in 1836 between Basingstoke and Old Basing. The cost of £7,500 was partly recouped by selling the houses for the poor owned by individual parishes. Although designed to house up to 400 paupers, it rarely held more than 150–200.[259] Many entered for short periods either when employment was lacking or young children were left to relieve the family finances.[260] Despite the aims of the 1834 Act and in common with the rest of England, most poor continued to be relieved outside the workhouse (out relief), in a generally constant ratio of 6:1. This was much cheaper than in relief. Most of the workhouse inmates were children, the elderly or disabled and were predominantly from agricultural, labouring or domestic service families.[261]

---

252 Above, Economic Hist., Thornycroft.
253 TNA, ED 74/3. The school closed in 1938 as the company faced financial difficulties. Above, Economic Hist., Thornycroft.
254 HRO, 46M74/PV2, 29.
255 Parl. Papers, 1803–4 (175), Poor Abstract, 451.
256 Parl. Papers, 1819 (224), 844.
257 Parl. Papers, various 1783 to 1827.
258 Poor Law Amendment Act 1834, 4 & 5 Will 4 c.76.
259 HRO, PL3/5/1.
260 Large, *Workhouse*, 17–18, 55–6.
261 HRO, PL3/5/1–29; TNA, MH 12/10669 to 10699.

In the workhouse, life was strictly prescribed by the poor law officials in London.[262] Everyone worked if able, usually at maintaining the establishment, and until the late 19th century, the elderly were often employed picking oakum. Frequently there were not enough able-bodied inmates to do all the work. The diet was boring, consisting mainly of gruel, bread and cheese but adequate. Later it was supplemented from the adjoining gardens and farm.[263] Basingstoke was unusual in educating its workhouse children from the outset, with elementary education and training in agriculture, domestic work, shoe making and sewing/tailoring. From 1898 the children attended Old Basing parish school.[264] Great effort was made to move children into productive work. From the late 1850s out relief declined as Basingstoke industries and the railway offered more employment.[265]

Outside the workhouse, the union provided basic subsistence, food, a doctor, help with child care, nursing and funerals and assistance with emigration to Australia, Canada and New Zealand. Around the turn of the century there was formal provision to send orphans away for a new life.[266] In 1921 there were only 105 inmates.[267] The workhouse system was abolished in 1929 but the infirmary continued to treat patients.[268]

Private Charity: Almshouses

Basingstoke was relatively well endowed with almshouses and this provision increased in the 19th century. Some founders provided stipends for residents. The oldest almshouses with stipends, situated on the south side and east end of London Street, were founded in 1607 by Sir James Deane.[269] They contained eight tenements for poor widows, six from Basingstoke and two from Ashe and Deane. They were endowed by a rent charge from the manor of Ashe. In 1798 and 1816 their stipends were increased following bequests.[270] Page's almshouses in Hackwood Road were founded in 1802 by Joseph Page of London who left provision originally for three houses behind Deane's for single people from the Congregational church,[271] managed by trustees from the church. Two almshouses were provided by John Burgess Soper, a former

---

262　Poor Law Commission became Poor Law Board in 1847 and Local Government Board in 1871.
263　Large, *Workhouse*, 71.
264　Large, *Workhouse*, 126–7.
265　Large, *Workhouse*, 108.
266　Large, *Workhouse*, 129–30.
267　*Census Report Hants*, 1921, 42.
268　The workhouse continued as a hospital. Adopted by the NHS in 1948 but demolished 1977 after North Hants hospital opened. In 1984 The Hampshire Clinic, a private hospital, was built on the site.
269　HRO, 148M 711/8/5/1–2.
270　Baigent and Millard, *Basingstoke*, 709.
271　*VCH Hants* IV, 140.

mayor and businessman, in Chapel Street close to the railway arch in 1891 but little is known about them.[272] In 1911 Walter John Smith, a corn merchant, established four houses in New Road as almshouses with an endowment to pay stipends. They were administered by a trust of family members, and later incorporated into Basingstoke municipal charity.[273]

Acton's Almshouses consisting of four units were built by James Acton *c*.1690. Residents lived rent free but received no stipends and were supported by poor law officials. The houses were renovated in 1800 and 1890.[274] Little Almshouses were originally located in New Street, relocated to Chapel Street and again in 1829 to Totterdown where there were three units for widows, supported by a small grant from the Pemberton gift.[275] Chapel Street houses were four unendowed units. Churchwardens and overseers nominated residents and the buildings were repaired by the overseers. They were sold before 1911 by order of the Local Government Board.[276]

Self-help and Friendly Societies

In the 19th century many societies were established to encourage providence, saving and self-help. For example, from 1825 the Basingstoke branch of the Hampshire Friendly Society provided medical assurance. Members contributed and wealthier citizens made donations to the society.[277] Similarly, from 1823 the Dorcas Clothing Society sponsored by the parish church encouraged the poor to save for clothing which was also subsidised by subscribers.[278] Basingstoke Provident Society was established in September 1840 to encourage saving. Initially 300 poor families deposited 1*d*. to 6*d*. a week. Wealthier families made donations or subscribed to the charity. From January 1841 poor families were provided with coal, blankets and clothing. Established in 1854, Basingstoke Provident Clothing Society encouraged the working classes to save so they could obtain winter clothing.[279]

St Thomas Home, Darlington Road

St Thomas Home became the diocesan penitentiary housing about 60 'friendless and fallen young women', when it transferred from Gosport in 1878. Many girls came to escape from prostitution or after being thrown out of their families. A few girls had illegitimate babies who were cared for elsewhere, while their mothers were educated

272 Willis Museum Search Room.
273 HRO, 63M83/B23/7; 32M84/70.
274 Willis Museum Search Room: Acton Almshouse file.
275 File C22A in Willis Museum Search Room; Baigent and Millard, *Basingstoke*, 709.
276 Baigent and Millard, *Basingstoke*, 709.
277 *HC*, 17 Jan. 1825, 4 Jan. 1841.
278 HRO, 46M74/PZ17.
279 *Salisbury and Winchester Jnl*, 4 Jan. 1841; *HC*, 4 Jan. 1841.

Fig. 28. St Thomas Home from Revd R. F. Bigg-Wither, History of St Thomas Home, 1887.

for a reformed life.[280] They lived and worked in one of five cottages linked by a covered corridor, two of which were laundries, two were for needlework, including sewing surplices and altar cloths, and one was a kitchen (Fig. 28). The girls, aged 13 to 22 in 1921, were trained for two years for domestic service or running homes of their own[281] by a kitchen matron, laundry matron and needlework matron. Industrial earnings especially for laundry helped to finance the home which was also funded by the diocese.[282] There was a chapel (from 1885), an infirmary and accommodation for the warden and sisters of St Thomas the Martyr, Oxford, who ran the home, assisted by volunteers. The second warden was Revd Reginald Bigg-Wither, who wrote a history of the home.[283] The bishop was visitor who, with a council of men, supervised the home. The sisters opposed having women on the committee.[284] Girls attended chapel, and many were baptised/confirmed. During the First World War the girls also grew vegetables.

Financial problems were evident by 1920 with inflated prices for food, fuel, gas,

280   Revd R.F. Bigg-Wither, *History of St Thomas Home. The Winchester Diocesan Penitentiary* (Basingstoke, 1887); HRO, 46M74/PZ26.
281   Bigg-Wither, *St Thomas*, 46.
282   HRO, 100M97/C1/1.
283   Bigg-Wither, *St Thomas*; Reavell, *South View*, 15–17.
284   HRO, 100M97/A8/1.

clothing and water and the cost of maintaining the cottages.[285] Despite an appeal fund, the home closed in 1927 owing to lack of both money and sisters to staff it.[286]

Boys' Garden Colony

The colony was based at South View House in Vyne Road. An initiative of London magistrate, Henry Chancellor, it was established in 1917 to equip adolescents, who had been placed on probation, with horticultural skills which they could subsequently use to gain employment. For their work experience the boys were employed at various nurseries in the town.[287]

First World War and its Aftermath

THE DAYS AROUND the British declaration of war on Germany on Tuesday 4 August 1914, were quite dramatic for Basingstoke. The town's three banks were closed from Saturday 1 August, reopening only on the following Friday afternoon. Grocery shops reported a run on sales, with some forced to close early on Wednesday 5 August because they were 'being besieged with heavy orders due to the war crisis'. Details of call up procedures were published immediately for Territorial Army members and reservists and on Thursday 6 August horses from farms around Basingstoke were brought into town for inspection and assignment for cavalry or draught purposes. Basingstoke station and the 'rail bridges along the line', were put under military guard and on Friday 7 August Major-General Sir William Knox set up a recruitment office in the town hall, having already recruited 67 of his hoped-for total of 200.[288]

Recruitment continued, with 300 men volunteering during the first month of the war. However, Knox considered this inadequate and claimed that Basingstoke was 'gun shy', provoking an adverse response from the mayor and other dignitaries.[289] Lord Curzon, tenant of Hackwood House, supported Knox's view, stating in November 1914 that, 'The war has not hit this place at all', while calling for 300 to 400 more recruits.[290] Men employed in assisting the war effort were considered, at least temporarily, to be in reserved occupations. These included Thornycroft workers producing army vehicles and the builders of Park Prewett Hospital, later requisitioned for military use, though many from both establishments had already volunteered.[291]

285 HRO, 100M97/C1/1.
286 HRO, 44M68/H3/1; *Census*, 1921; HRO, 100M97/A8/1.
287 R. Ottewill, 'The Boys' Garden Colony', *BAHS Newsletter*, No 231 (May 2020), 3–6.
288 *HBG,* 8 Aug. 1914.
289 *HBG,* 12 Sept. 1914.
290 *HBG,* 7 Nov. 1914. Curzon later served in Lloyd George's War Cabinet.
291 D.M. Smith, *Park Prewett Hospital. The History 1898–1984* (1986), 9–10; B. Clarke, *Thornycroft in Basingstoke,* quoting *Commercial Motor,* 13 Aug. 1914, 9.

Fig. 29. Cameron Highlanders marching down Station Hill in 1915. Courtesy of Alastair Blair.

A number of Thornycroft workers, subsequently released for enlistment, served in the Royal Army Service Corps in the mechanical transport battalions.[292] The opinions of Knox and Curzon were belied by the numbers of men who joined up. By 1916 well over 1,000 had enlisted voluntarily and the Basingstoke war memorial records 233 names of men who died.[293]

Basingstoke, with its direct road and rail transport links to London, to military establishments such as those in the Aldershot and Salisbury areas, and to the south coast ports, became a centre for the massing and subsequent dispersal of troops (Fig. 29). By 15 November 1914 about 900 troops of the 12th Hampshire Regiment were stationed in the town (Fig. 30).[294] These were joined the following month by various battalions from the Welsh, Cheshire and Worcester Regiments. In December it was estimated that roughly 5,400 troops were living in and around Basingstoke, which had 'now assumed the aspect of a military town'.[295]

Many were billeted in private houses at rates of 3*s.* per night for officers and 9*d.* for other ranks, with the stipulation that each man must have his own bed.[296] Other properties, such as the Salvation Army Temple,[297] the Liberal and Conservative

292 J.I. Thornycroft, *Half a Century of Thornycroft Progress and Five Years of War Work* (1919), (unpag., section entitled, *Motor Vehicles and Munitions*).

293 https://www.basingstoke.gov.uk/ww1 (accessed 1 Nov. 2019).

294 *HBG,* 21 Nov. 1914.

295 *HBG,* 12 Dec. 1914.

296 *HBG,* 15 Jan. 1915.

297 Below, Religious Hist., Salvation Army.

Fig. 30. First World War soldiers' camp on Basingstoke Common.

clubs were also commandeered. Provision of meals took place in the Drill Hall and mess tents sited in Goldings Park and Cannon's Meadow.[298] Later in the spring and summer months of 1915 even greater numbers of troops, estimated at 18–20,000 were accommodated in tented encampments on Basingstoke Common (Fig. 30) and in the fields surrounding the town.[299] Residents were urged to reduce gas consumption in the winter of 1914–15 owing to the heavy demand caused by the influx of troops.[300] In May 1915 three miles of pipes were laid to supply the tented camps with water.[301]

While waiting for transfer and deployment the troops took part in training exercises on Basingstoke Common, in the fields on the outskirts of the town and Pyle Hill near Newbury where trench digging exercises took place.[302] The Golf Club to the north of the station was used as a training airfield.[303] There were some notable troop inspections, such as that by King George V and Queen Mary at Hackwood House on 28 May 1915, followed by a further inspection by Lord Kitchener.[304]

As well as accommodation and training areas, Basingstoke supplied buildings for more leisurely activities. In 1914 Church Cottage was designated as The Soldiers' Institute to provide troops with rest and recreation[305] as did the Mechanics' Institute and halls at the Congregational, Immanuel and Primitive Methodist churches.[306]

298 *HBG,* 5 Dec. 1914.
299 *HBG,* 8 May, 25 Dec. 1915.
300 HRO, 19M65/B66.
301 *HBG,* 15 May 1915.
302 *HBG,* 8 May, 3 July 1915.
303 https://www.basingstokegolfclub.co.uk/page.aspx?pid=19055 (accessed 9 July 2019).
304 *HBG,* 25 Dec. 1915.
305 M. Oliver, *Church Cottage* (Basingstoke, 2007), 35.
306 *HBG,* 26 Sept., 21 Nov. 1914.

However, the pubs were obliged to close at 9 p.m. and soldiers had to be back in their billets 30 minutes later.[307] The pressure for accommodation lessened after conscription was introduced in 1916, as enlisted men frequently travelled directly to military training camps, for example that at Bovington, Dorset.

The welfare of wounded servicemen was an early concern in Basingstoke. From August 1914 the Cottage Hospital allowed Red Cross nurses to visit and, presumably, observe treatment. From December 1914 the Cottage Hospital treated military patients at a cost of 3s. 6d. a day.[308] By the end of August 1914 the Girls' High school

Fig. 31. West Ham House as a Red Cross hospital in 1916. Courtesy of Alastair Blair.

buildings were prepared as a 100 bed Red Cross Hospital, though whether it became fully operational is uncertain.[309] Several large houses were offered to the Red Cross Society for military hospitals. West Ham House, the home of Mrs Godfrey Courage, functioned as a hospital throughout the war, opening on 31 December 1914 with 25 beds occupied by patients transferred from the Cambridge Hospital, Aldershot. West Ham Hospital specialised in operations and electrical treatment and by the time it closed on 21 January 1919 there were 67 beds and 1,550 patients had passed through its care (Fig. 31).[310]

The building of Park Prewett Hospital began in 1913 as a second county mental hospital to augment the service supplied by Knowle Hospital, near Fareham. It was requisitioned to serve as the 4th General Canadian Hospital for troops from Salonika.

307 *HBG,* 28 Nov. 1914.
308 HRO, 144A12/1.
309 *HBG,* 29 Aug. 1914.
310 HRO, 173A12/A1/2/1 CD/292.

Patient numbers rose to over 1,000 by December 1917, with treatments administered, not just for battle wounds and shell shock, but also other medical conditions, some of which, such as malaria and dysentery, had been contracted while in Salonika.[311] The Canadians remained until July 1919.[312]

Meanwhile other initiatives contributed to the war effort. Basingstoke schoolchildren collected money, cigarettes, matches and clothes for wounded soldiers and provided entertainment for convalescent soldiers in West Ham Hospital. Following an appeal by the Ministry of Munitions, the town's schools also organised a collection of 2.5 cwt of horse chestnuts, a source of acetone for cordite production.[313] Just ten days after the outbreak of war a relief committee was set up to provide support for servicemen's dependants.[314] At the end of the war Basingstoke received a gift of a tank 'in recognition of the war savings donated by the people of the town.' The tank stood on the corner of Fairfields and Council Road from 25 August 1919 until the Second World War when, as with similarly donated tanks in other towns, it was removed and reused in the manufacture of armaments.[315] Belgian refugees began arriving in the town from September 1914, with eight being cared for at Audley Wood.[316] By January 1915 there were refugee centres in Albert House, Wote Street and premises in London Street and Church Street.[317]

The engineering and textile companies which had developed since the 1850s supplied the War Office. To fulfil the urgently required orders, Thornycroft expanded its premises and took on many more workers, of whom around 550 were women.[318] Such employment in manufacturing made a significant change for many women in Basingstoke in terms of income opportunity and gaining the vote.[319] Income received from billeting soldiers also made a small enhancement to some household budgets. Many female Red Cross volunteers moved into the town from Ireland, Wales, Jersey, Derbyshire and Norfolk to serve as nurses, ambulance drivers, clerks, cooks, housemaids, laboratory assistants and storekeepers. Some had previously served abroad in France, Salonika and Egypt.[320] At the end of 1915 the *Hants and Berks Gazette* claimed that the billeting of troops had 'substantially benefitted residents and tradesmen,' and that 1915 had been 'a year of unexampled prosperity due to abundance of employment.'[321]

311 M. Isted, *A Place Apart. The Story of Park Prewett Hospital,* (Tadley and District Hist. Soc., 2017), 21.

312 D.M. Smith, *Park Prewett Hospital. The History 1898–1984* (1986), 9–11.

313 HRO, 35M86/LB1, 10 Feb. 1918.

314 *HBG,* 15 Aug. 1914.

315 *HBG,* 7 Jan. 1985.

316 *HBG,* 26 Sept. 17, 26 Oct. 1914.

317 HRO, 19M65/B66.

318 Townsin, *Thornycroft,* 10.

319 Below, Politics, The Campaign for Women's Suffrage.

320 https://vad.redcross.org.uk/Volunteers-during-WW1 (accessed 8 July 2019).

321 *HBG,* 25 Dec. 1915.

However, these employment opportunities were transitory. Billeting tailed off from 1915; peace brought an end to munitions production; military hospitals closed, and women were expected to relinquish wartime jobs to returning ex-servicemen. When the war ended many men were also dismissed as demand for products fell.[322]

Unemployment in the early 1920s became a major problem for the town as elsewhere in Britain.[323] By October 1921, out of over 1,000 on the unemployment

Fig. 32. War Memorial unveiling in 1923. HRO, HPP38/0119.

register in the Basingstoke area, 632 men were available for full-time work.[324] Government policy under the Unemployment Insurance Act of 1920 provided 15*s.* a week for unemployed men (12*s.* for women) but for only 15 weeks. Thereafter, recourse had to be made for relief under the local poor law provision.[325] On 21 October 1921 a large deputation of men, many 'out of benefit' lobbied the meeting of the Basingstoke board of guardians. Councillor Pheby spoke on their behalf saying: 'I have 500 men outside who are practically starving.' Requests were made for benefit above government rates. The board of guardians responded quickly. They provided

322 Above, Economic. Hist., Thornycroft.
323 *HBG,* 17 Dec. 1921.
324 *HBG,* 19 Jan. 1921, 15 Oct. 1921, 12 Dec. 1925.
325 W.R. Garside, *British Unemployment 1919–1939. A Study in Public Policy* (Cambridge, 1990), 37–8.

additional assistance for those who had exhausted their 'dole', but to continue doing so, within months, the guardians had to borrow £5,500.[326]

The town council initiated public works to provide employment. These included the widening of Winchester Road and some of the work involved with preparing Goldings Park as the War Memorial Park.[327] The local Labour party stated that the burden of relief should be on central government as unemployment was a national problem.[328] Work on the War Memorial Park, providing gravel paths, a bandstand, a paddling pond and sports facilities for the public, brought temporary relief for some of the unemployed and the park became one of Basingstoke's abiding memorials to those who served in the 1914–18 war. In January 1919, following a public meeting a War Memorial Committee had been set up to organise the planning and funding of the project. Goldings, a Georgian house on London Road, was purchased along with its 18 a. park.[329] Thomas Burberry put up the sum of £10,500 to acquire the house and grounds until the council were able to raise enough funds, mainly by public subscription. By 1921 the £4,500 loan for the park was repaid and two years later an additional £2,000 enabled the newly commissioned War Memorial to be unveiled on Empire Day, 24 May 1923 (Fig. 32).[330]

Two war memorial chapels were built in Basingstoke churches. All Saints' church saw the completion of the first chapel, which was initially named the Warrior chapel, as it was built between 1915 and 1917 and consecrated before the end of the war.[331] Thereafter, the Memorial chapel of St Michael's church was completed and the consecration ceremony took place in September 1920.[332] Finally, in cemeteries in Basingstoke there are the graves and headstones of those buried locally who died from wounds or illness contracted while in service; in South View cemetery these number four Canadians, one Belgian, and 15 UK Commonwealth War Grave Commission graves, while in Worting Road cemetery there are 19 Canadian and nine UK Commonwealth War Grave Commission graves. To revise, slightly, Lord Curzon's 1914 statement, this place was hit by war.

326 Large, *Workhouse,* 160–161; *HBG,* 22 Oct. 1921.
327 *HBG,* 15 Oct. 1921; HRO 148M71/16/1/11.
328 *HBG,* 29 Oct., 12 Nov. 1921.
329 Above, Introduction, Landownership.
330 HRO, 148M71/16/1/11.
331 https://www.basingstoketeamparish.org.uk//all-saints-memorial-chapel (accessed 4 Nov. 2019).
332 Below, Religious Hist., St Michael's.

LOCAL GOVERNMENT, POLITICS AND PUBLIC UTILITIES

FOR LOCAL GOVERNMENT purposes, throughout the period covered by this volume Basingstoke was a municipal borough headed by a mayor. From 1872 until 1894, it was the designated Urban Sanitary Authority, taking over from the pavement commissioners, and from 1894 to 1920 it was the Urban District Council (UDC). From 1855 to 1929 members of the borough council also constituted a burial board.[1] In addition, between 1885 and 1903 there was a separately elected seven-member school board.[2]

Responsibility for the parishes that constituted the Basingstoke poor law union was exercised by a board of guardians established in 1835, initially with 41 members, four of whom represented Basingstoke parish, which increased to ten in 1896. This remained the position until 1930 when the total number of guardians was 47.[3]

At county level, until 1889 the magistrates at quarter sessions carried out administrative as well as judicial functions. Thereafter, Hampshire CC, on which there was initially one representative for Basingstoke borough, provided local government services for the county as a whole.

Apart from quarter sessions, all of the above were elective bodies with varying franchises as the qualifications relating to who could vote and stand for election were gradually extended. In the late 19th century one or two appropriately qualified women began to stand as candidates for election.[4]

As happened elsewhere, local politics was characterised by divisions over rate rises to finance spending on public services, such as water and sewerage, as well as by personality clashes. In addition, on occasion, riots and a typhoid epidemic challenged the authorities. Eventually, civic improvements were made with respect to the supply of water, gas and electricity and the treatment of sewage. Health provision, poor law administration, policing and the fire service developed to meet the needs of the growing town.

1   Below, Basingstoke Cemeteries and Burial Board.
2   Above, Social Hist., Education.
3   Below, Administration of Poor Law.
4   See, for example, R. Ottewill, 'Mrs Edith Mitchell: Basingstoke's First Female Guardian', *HFC Newsletter*, 81 (Spring, 2024), 19–21.

Municipal Government and Local Politics 1800 to 1835

P RIOR TO THE Municipal Corporations Act 1835, Basingstoke borough was
governed by a corporation, which was, in essence, a self-perpetuating elite. It
consisted of a mayor, seven aldermen and seven burgesses. The mayor was elected on
an annual basis by the members of the corporation from amongst the aldermen, with
the established practice being to select them by rotation. For his year in office, he was a
justice of the peace,[5] keeper of the gaol and presided at quarter sessions. An allowance
of £20 a year was paid, and the mayor could be removed from office by the aldermen
and burgesses if he governed badly. Aldermen were elected from amongst the burgesses
who were elected from the householders of the borough.[6] The officers of the corporation
were a high steward, recorder, town clerk, two sergeants at mace, two constables and a
town crier. Income for 1832–33 was £921 3s. 4d. of which £700 was rent from an estate
in Maidenwell, Lincolnshire. The largest item of expenditure was £251 13s. 4d. paid to
charities, which included £60 for four poor scholars attending university and £45 for the
poor of Basingstoke.[7] Between 1782 and 1805 the corporation had also invested £700
in Basingstoke canal shares. In 1829 an Act of Parliament permitted the enlargement of
the Market Place and the erection of a replacement and very commodious town hall.
Just over £3,600 was spent on purchasing properties on the site of the new town hall,
while the building costs were £3,900. It was opened in 1832. To meet these expenses the
corporation needed to borrow £4,300. By 1835 it was said that the town was improving
in trade and the management of local affairs and the administration of justice deserved
the confidence of the townspeople.[8]

Municipal Government and Politics 1835 to 1925

T HROUGHOUT THIS PERIOD, a key role in the municipal affairs of towns like
Basingstoke was played by local businessmen, many of whom were shopkeepers -
a situation which was sometimes referred to, perhaps disparagingly, as a 'shopocracy'.[9]
Their involvement reflected the fact that they were the largest group of ratepayers

---

5   And for the year following.
6   Parl. Papers 1835 (116), *First Report of the Commissioners appointed to enquire into the
     Municipal Corporations of England and Wales. Report on the Town of Basingstoke.*
7   Parl. Papers 1835 (116), 1103–4.
8   Much of the detailed information in this section has been extracted from Parl. Papers
     1835 (116), 1099–1107.
9   Term coined during the 19th century to refer to shopkeepers as a 'social class': See
     E.P. Hennock, *Fit and Proper Persons: Ideal and Reality in Nineteenth-Century Urban
     Government* (London, 1973), 318.

and keen to protect their interests. From the 1840s onwards an increasing number were Nonconformists, who were primarily motivated by what, in the context of large towns, such as Birmingham, was regarded as civic duty.[10]

Under the provisions of the Municipal Corporations Act 1835, the new Basingstoke municipal borough council consisted of four aldermen, who served for six years, and 12 councillors for three years. The aldermen were elected by the councillors, usually but not exclusively from their number. One-third of the councillors were elected annually under a system known as partial renewal. Casual vacancies were filled at by-elections. The franchise was restricted to burgesses who were male occupiers of domestic or business property who lived within the borough or within a seven mile radius and had paid all their rates by 31 August. In addition, since Basingstoke was not divided into wards, electors had to own real or personal property worth £500, or land assessed at £15 or more.[11] The burgess roll initially numbered 198 but by the late 1860s this had increased to nearly 600.

Under the provisions of the Municipal Franchise Act 1869 the burgess qualification was extended by changing the residence qualification, enabling those living within a 15 mile radius of the borough to stand and, most radically, giving women the vote in local elections, by determining that words referring to 'the masculine gender' also applied to unmarried females.[12] Of the 727 burgesses on the 1869 roll, approximately 90 were women.[13] As the population grew and the franchise was extended, so the number of burgesses increased to 5,711 in 1925.

1835 to 1871

As elsewhere the main aim of most council members was to keep the rates as low as possible, so any policy initiatives tended to be reactive rather than proactive.

For annual elections, fairly reliable data are available for 30. Of these, just under half, 14, were uncontested. For the remainder, there were two or more candidates per seat on just three occasions. The most competitive election was in 1844 when there were nine candidates for the four seats. As usual, electors favoured the councillors they knew and the three sitting councillors seeking re-election were all successful.[14] It was not until 1851 that a sitting councillor seeking re-election, Edward Adams, a brewer, was defeated. Moreover, this only occurred in five other years in this period. For election to the aldermanic bench, resignation and death were more significant causes of councillor turnover than electoral defeat.

10   A. Reekes & S. Roberts, *George Dawson & his Circle. The Civic Gospel in Victorian Birmingham,* (Merlin Press, 2021), 10.

11   Municipal Corporations Act 1835, 5 & 6 Will 4 c. 76.

12   Municipal Franchise Act 1869, 32 & 33 Vic c. 55.

13   HRO, 148M71/1/2/1/12.

14   These were Nicholas Greene, a solicitor; William Glover, a plumber and glazier and George Penton, a brewer. *RM,* 16 Nov. 1844.

Notwithstanding the council's relative quiescence, various issues and concerns surfaced at election time. One was the religious affiliation of candidates, with membership of the established church appearing to be essential for election in the early years, despite the repeal of the Test and Corporations Acts in 1828. Indeed, the first known Nonconformist to stand, Richard Wallis, a Quaker and by occupation a wagon-master, was only successful on his fourth attempt at a by-election in November 1841.[15]

A second factor was a clash of economic interests particularly within the brewing industry. At a by-election in April 1842 the May family, two members of which were already councillors, sought to undermine the candidacy of fellow brewer, Edward Adams, by supporting William Paice, a cabinet maker, who won the contest.[16]

A third factor was the clash of personalities. These were very much to the fore in the many 'squibs' and some of the election literature that sought to cast unwarranted aspersions on the character of candidates, a key feature of municipal elections during the mid-Victorian era. [17]

A fourth factor, which increased in importance as the century wore on, concerned differences over policy issues. These included drainage and infrastructure improvements and their impact on the rates. In 1860, for example, two candidates who were not serving councillors at the time, Charles Barton, a butcher, and Edward White, a tailor, benefited from antipathy towards an increase in the paving rate.[18] Five years later, in 1865, there were six candidates and at the heart of the contest was the struggle between those who were in favour of sewerage installation and those opposed to it, leading to the first election riot.[19] The outcome was a victory for the 'non-drainage party'.[20]

Lastly, although municipal elections were generally characterised by an absence of 'party spirit', with most councillors being Conservatives, on occasions party politics did come to the fore. For example, in 1859 three candidates stood in the Liberal interest and three in the Conservative, together with one non-aligned candidate.[21] Although all three Liberals - Arthur Angell, a draper, Arthur Wallis, an iron founder and Quaker, and John Williams, a grocer, were successful, it was one of the Conservative candidates, the brewer, Thomas May, who topped the poll.

1872 to 1925

After 1872 and the introduction of the secret ballot, local politics were enlivened by ongoing disagreement over spending on public amenities, such as sewerage and water

---

15　He had previously been defeated at a by-election held on 16 Nov. 1838 and in the annual elections of 1839 and 1840.

16　*BC*, 7 May 1842; *RM*, 23, 30 Apr. 1842.

17　See, for example, *HC*, 8 Nov. 1851, 1 Nov. 1856.

18　*RM*, 3 Nov. 1860.

19　Below, Riots and Disorder.

20　*RM*, 4 Nov. 1865.

21　*RM*, 5 Nov. 1859.

supply. In Basingstoke there was also discord associated with temperance, exacerbated by the Salvation Army's arrival.

During this period elections were far more likely to be contested. Of the 50 annual elections only eight were unopposed. The most competitive was in 1888 when there were ten candidates, while the biggest upset was in 1890 when four councillors seeking re-election were all defeated for a variety of reasons.[22] Of the 35 casual vacancies filled at by-elections, 23 were due to the councillor being elected to the aldermanic bench, seven to the councillor's resignation and five to his death, with there being contests in about 20 instances. During the First World War vacancies were filled by co-option.

Of the factors that influenced the outcome of elections before 1871 a number continued to apply, such as personality clashes. Another development was the emergence of political organisations, such as the Ratepayers' Protection Association. Initially established in 1874, its principal objective, like similar pressure groups in other towns, was a reduction in the public expenses of the town and supporting municipal candidates who favoured this course of action. After a long period of quiescence, it came to the fore in the first decade of the 20th century.[23]

A particularly notable election was that of 1881, fought at the height of the unrest surrounding the arrival of the Salvation Army, which had antagonised the brewing industry with its support for teetotalism. This was contested by four Conservative churchmen, broadly supportive of the brewers and four Liberal Nonconformists all of whom were advocates of temperance.[24] The four Conservatives secured a narrow victory, but despite the result there was a serious riot and destruction of property by a mob.[25]

Although the party political and denominational affiliation of candidates continued to play a part in elections, a number eschewed party labels and, in the main, the affairs of the council were conducted in a non-partisan manner. For example, in 1887, despite the majority of councillors being Conservatives, the unanimous choice for mayor was Thomas Maton Kingdon an ironmonger, a Congregationalist and a prominent member of the Liberal Party.[26]

When there were sharp divisions over matters of policy, these were not necessarily along party lines. During the 1890s, matters that were raised by some candidates and the press at elections included the provision of allotments and the level of rents;[27] the consecration of a new portion of the cemetery;[28] the proposed

22   R. Ottewill, 'The Municipal Election Upset of 1890', *BAHS Newsletter*, 235 (May, 2021), 3–8.
23   *HC*, 7 Nov. 1874.
24   Below, Election Riots.
25   *HBG*, 5 Nov. 1881; Clarke, *Riots: 1880–1883*; below, Election Riots.
26   *HBG*, 12 Nov. 1887.
27   *HBG*, 5 Nov. 1892, 3 Nov. 1894, 19 Oct. 1895, 30 Jan. 1897.
28   *RM*, 3 Nov. 1894; *HBG*, 24 Oct. 1896.

new water works;[29] and the implementation of the Housing of the Working Classes Act.[30]

Procedural issues could also prove controversial. In 1892 John May (Fig. 23) resigned his aldermanic seat so that he could contest the election. He topped the poll, only to be re-elected alderman, thereby necessitating the expense of a by-election.[31] Statements by candidates could also give rise to dissension. In 1898, for example, Thomas Maton Kingdon was criticised for complaining that those who did not pay rates could still vote.[32] It seemed to be a criticism of working-class voters who were becoming a significant component of the municipal electorate. This nearly lost him his seat: he held on by just three votes.

In the early years of the 20th century, the level of rates continued to preoccupy candidates and electors. Thus, in 1905 the Ratepayers' Protection Association nominated two candidates: Frederick Prance, a solicitor, and Edwin White, a timber merchant, who topped the poll.[33] In the following years Association candidates continued to enjoy electoral success and influence. Although there was a contest in 1914, given that it took place during the early stages of the First World War, it is perhaps unsurprising that it 'was conducted in a very amicable spirit and with very little excitement.'[34]

After the war, party politics emerged in a different guise. In June 1919 two members of the local Labour Party, George Pheby, a locomotive engine driver, and Frederick Tollerton, an engineer's storekeeper, became councillors in an uncontested by-election.[35] At the annual election on 1 November there were four official Labour candidates - George Pheby; Russell Howard, a railwayman and trade union organiser; Francis Lewis, a licensed victualler and G.J. Simmons, a platelayer. Of these only the first two were successful.[36] Re-elected in 1922, George Pheby was Basingstoke's first Labour mayor serving for the municipal year 1924–5.[37] During his term of office he was elected to the aldermanic bench but was 'deposed' in 1926.[38] Although other Labour Party candidates frequently contested municipal elections, they were not often successful. Electors feared the impact of their commitments on the rates. These included building more council houses using direct labour; setting up clinics and welfare centres for mothers and children, and the municipalisation of the gas undertaking. But Russell Howard, despite being defeated in 1922, regained his seat in 1926 and later became an alderman, the mayor

29   *HBG*, 3 Nov. 1894, 19 Oct. & 9 Nov. 1895, 24 Oct., 7 Nov. 1896.
30   *HBG*, 5 Nov. 1898.
31   *HBG*, 22 Oct. 1892.
32   *HBG*, 5 Nov. 1898.
33   *HBG*, 4 Nov. 1905.
34   *HBG*, 7 Nov. 1914.
35   *HBG*, 21 June 1919.
36   *HBG*, 8 Nov. 1919.
37   *HBG*, 15 Nov. 1924.
38   *HBG*, 13 Nov. 1926.

from 1933–4 and was awarded the Freedom of the Borough in 1958.[39] Russell Howard Park, named after him, opened in 1967.[40]

Campaign for Women's Suffrage

THE ISSUE OF votes for women was occasionally discussed at local meetings in the late 19th century, but a Basingstoke branch of the National Union of Women's Suffrage Societies (NUWSS), was not established until November 1908.[41] The NUWSS advocated using peaceful measures to gain support rather than adopting the direct action favoured by the Suffragettes. From then until the outbreak of the First World War advocates of women's suffrage met frequently in Basingstoke, as did their opponents. The most renowned of these opponents were Miss Mary Angela Dickens (a granddaughter of Charles Dickens) of the Women's National Anti-Suffrage League, who spoke in February 1909[42] and Leo Maxse, editor of the *National Review*, in February 1911.[43]

National figures advocating women's suffrage who spoke in Basingstoke included, in 1910, Mrs Millicent Fawcett, the president of the NUWSS[44] and in 1912, Miss Margaret Ashton, Manchester's first female city councillor.[45] Among the local leadership were Mrs Conran, Mrs Isabella Raynbird and Miss Dorothy Edwards. The last two were members of a deputation which in July 1912 met Arthur Clavell Salter, the Conservative MP for Basingstoke who was reasonably sympathetic to the cause.[46] His moderate stance chimed with that of most local supporters of women's suffrage. Mrs Pankhurst's Women's Social and Political Union (the Suffragettes) had few supporters in the town. There are no records of any direct action in Basingstoke and only one incident of any notoriety. At an open-air meeting held in the Market Place in the summer of 1911, the speaker, a leading suffragette, Mrs Leigh, was hit on the head by a stone while speaking. However, without hesitation she grabbed the culprit, a boy, and made him give a public apology before continuing with her speech.[47]

The final recorded meeting of the Basingstoke Women's Suffrage Society was held on 31 July 1914. Following the declaration of war, four days later, all campaigning for

39   https://www.basingstoke.gov.uk/freedom-of-the-borough#elem_18581 (accessed 20 July 2024); above, Economic Hist., Trade Unions.
40   HRO, 148M71/1/3/50, 560.
41   For a detailed discussion of the local campaign see R. Ottewill, 'Campaigning For and Against Women's Suffrage in Edwardian Basingstoke', *The Local Historian*, 51 (1) (Jan. 2021), 27–35.
42   *HBG*, 6 Mar. 1909.
43   *HBG*, 18 Feb. 1911.
44   *HBG*, 29 Oct. 1910.
45   *HBG*, 9 Nov. 1912.
46   *HBG*, 20 July 1912.
47   F. and E. Pethick Lawrence (eds), *Votes for Women*, 30 June 1911.

women's suffrage was suspended. There appears to be no further record of organised campaigning after the war. During the early 1920s women made their initial appearance as municipal election candidates. The first was Mrs Edith Alice Weston in November 1920. She stood for the Labour Party at a by-election but was heavily defeated.[48] The first successful female candidate was Mrs Sylvia Hoare, a Conservative, in 1924.[49]

Parliamentary Representation

IN THE YEARS leading up to the 1832 Great Reform Act, Basingstoke remained part of the Hampshire County constituency represented in parliament by two MPs, who were usually members of the Heathcote and Chute families. The 200 Basingstoke electors (40s. freeholders) voted in Winchester in the rare event of a contested election in the constituency.

From 1832 to 1885 Basingstoke was part of North Hampshire constituency whose most distinguished MP was Charles Shaw-Lefevre. First elected for the old Hampshire constituency in 1831, he was Speaker of the House of Commons from 1839 to 1857.

After the 1885 Redistribution of Seats Act, Basingstoke became the centre of a smaller constituency, Hampshire North, consisting of Basingstoke borough and the two Petty Sessional Divisions of Basingstoke and Odiham. From 1885 the seat was held by a Conservative but Basingstoke itself was regarded as a 'Liberal stronghold with a manufacturing population and a well-established Nonconformist element'.[50] The first MP was George Sclater-Booth, who secured a majority of 1,579 over his Liberal opponent at the 1885 general election. He was elevated to the peerage as Lord Basing in 1887. His successor from 1887 Arthur Frederick Jeffreys, a local landowner, had acquired Burkham House just over the constituency boundary in 1881–2.[51] Re-elected at successive elections, in January 1906 he just held the seat by 120 votes over his Liberal opponent, Harry Verney but he died a few weeks later. The victor in the ensuing by-election was Arthur Clavell Salter who secured a majority of 259 over Verney. But for the intervention of a third contestant, the self-styled 'Independent Liberal, Free Trade and Labour Candidate',[52] T. Ernest Polden, who secured 467 votes, the result might have been different. Comfortably winning at the January 1910 general election and being unopposed in December 1910, Salter, a London-based lawyer, remained MP until his elevation to the bench in October 1917. His successor was Auckland C. Geddes, an academic and soldier and already a minister in Lloyd-George's war-time government.[53]

48   *HBG*, 20 and 27 Nov. 1920.
49   *HBG*, 25 Oct. 1924, 8 Nov. 1924.
50   H. Pelling, *The Social Geography of British Elections 1885–1910* (London, 1967), 129, 134.
51   http://research.hgt.org.uk/item/burkham-house/ (accessed 30 July 2024).
52   *HBG*, 3 Mar. 1906.
53   G.R. Searle, *A New England? Peace and War 1886–1918* (Oxford UP, 2004), 711.

After 1918 Basingstoke constituency included the borough of Andover and rural districts of Andover, Basingstoke, Kingsclere, Stockbridge and Whitchurch. Auckland Geddes resigned in 1920 on his appointment as British Ambassador to the United States of America and at the ensuing by-election the Conservative, Richard Holbrook, held the seat against opposition from Liberal and Labour candidates. Holbrook was a newspaper proprietor and already aged 70 when first elected (Fig. 33).

Fig. 33. Announcing the election results from the town hall in 1920.

At the general election of December 1923 there was no Labour candidate and the Liberal, Reginald Fletcher, gained the seat with a very slim majority. A few months later in October 1924 there was a Labour candidate, who split the anti-Conservative vote, and Richard Holbrook regained the seat with a substantial majority. Thus, the Liberal victory was short-lived as the Conservatives then held it at every election until 4 July 2024 when Labour won the seat.[54]

Riots and Disorder

The Salvation Army Riots/Massagainians

Riots in Basingstoke against the Salvation Army in the 1880s gave rise to questions in the House of Commons, the publication of a parliamentary paper, *Basingstoke*

---

54   F.W.S Craig (ed.), *British Parliamentary Election Results, 1918–1949*, Chichester Parliamentary Research Services (1983), 364.

Disturbances, and headlines in the national press.[55] Basingstoke was one of the earliest towns with anti-Salvation Army riots which occurred in 60 urban centres, mainly from 1882 to 1884.[56] The Salvation Army arrived in Basingstoke in September 1880.[57] Their militant campaign against the consumption of alcoholic drinks, which was supported by the *Hants and Berks Gazette*, Nonconformist churches and various temperance societies including Church of England ones, was seen by the brewers and publicans and their employees as a threat to their livelihood, and by their customers as a threat to their enjoyment. From October 1880 to March 1881, attacks on the Salvationists and their supporters by the self-styled Massagainians intensified.[58]

On the afternoon of Sunday 20 March 1881, the so-called Battle of Church Square took place. General Booth complained to the Home Secretary that one man had his arm broken, another his jaw broken and that many were brutally kicked and seriously injured'.[59] The police and other witnesses estimated that there were about 3,000 people crowded into the Square, many of whom were involved in the fighting.[60]

At a demonstration against the Salvation Army a week later, the mayor read the Riot Act and asked the Royal Horse Artillery to clear the streets.[61] Reports of the proceedings of the town council, the watch committee and the magistrates showed that the Salvation Army had caused bitter arguments within each of those bodies.[62] In August 1881 the magistrates were presented with two petitions. One was signed by the vicar of Basingstoke and 498 others, calling for the Salvation Army processions to be banned as they, and the band of rough music that followed them, were disturbing the peace of the town and impeding those trying to go to church. The other petition was signed by the minister of the Congregational church and 613 others calling for the processions to be properly protected.[63] During the disturbances against the Salvation Army, Basingstoke's seven policemen struggled to preserve the peace of the town.[64]

Later that month the Captain of the Salvation Army took out a private prosecution against a group of Massagainians, ten of whom were sent to Winchester gaol for 14

55   *Pall Mall Gaz.*, 27 Mar. 1881, *London Daily News*, 19 Mar. 1881, *Globe*, 6 Mar. 1882, *Morning Post*, 9 Aug. 1882. Clarke, *Riots 1880–3*, (BAHS, 2010).

56   V. Bailey, 'Salvation Army Riots, the Salvation Army and legal Authority in the provincial Town', in A.P. Donajgrodski (ed.), *Social Control in Nineteenth Century Britain* (Croom Helm, 1977).

57   K. Clements, *Two Feeble Women: the Early History of the Salvation Army in Basingstoke* (No publisher noted, *c*.1995).

58   The origin of this name is unknown.

59   TNA, HO, 45/9607/A2886.

60   *HC*, 26 Mar. 1881; *HBG*, 26 Mar. 1881, 9 Apr. 1881, 16 Apr. 1881, 7 May 1881, 14 May 1881; *Report of the Proceedings before the Magistrates, on May 3rd and 9th, 1881* (no publisher noted).

61   *HBG*, 9 Apr. 1881.

62   *HBG*, 9 Apr. 1881, 10 Sept. 1881.

63   Parl. Papers 1882 (132), *Basingstoke Disturbances*.

64   B. Clarke, *Drunkards, Thieves and Rioters and the Basingstoke Borough Police 1836–1889* (BAHS, 2015), 83–92.

days. When their sentence was over the town corporation let the Corn Exchange for a great banquet to welcome the 'Massagainian Martyrs' home.[65] This led to further headlines in the national press[66] and questions in Parliament.[67] Hostilities continued throughout 1882, but when it became obvious that the Salvation Army posed no real threat to the beer trade, the attacks gradually petered out. By the end of 1883 any organised harassment of the Salvation Army in Basingstoke had ceased.[68]

Election Riots

The municipal election in 1865 turned into a fiercely contested struggle between those who were in favour of an improved system of drainage being carried out, and those who opposed it on cost grounds.[69] Both parties treated their more boisterous supporters with beer who then gathered in the Market Place pelting passers-by with paper bags filled with flour, red ochre, lime and other materials.[70] There was another disturbance in 1869 when a mob threw paper bags containing red ochre and lamp black in the Market Place,

Fig. 34. Hillside House, Vyne Road, after the 1881 election riot. Hampshire County Council. Provided by Hampshire Cultural Trust, 2025.

65   *HBG,* 24 Sept. 1881.
66   *Pall Mall Gaz.,* 22 Sept. 1881; *Daily News, Morning Post,* and *Standard,* 23 Sept. 1881.
67   House of *Commons Debates* 16 Mar. 1882, Vol. 267, cols 1016–7.
68   A detailed account is in Clarke, *Riots 1880–83;* above, Social Hist., Temperance.
69   Above, Municipal Government.
70   *HC,* 4 Nov. 1865. Red ochre was frequently used by rioters to stain opponents' clothes.

broke a number of windows and set fire to a corn rick in Winchester Road.[71]

The municipal election in November 1881 was the first time since the March riots and the August petitions that the divisions in the town concerning the Salvation Army could be translated into votes.[72] On election night a group of about 200 Massagainians smashed one of the large plate glass windows of the Old Angel Temperance Café (Fig. 12)[73] that was being used as the headquarters of the pro-Salvation Army party. Then they went on the rampage, roaming round town breaking windows and causing damage to the homes and property of the Salvation Army's supporters. At Hillside in Vyne Road, the home of the magistrate, John Burgess Soper, they smashed all 12 windows and broke the blinds (Fig. 34).[74]

Bonfire Night Disturbances 1850s and 1860s

The 1815 Basingstoke Paving Act banned fireworks and bonfires in the streets but special constables were needed in the mid 19th century to assist the police in keeping order, as for example in 1849 when some 200 young men and boys marched through the town letting off fireworks and throwing stones. They smashed a number of lamps and windows, and a firework set fire to the thatch of a cottage.[75] In the 1850s and 1860s there were Bonfire Night disturbances nearly every year involving up to several hundred people letting off fireworks and lighting bonfires. In 1857 they smashed the windows of the police station.[76]

Public Health and Utilities

Policing and Administration of Justice

From 1815 policing the borough was the responsibility of the pavement commissioners[77] who appointed a watchman stationed in a watch box under the town hall, to patrol the central streets. From 1818 he had an assistant.[78] This policing was considered inadequate by 1835.[79]

---

71   *HA* and *RM*, 6 Nov. 1869.
72   Above, Salvation Army Riots.
73   Above, Social Hist., Temperance.
74   TNA, HO 45/9607/A2886; *HBG,* 5 Nov.1881; Clarke, *Riots 1880–83*, 83–4.
75   *RM*, 10 Nov. 1849, 17 Nov. 1849.
76   *RM*, 7 Nov. 1857, 9 Nov. 1861, 8 Nov. 1862, 7 Nov. 1868; *BC*, 1 Nov. 1864; for Swing riots, above, Economic Hist, Agriculture.
77   Below, Pavement Commissioners.
78   HRO, 148M71/1/5/7/1, 81–3.
79   Parl. Papers, 1835 (116), 1102.

Fig. 35. Basingstoke Borough Police in 1889. Hampshire County Council. Provided by Hampshire Cultural Trust, 2025.

Borough Police

As a result of the Municipal Corporations Act 1835 Basingstoke corporation formed a watch committee which appointed a borough police force (Fig. 35),[80] consisting of one day constable or superintendent and two night constables, trained for the first month by a Metropolitan police officer.[81] The superintendent was also keeper of the town gaol in New Street,[82] where the keeper's house became the police station.[83]

In 1839 the Hampshire Constabulary was founded. The Basingstoke division was responsible for policing the parishes outside the borough and had its police station in Wote Street (later in Mark Lane). The borough council resisted attempts to merge the forces.[84] Within Basingstoke in 1848 an extra police constable was recruited funded by the board of guardians, to search vagrants coming into the town.[85] But the borough police were struggling. Despite increasing the number of policemen to five by 1863,

80 5 & 6 Wm. IV, c.76; HRO, 148M71/1/6/2, 19 Jan. 1836.
81 HRO, 148M71/1/6/2, 26 Jan. 1836.
82 Also known as bridewell or house of correction.
83 HRO, 148M71/1/6/2, 30 Jan. 1836.
84 HRO, 148M71/1/6/2, 31 Dec. 1839; *RM*, 16 Nov. 1850, 20 May 1854, 23 Feb. 1856, 9 Oct. 1875.
85 HRO, 148M71/1/6/2.

the Inspector of Constabulary reported that the borough was too large for so small a force.[86] Two more police officers were appointed in 1871 and the force received a government grant from 1872.[87]

In 1887 the watch committee appointed an additional constable so that the outlying districts could be given more attention.[88] This brought the total up to eight. As a result of the Local Government Act 1888, the borough force ceased to exist and became part of the Hampshire Constabulary.[89]

Law and Punishment

Basingstoke magistrates held quarter sessions in the town hall until Easter 1836. Minor offenders found guilty of assault or small thefts were bound over to keep the peace, fined, whipped or confined for brief periods (up to four weeks) in the house of correction (town gaol) in New Street. Those accused of serious crimes were sentenced to transportation,[90] imprisonment in the county gaol in Winchester for a few months, often with hard labour, or to await the assizes.[91] Bastardy orders and other management of the poor occurred at the quarter sessions until 1834.[92]

The Municipal Corporations Act 1835 provided that any borough wishing to carry on holding quarter sessions had to petition the king making their case.[93] Basingstoke petitioned but was rejected and its sessions finished in May 1836.[94] Winchester petitioned successfully for a separate quarter sessions.[95] Basingstoke accused were tried at Winchester from 1836. Basingstoke County Court division in the town hall in 1859 covered all the parishes of the Basingstoke and Hartley unions.[96]

Throughout the 19th century, magistrates in petty sessions served as the licensing authority for alehouses and clubs with bars. They managed the highways and dispensed justice for minor offences such as assault, theft and non-payment of poor rates or tithes. They continued until the 1970s when they were replaced by magistrates' courts.[97]

86   Parl. Papers, 1864 (28) *Reports of the inspectors of constabulary for the year ending 29 Sept. 1863*, 112.

87   Parl. Papers, 1873 (16) *Reports of the inspectors of constabulary for the year ending 29 Sept. 1872*, 219.

88   *HBG*, 8 Oct. 1887.

89   51 & 52 Vict. c.41 ss.39 and 118(16); *HBG*, 16 and 30 Mar. 1889.

90   HRO, 8M62/31.

91   HRO, 8M62/31.

92   HRO, 8M62/31.

93   5 & 6 Will 4, c.76.

94   *HA*, 9 Apr. 1836, 30 July 1836.

95   HRO, Q23/6/3–4.

96   *Kelly's Dir.* (1859), 487.

97   HRO, 8M62/30; 77M82/XP46, 47; 44M69/G3/1014.

Administration of the Poor Law

Until 1834 magistrates and parish overseers managed the poor. Under the 1834 Poor Law Amendment Act a board of guardians, elected by each parish, ran the Basingstoke poor law union, comprising Basingstoke, Old Basing and 35 surrounding parishes.[98] In addition to centralised care of the poor in its 37 parishes, and the building of a new large workhouse,[99] it began the process of levying a local rate based on the valuation of properties. Four, soon reduced to three, relieving officers determined admittance to the workhouse and the payment of out relief in each district. The board also became the responsible body for civil registration of births, deaths and marriages after 1837, and for nuisances, medical care, mass vaccination and other civic matters.[100] Medical officers cared for the poor inside and outside the workhouse and reported on nuisances. The workhouse was managed by married couples, appointed as master and matron. A schoolmistress taught the children.[101] Poor law unions, supervised by central government, prefigured modern local government. Following the 1894 Local Government Act, women could stand for election as guardians and Mrs E. Mitchell did so successfully in 1896, followed by Mrs Raynbird in 1899.[102] In 1925 equal numbers of men and women were elected guardians.[103] The board of guardians maintained its care of the poor until 1929.[104] They also acted as the Rural Sanitary Authority for the non-Basingstoke parishes from 1875, and later the Rural District Council from 1894.[105]

Pavement Commissioners

The Basingstoke Paving Act of 1815 was the first local initiative to pave, light, clean, improve and clear obstructions from the urban area streets and paths which were described as 'ill paved, ruinous and dangerous'.[106] The 85 pavement commissioners appointed by the Act were empowered to raise limited rates to implement it in the area of half a mile radius from the town hall. The commissioners could choose replacements, all of whom had to have land or wealth.[107] Map 4 shows

98   Large, *Workhouse*, 17, 22.
99   Large, *Workhouse*, 27–31.
100   HRO, PL3/5/ series.
101   Large, *Workhouse,* 25–7, 49–51, 63.
102   HRO, PL3/5/24.
103   *HBG*, 11 Apr. 1925.
104   HRO, PL3/5/ series.
105   Large, *Workhouse*, 146.
106   HRO, 148M71/1/5/7/1. An Act for Paving the Footways and Crosspaths, and Lighting, Watching, Cleansing, Widening and otherwise Improving the Streets, Lanes, and other public Passages and Places in the Town of Basingstoke, in the County of Southampton (1814–15), 55 Geo. III, c. 7.
107   HRO, 148M71/1/5/7/1. After the initial period only a few of the commissioners transacted business, generally five or seven.

the development of the town between 1762 and 1930 with the area to the north of the railway being outside the scope of the Act. In 1868 the rateable area was extended to all the urban area.[108] By 1817 the Market Place was paved followed by Wote Street, Winchester Street and Church Street. Later the cross passages such as Potters Lane and Caston's Alley were paved. Pavements were built as new buildings were constructed, for example around the new town hall in 1833[109] and as housing developed along Station Hill, Chapel Street and Hackwood Road.[110] The pavement commissioners ceased work on 20 December 1872 when their responsibilities passed to the Urban Sanitary Authority.[111]

Residents had to improve the drainage of water from their roofs via gutters, downpipes and spouts.[112] From the 1820s there were concerns about the adequacy of drainage from Winchester and London Streets and the Market Place down to the river Loddon. By January 1839 an underground barrel drain, or common sewer, had been installed along the length of London Street and part of Winchester and Church Streets.[113] There was also a drain down Wote Street that improved the water flow to the top pound of the canal. Originally this was intended only to take surface water but in later years effluent from water closets found its way into the drain.[114]

Householders were required to sweep the pavement in front of their houses each morning and from March 1821 contracts were agreed for cleansing the streets and public passages.[115]

Water Supply

The river Loddon rose from two springs in the west and merged below the town. At its widest part at Wote Street bridge it was about 12ft wide.[116] For the first half of the 19th century water was drawn from numerous wells around the town.[117]

The 1848 Public Health Act empowered the setting up of a local board of health when the death rate was 23 per 1,000 persons. However, with sufficient local support, residents could petition for a local board of health even before that level had been reached. In response to a request from anxious ratepayers, William Ranger, Superintending Officer of the General Board of Health, inspected Basingstoke in

108 HRO, 148M71/1/5/7/2, 91.
109 HRO, 148M71/1/5/7/1, 155.
110 HRO, 148M71/1/5/7/2, 4.
111 HRO, 148M71/1/5/7/2, 142–6; L. Rosenthal, 'Owners', 14.
112 HRO, 148M71/1/5/7/1, 32, 136–137.
113 TNA, MH 12/10688; HRO, 148M71/1/5/7/1; TNA, 148M71/1/5/7/1.
114 Ballard's Report upon the Sanitary Condition of Basingstoke, 1871; above, Canal, Sewage Issues.
115 HRO, 148M71/1/5/7/1, 99–100.
116 TNA, MH 12/10683 Ballard's Report.
117 TNA, MH 12/10683 Ballard's Report.

1853[118] and reported that it was 'plentifully furnished' with water for an agricultural town dependent on pumps and wells[119] but some, as in many English towns, were contaminated and unfit for domestic use.[120] Ranger estimated the local death rate at 17 per 1,000,[121] much lower than in more industrial towns.[122] He concluded that a new waterworks would be beneficial but did not merit the cost. Basingstoke corporation asked the central board to leave Basingstoke alone.[123]

As industry developed and the population increased, the situation worsened. In 1866 and 1871, the district medical officers working for the board of guardians stated that the water, particularly in the central and lower areas of the town, was often polluted with sewage and totally unfit for use.[124] The mortality rate had increased greatly to 22 per 1,000, close to the level when central government could have intervened.[125] However, most of the town's ratepayers objected to any increases in their rates so the corporation took no action. Such resistance was common throughout England as in Winchester.[126] No improvements were made until 1871 when the Basingstoke and Eastrop Waterworks Company Ltd was formed.[127] The company built a reservoir at Darlington Road, South View, in the highest part of the town north of the railway on land purchased from J.B. Soper to supply Basingstoke and the parish of Eastrop.[128] The Waterworks company contracted with the Corn Company, who had a well and a steam mill in Steam Dell, Totterdown, Reading Road, south of the railway, to use the water from the well and steam power from the mill to pump water to their reservoir.[129] The reservoir delivered an average daily supply of 360,000 gallons. The quality and quantity of the water in the reservoir was regularly criticised.[130]

The Urban Sanitary Authority purchased the water company in 1881 but disputes over costs delayed the takeover until 1884, after which supply was funded by a water rate.[131] The growing population and newly installed sewerage system (1879), led to

---

118 TNA, MH 13/17/220, f.523, 585.
119 TNA, MH 12/10688 Ranger's Report.
120 TNA, MH 12/10688 Ranger's Report; C. Hamlin, *Public Health and Social Justice in the age of Chadwick* (Cambridge, 1998).
121 TNA, MH 12/10688 Ranger's Report.
122 TNA, MH 13/17/220, f.585; TNA, MH 12/10688 Ranger's Report.
123 TNA, MH 13/17/220, f.585.
124 TNA, MH 12/10683.
125 TNA, MH 12/10683.
126 W.H. Boorman, 'Health and Sanitation in Victorian Winchester or: the triumph of the Muckabites' *Proceedings of the HFC,* 46 (1990), 161–180.
127 HRO, 148M71/1/5/7/2, 120; 148M71/1/5/61/2.
128 TNA, BT 31/1570/5130; HRO, 148M71/5/61/1.
129 HRO, 148M71/1/5/61/1, 13. The Corn Company was more correctly known as Raynbird, Caldecott, Bawtree, Dowling & Co Ltd, listed in trade directories at the time as corn, seed, manure and oil cake merchants.
130 B. Clarke, *The Great Basingstoke Typhoid Epidemic* (BAHS, 2017), 2, 13–15.
131 HRO, 148M71/1/5/61/8, 13; *Hants. Telegraph & Sussex Chronicle,* 22 Nov. 1882.

more houses demanding water.[132] An epidemic of pustular tonsillitis in 1894–5 was blamed on the water and Dr Farrar, medical inspector of the Local Government Board, said 'the town well can never be trusted again'.[133]

A severe outbreak of typhoid in autumn 1905 was caused by pollution of the well from a leaking main sewer.[134] On 16 September the first case of typhoid was notified.[135] By the end of the epidemic, 170 Basingstoke residents had caught typhoid and ten outside the town contracted the disease whilst in Basingstoke.[136] Fifteen victims died.[137] Residents were told to boil all water. The reservoir and mains were disinfected.[138] The council set up a sick relief fund for typhoid patients. It received £730 14s. 2d. which it spent relieving 163 sufferers and families.[139]

The council had already identified a site for a new well at West Ham, north of Worting Road between the Basingstoke and Alton Light Railway and the LSWR lines.[140] This was west of the polluted built-up area and capable of yielding over 900,000 gallons of pure water a day.[141] The pumping station was opened in 1906, at a cost of nearly £20,000.[142] As part of the works, new piping was laid to the Darlington Road reservoir and a new 240,000–gallon reservoir, constructed on higher ground in Cliddesden, was operational by 1907.[143] The death rate in Basingstoke in 1906 was only 10.8 per 1,000.[144] The council reported in June 1922 that the town now had a water supply second to none and the health of the town was good.[145]

Sewerage

Under the 1815 Basingstoke Paving Act[146] all private drains which discharged into the public sewers had to be in good repair and cleansed at the cost of the owners.[147] These were monitored by the sanitary inspectors. In 1853 Ranger reported that there were sewers in many of the streets but privies and water closets were not connected

132 HRO, 148M71/1/5/32/15; below, Sewerage.
133 HRO, 148M71/1/5/32/15.
134 *The Times*, 17 Sept. 1906; HRO, 148M71/1/5/32.
135 HRO, 148M71/1/5/32/7.
136 *HBG,* 29 Sept. 1906.
137 HRO, 148M71/1/5/32/7.
138 *HBG,* 14 Oct. 1905.
139 *HBG*, 30 June 1906.
140 HRO, 58M74/BP2112; TNA, HLG 6/991.
141 HRO, 148M71/1/5/32/2.
142 *The Times*, 22 Apr. 1907; HRO, 148M71/1/5/32/15; *HBG*, 9 Dec. 1905. The works were visible from the railway in 2024.
143 *The Times*, 22 Apr. 1907.
144 *The Times*, 22 Apr. 1907; HRO, 58M74/BP2112.
145 *HBG*, 10 June 1922.
146 HRO, 15M84/Z1/51.
147 HRO, 76M86/20.

to them. Many householders discharged their sewage on to the road surface or into cesspits or ditches. In 1871 Ballard, medical officer for the Local Government Board, reported that wells throughout the town were contaminated by surrounding cesspits from which excrement seeped into the chalk: 'In short, throughout the town people are unwittingly drinking their own excrement'.[148] Untreated sewage found its way into the river Loddon and the canal. The situation worsened with the collapse of the canal tunnel at Greywell, as the static water in Basingstoke and Old Basing became stagnant, polluted and fetid.[149]

From 1872, the new Urban Sanitary Authority[150] initially tried the low-cost options favoured by ratepayers, including a contract with the Town Manure Company to dispose of sewage; a new water cart to cleanse the streets and a cart to collect night soil. But following the Public Health Act 1875 they were forced to build a sewage treatment works on Basing Road. After almost 23 years of debate 13 a., known as Cowdrey's Down, were purchased from Lord Bolton[151] as well as a site next to the gas works in Eastrop for a pumping station.[152] The Local Government Board loaned £18,000 towards the cost.[153] The pumping station in Basing Road, comprising a steam engine, boiler, sewage pipes, mixing rooms, lime and coal stores and a cottage, was opened in 1879, far enough from the town well to avoid contamination. [154]

It later emerged that the pipes were poorly installed with unsealed joints.[155] The sewage was treated with lime, tar and salts of magnesium using the Hille's process previously used in Wimbledon.[156] The sludge initially consisted of 95 per cent water and proved difficult to cart away. It was later pressed into dry cakes, free from smell and easier to transport, for sale to local farms.[157] The effluent containing manurial properties was pumped 110ft to a tank just east of the railway line on Swing Swang Lane. A system of broad irrigation was used on a rotational basis. Crops of mangolds and rye grass were grown at intervals on the resting plots to be sold to cover the working expenses of the pumping station.[158] The thin layer of soil on the chalk was regularly ploughed to assist the water to filter naturally through the bedrock into the river Loddon.[159]

---

148 TNA, MH 12/10683, Ballard's Report upon the sanitary condition of Basingstoke, 1871, 2.

149 TNA, MH 12/10688; above, Introduction, Canals, Sewage Issues.

150 The borough council acted as the Urban Sanitary Authority.

151 OS 6" XVIII.NE 1912.

152 HRO, 148M71/1/7/1; HRO 8M62/71.

153 HRO, 148M71/1/7/1; HRO 8M62/71.

154 Parl. Papers, 1907, [Cd. 3656], XXV.1, 90–93.

155 Parl. Papers, 1907, [Cd. 3656], XXV.1, *Farrar's report on Drainage, Excrement and Refuse Disposal*, 90–93.

156 HRO, 58M74/144.

157 HRO, 58M74/144.

158 HRO, 148M71/1/7/1.

159 HRO, 148M71/1/5/32/15; B. Butler (ed), *The Dream Fulfilled, Basingstoke Town development 1961–78* (Gollancz, 1980).

After the 1905 epidemic, Dr Farrar reported that nearly all houses in the town were provided with outdoor water closets apart from a few houses in Cliddesden and some cottages built for the GWR employees in South View. Subsoil drainage was separated from sewage and leaky pipes were mended.[160]

With the influx of troops during the First World War, a further 14 a. were leased from Lord Bolton; in 1919 this plus an additional 41 a. was purchased from him for £6,500. This brought the total area for irrigation to 77 a. Further extensions to the farm and improvements were carried out in 1922.[161] The net cost of the pumping operation for that year was reduced by the sale of crops totalling £290 some of which fed the entire borough's team of working horses.[162] All new build houses were connected to the sewage system by 1925. With the addition of some individual street extensions, this system continued into the 1960s.

Medical Services

In 1828 five surgeons served the 3,165 residents of Basingstoke, reducing to three in 1851 and increasing to five again by 1871 for a population of 5,574 and reducing again to four in 1881.[163] Before 1834 the parish vestry employed local doctors when needed to care for the poor who could not afford doctors' fees.[164] From 1835 the Basingstoke poor law union employed doctors to provide medical care for all the poor including surgery, accidental injuries and midwifery consultations. Initially, two doctors worked for Basingstoke union: Edward Covey and John Nicholls, each on a stipend of £170 a year.[165] The union also paid an annual subscription to the county hospital in Winchester for treatment of the poor.[166]

The guardians of Basingstoke union also contracted medical officers to cover its various districts.[167] In 1878 a salary of £85 a year was offered exclusive of the authorised fees for surgical and midwifery cases and for visiting lunatic paupers. The medical officer was usually also the medical officer of health and public vaccinator for his district for which he received a further £38 18s. 6d. a year. From 1840, smallpox vaccination was freely available to the poor of Basingstoke union. In 1853 vaccination became compulsory for all infants less than four months old.[168] In 1897, the union bought supplies of the antitoxin for treating diphtheria.[169] Cod liver oil, and quinine for endemic malaria, known as ague, were

160 Parl. Papers, 1907, [Cd. 3656], XXV.1, 90–93.
161 *HBG*, 14 Oct. 1922.
162 *HBG*, 5 May 1923.
163 *Census*, 1851, 1871, 1881.
164 HRO, 46M74/PV2, 1817–1841.
165 HRO, PL3/5/1, 1835–1836.
166 HRO, PL3/5/ series.
167 Large, *Workhouse*, 86.
168 HRO, PL3/5/8, 1850–4.
169 HRO, PL3/5/23, 1897–99.

routinely made available to the poor by 1866[170] and this continued to the end of the poor law system in 1929.

Under the 1911 National Insurance Act workers who earned less than £160 a year contributed 4*d*. a week to receive medical care including for tuberculosis and some sick pay and maternity benefits. Their families however were not covered by this scheme and had to pay for medical care.

The workhouse had an infirmary wing to care for sick residents which had 40 beds in 1848. In 1900 the guardians built a separate infirmary block about 200 yards from the main building. This functioned as a hospital after the abolition of the workhouse in 1929 and still received patients until the North Hampshire Hospital opened in 1974.[171]

Cottage Hospital

In 1867 Wyndham Portal, a paper mill owner from Overton, suggested building a cottage hospital for the poor of Basingstoke. The hospital with eight beds was eventually built on Hackwood Road in 1879 at a cost of £1,160, paid for by subscriptions.[172] No patients with infectious diseases, such as tuberculosis, were admitted. Subscriptions, donations, parish and friendly society payments covered most treatments. Patients had to be recommended for admission either by a subscriber, individual or local parish council; or they, or their employer, paid the fees of between 2*s*. and 8*s*. a week.[173]

Local doctors with a resident matron cared for the patients.[174] In the first year 45 patients were treated. In 1901–2 soldiers injured in the Boer war were transferred from Netley Military Hospital near Southampton.[175] In 1904–5, 110 patients were treated staying for an average of 26 days. Patients paid a total of £90, and subscribers and donations covered £240.[176] Annual financial statements listed subscribers, donations and collections in churches, together with each patient by residence, mainly Basingstoke and nearby rural parishes; condition; outcome, but not name. In some years funds were overstretched.[177] More nursing staff were recruited as patient numbers increased.[178] Between 1914 and 1918, 17 beds were used for injured soldiers of whom 133 were treated in the first year.[179] In the same years a Red Cross Hospital for wounded soldiers in West Ham House on Worting Road treated between 1,600

170 HRO, PL3/5/12, 1865–9.
171 Large, *Workhouse*, 163–5.
172 HRO, 8M62/6.
173 See for example HRO, 35M56/1, 8M62/6.
174 HRO, 144A12/1.
175 HRO, 8M62/6.
176 HRO, 35M84/56/1.
177 HRO, 8M62/7.
178 HRO, 8M62/7.
179 HRO, 8M62/6, 7.

and 1,700 patients, performed 82 operations and had only four deaths.[180]

After the war, fundraising events helped pay for improvements and extensions, including employing a surgeon. New wards, one private; an X-ray department, an ophthalmic department, a children's ward and accommodation for nurses were added by 1925 when its name was changed to Basingstoke Hospital. 795 inpatients and 366 outpatients were treated from 1 June 1925 to 31 May 1926 by five doctors and surgeons at a cost of £3,518, over three-quarters of which was met by donations and subscriptions.[181]

Fig. 36. Park Prewett Hospital.

Hospitals for Infectious Diseases

From 1800 to 1880 there was a series of pest houses in Basingstoke.[182] An infectious diseases hospital opened in 1880. In 1899 it was replaced by a purpose-built brick isolation hospital on Kingsclere Road which had 40 beds in 1905.[183] During a smallpox outbreak in 1902 a small, corrugated iron smallpox hospital was also erected on Kingsclere Road. Typhoid patients in 1905 were nursed in both these fever hospitals.[184]

Hospitals for Psychiatric Illness

Basingstoke union treated the mentally ill who could be admitted to the workhouse or sent to an asylum if they were dangerous. In 1898 as the County Lunatic Asylum

180 *HBG*, 29 Mar. 1919.
181 HRO, 8M62/6; 35M84/56/5.
182 Stokes, *Basingstoke*, 84.
183 HRO, 148M71/1/5/32/2, 16 Nov. 1905.
184 HRO, 35M84/66.

at Knowle near Fareham was becoming overcrowded, Hampshire County Council purchased a site at Park Prewett, north of the town, where a hospital was eventually built in 1917. Initially used as a Canadian military hospital, it opened as Park Prewett Psychiatric Hospital in 1921 (Fig. 36).[185]

Cemeteries and Burial Board

In 1853 William Ranger reported that there were six burial grounds in Basingstoke: at the parish church; the Liten (burial place of the Sandys family) in the ruins of the Holy Ghost chapel; London Street belonging to the Independent Chapel; the Quaker grounds in Totterdown and Wote Street; and one attached to Lady Huntingdon's Chapel.[186] There was no dedicated burial ground for Roman Catholics.

The Basingstoke Burial Board was formed in 1855 and purchased an additional 3 a. of land adjoining the Liten from the trustees of Charles May.[187] This became known as South View Cemetery.[188] The existing burial grounds were all closed under the order of the Secretary of State in 1856.[189] Foundation stones were laid at South View in October 1857 for two separate chapels, built in Victorian High Gothic style; one for Episcopalians who were granted just over half of the new ground; the rest was for Nonconformists.[190] By 1870 the two chapels were in poor condition and continued to require repairs until at least 1922.[191] They were demolished in the 1950s.[192] South View was closed to new burials c.1912 but in 2024 was still available for the interment of some ashes.[193] Notable Basingstoke residents buried at South View include Thomas Burberry clothing manufacturer, Alfred Milward of Milwards Shoes and John Mares of the Manor House, a wholesale clothier.[194]

As space was running out in South View, the Burial Board purchased 25.5 a. of Salisbury Field, Worting Road in 1910 from Mr E.B. Radford at a cost of £5,200 for a new cemetery which opened in 1913.[195] Initially just 10 a. were laid out with gardens

185 HRO, 279M87; above, Social Hist., First World War and its Aftermath.
186 TNA, MH 12/10688 Ranger's Report.
187 *RM,* 28 Dec. 1855; *P.O. Dir*. (1867), 481–2.
188 HRO, 21M65/20F/19.
189 *HA*, 16 June 1855.
190 *HA*, 31 Oct. 1857; *P.O. Dir.* (1867) 481–2; Reavell, *South View*, 10.
191 *HBG*, 12 Aug. 1922.
192 Reavell, *South View, 10.*
193 Pers. Comm. (17 June 2024) from the cemetery manager confirmed that ashes placements still occurred at South View Cemetery but only in existing graves that were already owned.
194 http://www.friendsofthewillis.org.uk/index.php/history/basingstoke-history-hr (accessed 27 June 2017). Above, Economic Hist., The Clothing Industry; Introduction, Substantial Individual Houses.
195 HRO, 148M 1/9/1; TNA, HLG 6/992; South View Conservation Group, *A Guide to the Cemetery Landscape & Design. Walk 4. https://holyghostcemetery-basingstoke.org.uk/wp-content/uploads/2012/08/Walk4LandscapesWEB.pdf* (accessed 26 Sept. 2024).

and burial plots with the remainder to be let for agricultural purposes.[196] A chapel was built in the centre of the plot. Worting Road cemetery had space for 11,753 grave plots, considered sufficient for 45 years but was still in use in 2024.[197] In 1913 it was divided into 478 plots for Roman Catholics, 6,491 for Church of England and 4,784 for Nonconformists.[198] Burials were accepted from Basingstoke and Eastrop.[199]

In 1867 the Quakers purchased 1,000 sq. yds of land for £100 in the south-east corner of the Liten from the GWR. The money was raised by subscriptions from prominent Quaker families in the town: Steevens, Wallis, Meatyard and Hooper.[200] Between 1873 and 1949 22 of the 42 headstones were dedicated to members of the Wallis family.[201]

Gas Supply

The pavement commissioners in January 1834 gave the newly formed Basingstoke Gas and Coke Company permission and £120 a year to install mains and pipes to light the public streets and private buildings. As decreed by the 1815 Paving Act the lighting would only cover seven months of the year and exclude the five nights of each full moon.[202] The company built a gasholder on Gasworks Road, Norden (Norn) Hill (Fig. 37). As demand increased another was built in 1862 north of the existing one at a cost of £1,300. A telescopic gasholder followed in 1869–70. A new double lift telescopic gasholder was commissioned in 1896. With a capacity of 122,000 cu. ft it cost £2,368. The gasworks were enlarged in 1875–6 and upgraded in the 1880s.

Initially some 150 private lights were supplied, increasing to 169 by 1836 and 4,500 by 1874.[203] The LSWR was supplied with gas for lighting its station and approaches in 1839 and the GWR in 1848.[204] From 1845 prices reduced as demand increased.[205] From the 1870s onwards, requests for gas were received from industry, institutions and domestic customers. From 1880, lanterns on public lights were replaced by globe lamps.[206]

Following a request from the pavement commissioners, street lights were lit all year without regard to the full moon from 1871. In the 1880s public lights were

196 TNA, HLG 6/992.
197 TNA, HLG 6/992.
198 TNA, HLG 6/992. In 2024 it was no longer limited to the three categories. https://www.basingstoke.gov.uk/content/page/51099/23412%20Worting%20Road%20Cemetery%20map%20-%20proof%203.pdf (accessed 19 Sept. 2024).
199 TNA, HO 45/10579/181495.
200 HRO, 24M54/313.
201 HRO, 24M54/494/1; *HA*, 10 Dec. 1881.
202 HRO, 76M86/20; 148M71/1/5/7/1, 165–6.
203 HRO, 19M65/B63, B64. The Gas Company recorded the number of lights supplied. Numbers in each house varied.
204 HRO, 19M65/B63.
205 HRO, 19M65/B63.
206 HRO, 19M65/B64.

Fig. 37. Gas works, Norn Hill in 1925.

installed in South View, Southern Road, Hackwood Road and London Road. New houses at South View were connected to gas as they were being built and fitted with gas boilers and cookers, which provided a rental income to the company. In 1887 the company was incorporated as the Basingstoke Gas Company.[207] Contracts for maintaining the street lamps continued with the Urban Sanitary Authority, with four large lamps burning from sunset to sunrise in the centre of the town (including Market Place and Church Square), in 1892.[208] From 1901 all public lights were fitted with incandescent burners. In 1905 a central office and showroom opened in Church Street.[209] A high pressure gas main was installed in Winchester Street, Market Place, London Street, and Church Street in 1913.[210]

From 1914 demand for gas for industrial and domestic purposes increased and a new gas holder was commissioned. Many difficulties were experienced owing to lack of manpower and horses in obtaining coal and cartage until a borrowed steam wagon proved satisfactory and one was later purchased from Wallis and Steevens at a cost of £539 13*s.* 3*d.* By 1917 gas consumption for lighting was down owing to wartime restrictions and increasing use of electricity, but was still increasing for heating and power.[211]

207 HRO, 19M65/B64.
208 HRO, 19M65/B65.
209 HRO, 19M65/B65.
210 HRO, 19M65/B66.
211 HRO, 19M65/B66.

Electricity gradually supplanted gas for public lighting. In 1919 the corporation took over maintenance of the remaining gas lights.[212]

Electricity Supply and Street Lighting

From the 1890s Basingstoke council, encouraged by Thornycroft and the LSWR, considered providing electricity. In 1913, with Board of Trade approval, it erected a generating plant in Brook Street. The gas company, one of the biggest ratepayers, opposed this move claiming unfair competition and offered to supply electricity as well as gas[213] but the council went ahead.[214] The cost of construction and electrical equipment came to £13,000.[215] The supply of electricity started at the end of 1914. Street lighting in the compulsory area of the four main streets (Winchester, London, Wote and Church) was then powered by electricity.[216] Distribution to the rest of the centre, the town boundary, Old Basing and Sherborne St John soon followed.[217]

Firefighting

In 1838 there were three fire engines with buckets and ladders belonging to the town: two engines were held at St Michael's church, and one at the town hall. The watch committee set up a fire brigade with a superintendent, three engineers and twelve firemen (Fig. 38).[218] The engine would be sent to any parish near Basingstoke on receipt of a signed undertaking to pay £2 plus expenses per engine.[219] A new fire engine was purchased in 1861 to operate alongside the two others, dating from 1735 and 1800.[220] In 1838 the Norwich Union Fire Office provided another engine managed by their agent, William Glover, a plumber and painter, at his premises in Winchester Street.[221]

In 1868 responsibility for the fire brigade transferred to the fire brigade committee of the council.[222] In 1871 the Basingstoke and Eastrop Waterworks Company Ltd approved tenders amounting to £621 to provide iron pipes, sluices, cocks and high-pressure hydrants for use in case of fire and for watering the sewers and flushing

212 HRO, 19M65/B66.
213 HRO, 19M65/B66.
214 *HBG*, 16 Nov. 1912.
215 Willis Museum, Folder 6, *Borough of Basingstoke – Electricity*.
216 HRO, 19M65/B66. Compulsory order set out by pavement commissioners.
217 HRO, 68M72/DDC70.
218 HRO, 46M89/20; 148M71/1/6/2, 1 May 1838.
219 HRO, 148M71/1/6/2, 28 May 1838.
220 HRO, 148M71/1/6/3 1 July 1859, 2 Jan. 1860, 1 Apr. 1861 and 1 July 1861; *HBG*, 16 May 1891.
221 *HA*, 17 Feb. 1838.
222 HRO, 148M71/1/3/13, 9 Nov. 1868, 22 Dec. 1868.

Fig. 38. Volunteer Fire Brigade 1887. Superintendent John Burgess Soper has a white beard. Hampshire County Council. Provided by Hampshire Cultural Trust, 2025.

down drains.[223] By 1883 52 hydrants had been placed round the town.[224] A major advance occurred in 1891 when a steam-powered fire engine capable of projecting water more than 160ft was purchased from Messrs Merryweather for £400: £200 raised from subscriptions and £200 from the rates.[225]

In 1911 the Basingstoke brigade consisted of a president, captain, deputy captain, chief engineer, one additional engineer, two sub-engineers, ten firemen and a secretary. Although it was a purely voluntary brigade, the Council provided the clothing and the apparatus.[226]

From 1913 the efficiency of the fire brigade improved, as supported by Overton parish council and Basingstoke RDC, the UDC purchased a motor fire engine and commissioned a new fire station in Brook Street to house it. The fire engine christened 'Amy' in honour of the mayor's wife, was built by Dennis Brothers of Guildford and cost £888.[227] It had a maximum speed of 12 mph, carried ten firemen and a 35ft. telescopic ladder. Its 1,200ft. hose could pump up to 300 gallons of water a minute.[228]

223 HRO, 148M71/1/5/61/1.
224 HRO, 148M71/1/5/61/8.
225 *HBG*, 16 May and 19 Dec. 1891.
226 TNA, HO 45/10664/214369.
227 Dennis Brothers were established in 1895 and played a similar role to Wallis and Steevens and Thornycroft in the economy of the towns. https://www.dennissociety.org.uk/history.html, (accessed 20 Sept. 2024).
228 *HBG*, 8 Nov. 1913.

RELIGIOUS HISTORY

A T THE BEGINNING of the 19th century there were two places of worship for members of the Church of England, St Michael's, Basingstoke's parish church, and St Mary's, in the adjoining parish of Eastrop. For Nonconformists, there was an Independent chapel, a Countess of Huntingdon's Connexion chapel and a Quaker meeting house. All were situated in or near the town centre.

To meet the spiritual needs of the rapidly increasing population and reflecting the impact of the Oxford Movement on the Church of England[1] and the Evangelical Revival within Nonconformity,[2] by 1925 the number of churches, chapels and other places of worship in the town had increased to 20 (Table 10 and Map 7). There was also a Jewish congregation which met in the old Flaxfield College building.

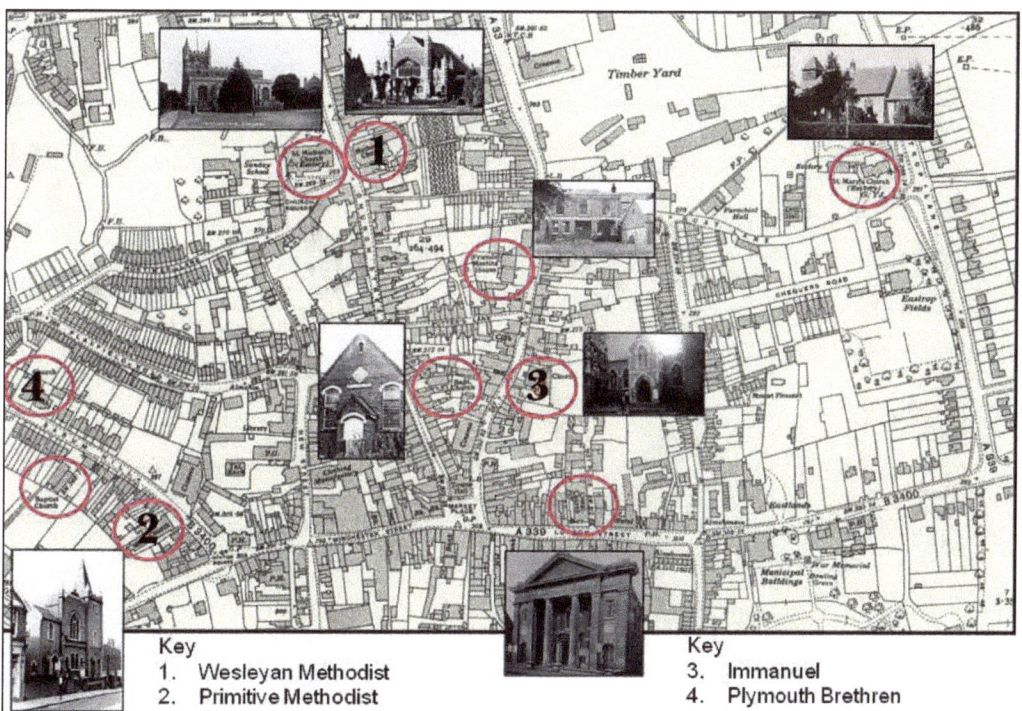

Key
1. Wesleyan Methodist
2. Primitive Methodist

Key
3. Immanuel
4. Plymouth Brethren

Map 7. Basingstoke town centre churches and chapels, 1910. © Roger Ottewill.

1   S.J. Brown, P. Nockles, J. Pereiro (eds), *The Oxford Handbook of the Oxford Movement* (Oxford, 2017).
2   D. Bebbington, *Evangelicalism in Modern Britain: A History from the 1730s to 1980s* (London, 1989).

Description	Location
Church of England	
St Michael's church	Church Street
All Saints	Southern Road
Mission room (St Michael's)	May Street
Mission room (St Michael's)[a]	Reading Road
St Mary's	Eastrop
Nonconformist	
Baptist (Strict/Particular/Ebenezer) chapel	Church Street
Baptist church (Open)	Sarum Hill
Brethren	Southern Road
Congregational[b] church	London Street
Congregational chapel	Worting Town End
Congregational hall[c]	May Street
Countess of Huntingdon's Connexion church[d]	Wote Street
Essex Hall (Brethren)	Essex Road
Friends' meeting house	Wote Street
Methodist (Primitive)	Sarum Hill
Methodist (Wesleyan)	Church Street
Methodist (Wesleyan)	Kempshott Village
Salvation Army barracks	Reading Road
Working Men's mission[e]	George Street
Roman Catholic	
Holy Ghost church	Sherborne Road

Notes
a. *Known as St Andrew's church from the early 20th century.*
b. *During the course of the 19th century the term Independent was gradually superseded by Congregational.*
c. *Previously the Railway mission.*
d. *Variously referred to as chapel and church. Known as Immanuel church from 1894.*
e. *Opened in 1905.*
Source: *Kelly's Dir. Hants 1923 and 1927.*

Table 10. Churches and chapels of Basingstoke in 1925

Between 1800 and 1925 a number of Nonconformist 'causes' failed to establish a permanent presence in the town. There was, for example, an Independent chapel in New Road from 1846 until the 1880s and a Bible Christian chapel during the 1870s.[3]

3   R. Ottewill, 'Bible Christians in Basingstoke', *BAHS Newsletter*, 243 (May 2023), 10–14.

The relative strength of the various denominations can be gauged from the 1851 religious census and surveys of churchgoing undertaken by the *Hants and Berks Gazette* in 1882 and 1903 (Table 11).

Denomination(s)	1851			1882			1903		
	Tot[a]	AdTot[b]	%[c]	Tot[a]	AdTot[b]	%[c]	Tot[a]	AdTot[b]	%[c]
Church of England	1557	1278	29.5	1242	1030	15.1	1677	1417	14.1
Nonconformist	1789	1538	35.6	2809	2359	34.6	2674	2269	22.5
Roman Catholic	---	---	---	112	95	1.4	99	80	0.8
Totals	3346	2816	65.1	4163	3484	51.1	4450	3766	37.4

Notes
a. Tot = total number of enumerated worshippers
b. AdTot = Adjusted total to take account of the double counting of those attending more than one service reducing the figure by just over one third (36%).[4]
c. % = adjusted total as a percentage of the combined population of Basingstoke and Eastrop in 1851 (4325); 1881 (6822) and 1901 (10076) respectively.
Sources: Vickers, The Religious Census of Hampshire 1851 HRS, 12, 1993; Hants and Berks. Gaz., 18 Feb. 1882; and Hants and Berks. Gaz., 21 Mar. 1903.

Table 11. Statistics relating to churchgoing

These figures highlight two major trends. First, the percentage of the population worshipping on the day of the census/survey fell from approximately two-thirds in 1851 to just over a third in 1903. This trend probably continued into the inter-war period even though the churches remained influential community institutions. Second, while Nonconformists outnumbered members of the Church of England, after 1882 the gap between them narrowed.[5]

Relations across the Established Church/Nonconformist divide during the period under review were

Fig. 39. Revd Dr Harry Boustead, vicar of Basingstoke (1905–1936). Hampshire County Council. Provided by Hampshire Cultural Trust, 2025.

4   R.M. Smith (ed.), *The Religious Life of London* (London, 1904).
5   The use of church attendance statistics raises many issues see, for example, C. Field, 'The 1851 Religious Census of Great Britain: a Bibliographical Guide for Local and Regional Historians', *The Local Historian*, 27.4 (1997), 194–217.

generally amicable but were strained at times. Some vicars of St Michael's, such as Dr James Elwin Millard (incumbent from 1864 to 1891), were relatively supportive in their dealings with Nonconformist ministers, and collaborated on issues, such as temperance, and on charitable initiatives. By contrast, Revd Harry Boustead (1905–36, Fig. 39) was at first markedly hostile towards Nonconformists but seems to have mellowed gradually in his attitude. The rectors of Eastrop, who represented the evangelical wing of the Anglican Church, generally worked closely with Nonconformist ministers.

Amongst the principal Nonconformist denominations, a strong spirit of collegiality prevailed, as they sought to give expression to their shared evangelical convictions. Co-operation was evident in united acts of worship, joint missions and fund raising, as well as campaigning on matters of common concern with temperance again to the fore and, for some denominations, opposition to the highly controversial Education Act 1902.[6]

Regarding the population at large, relations were generally harmonious. The one exception was the unrest between 1880 and 1882 accompanying the arrival of the Salvation Army in the town.[7] In the main this did not prejudice the part played by many leading figures in churches and chapels in securing the town's economic prosperity and in civic affairs. The clergy were well-regarded members of the community. Through the many activities that churches sponsored, they contributed not only to the spiritual wellbeing of the town but also to its social life and welfare provision.[8] Places of worship were also prominent features of the town's built environment.[9]

Church of England

Religious Life in the Parish of St Michael's, Basingstoke

In 1800 the parish of Basingstoke was a large one which included Old Basing village and Up Nately. The history is complex, resulting from the status of Old Basing as a minster church before the Norman Conquest, with dependent chapelries including Basingstoke. By 1244, the town had become more important than the village of Old Basing and the vicarage was transferred there by the bishop of Winchester.[10] From

---

6   R. Ottewill, 'A Brotherly Spirit: Free Church Collaboration in Basingstoke c.1860 to 1939', *The Local Historian*, 53 (1), (Jan. 2023), 50–67. R. Ottewill, 'An Act of Iniquity' *Basingstoke and the Education Act 1902* (Basingstoke, 2019); above, Social Hist., Education.

7   B. Clarke, *The Basingstoke Riots: Massaganians v The Salvation Army 1880–1883* (Basingstoke, 2010); above, Local Govt., Riots and Disorder.

8   Above, Social Hist., Social Activities of Religious Organisations.

9   Above, Introduction, Built Character.

10   Hare, *Medieval Basingstoke,* 77–8.

1485 Magdalen College Oxford were patrons of the living. In 1864 Basingstoke and Old Basing became separate parishes.

The vicar of Basingstoke in 1800 was Revd Dr Thomas Sheppard. Inducted in 1768, he held the living until his death in 1814.[11] He also held the living of Quarley from 1762, and had family property in Amport, the neighbouring parish, where he is buried in a family plot outside the north door of its church.[12] He was not therefore permanently resident in Basingstoke and had curates to assist him. In 1800, for example, Revd David Owen is shown as curate for Basingstoke and Revd John Lewis for Old Basing and Up Nately.[13] Basingstoke was a good living, well able to support assistant clergy especially after enclosure allowed agricultural improvements.[14] Dr Sheppard, as a private landowner, favoured enclosure, and acted as an enclosure commissioner in other parts of Hampshire. An anonymous letter accused him of being a 'wolf in sheep's clothing' for supporting the enclosure of Basingstoke's common fields to the detriment of his flock.[15]

In 1773 Revd Samuel Kilner noted that Basingstoke had 'two sermons every Sunday and a lecture every Thursday';[16] Old Basing had two services 'but only one sermon every Sunday, for which the vicar paid a curate'; and Up Nately only had a service once a month conducted by the vicar.[17] As was usual at this time, there was no great stress on regular Holy Communion or confirmation services. In 1783, the bishop, Brownlow North, had visited the parish and performed a service of confirmation for between three and four thousand people, the first such service in 18 years.[18]

At his death, Sheppard left generous bequests to the poor and for the education of children, to which his widow and executrix, Sophia, added.[19] Those relating to Basingstoke are recorded on a charity board in the church. During his life, he applied the rent from Winklebury farm (£15) to the maintenance of the Sunday school and the purchase of books.[20]

In July 1814 Revd James Blatch was presented as Dr Sheppard's successor.[21] Also appointed lecturer, he held both offices for a long period and served as rural dean

11   CCED personal ID 108769.
12   HRO, 21M65/E7/3/1/43; Pevsner, *North Hampshire*, 128–31.
13   HRO, 21M65/B1/126. Bishop's Visitation Return.
14   After the Commutation of Tithes, the sum for vicarial tithes was £497 11*s*. for Basingstoke and £475 for Old Basing.
15   HRO, 11M94/7. Exact date not known, probably *c*.1782–86.
16   Post-Reformation, benefactors such as Sir James Deane and Richard Aldworth left money to pay for a qualified lecturer, appointed by the town, to instruct the people in their faith. By 1800 this was usually the incumbent.
17   Baigent and Millard, *Basingstoke*, 650.
18   Entry in the parish register of Ashe, quoted in Baigent and Millard, *Basingstoke*, 534.
19   TNA, PROB 11/1554/218.
20   Listed with the town's charities, published by curate the Revd Woollnough in 1866; re-printed by *HBG*, 20 Jan. 1933.
21   HRO, 21 M65AZ/2.

from 1829 to 1848. He lived in the rectory as a bachelor and in 1861 had three servants living there to look after him.[22] He worked with Dr Sheppard's widow to carry out her husband's bequests, and like his predecessor, had an interest in education, serving on the board of the National school. He also had curates to assist him, notably Revd Edmund Yeadon from 1828 until his death aged 70 in 1865. Both were commemorated in a west window showing the four evangelists erected by parishioners and friends.[23] Included in Blatch's dedication was: 'he gave largely of his substance and cared for the poor'.[24] James Lunn, one of the last Blue Coat school boys, remembered as a child that the vicar would give a copper to the girls who curtseyed when he met them in the street, and a 'fairing' of threepence or sixpence on fair days.[25] There is little documentary evidence of church life in this period, but in 1851 there were 467 adults and 229 children at the morning service and 448 adults and 233 children at the afternoon – there being no evening service.[26] In Blatch's time 'services were conducted in the old style – the psalms, instead of being chanted, were read in alternate verses'.[27] There was music and a children's choir in the west gallery with the girls in front in red capes and straw hats.[28] Although innately conservative, especially towards the end of his ministry, he had been extremely generous to his parish, most notably when the major restoration programme of 1839–41 severely overran its estimate - meeting the shortfall from his own funds.[29] He also donated a handsome flagon to St Michael's and plate to St Mary's Old Basing and other gifts, including fine Vulliamy tower clocks to both churches, Basingstoke's in 1843.[30] Both Dr Sheppard and Revd Blatch have their coats of arms painted on shields on the nave roof corbels. Revd Blatch was active until the end of his life, chairing a parish vestry meeting shortly before his death aged 90 in 1864.[31]

When the parish was divided in 1864 the new vicar of St Michael's was Revd Dr James Elwin Millard (Fig. 40) from Oxford, where he had been master of Magdalen school for many years. His interest in education continued in Basingstoke. Seeing that infants were not well catered for, he opened an infants' school in Church Cottage in 1865 and made his barn at the rear of Church Cottage available for a girls' school in 1870, both part of the National school's provision.[32] Arriving as a bachelor he married Dora Frances Sclater of Hoddington House, Upton Grey, in 1866 and they had a family of seven children.

22 *Census*, 1881.
23 See commemorative plaque at the west end of the church.
24 Baigent and Millard, *Basingstoke*, 95.
25 James Lunn, *HBG*, 29 May 1936.
26 *Religious Census, 1851.*
27 G. Woodman, 'Reminiscences of Basingstoke 70 years ago', *HBG*, 6, 13 Mar. 1926.
28 James Lunn, *HBG*, 29 May 1936.
29 Below, Religious Buildings.
30 Plaque on the clock in the ringing chamber.
31 HRO, 46M74/PV2.
32 HRO 46M74/PZ1, PZ12; above, Social Hist., Education.

Fig. 40. Revd Dr James Elwin Millard with school teachers. Hampshire County Council. Provided by Hampshire Cultural Trust, 2025.

He was a churchman greatly influenced by the ideas and practices of the Oxford Movement and pursued many initiatives to help his parishioners, both practically and spiritually. Much information about the life of the church at this time can be gained from the parish magazine which he instituted in 1865.[33] This lists many more services than previously, both daily and weekly, as well as occasional offices.[34] Dr Millard wrote the content and subsidised the cost, and his energetic and reforming voice can almost be heard. Like his predecessor he was appointed lecturer. In 1865, there were two curates, Revd J.B.W. Woollnough and Revd W.J. Burdett, an organist and choir of over 20 men and boys for Sunday services. There were also bible classes and confirmation classes.[35] In 1870 Dr Millard established the Guild of St Michael for the mutual support and encouragement of new communicants in their religious life and practice, and for the promotion of church work in the parish.[36] Members were of great assistance in the vicar's efforts to reach everyone in the parish and helped with the establishment of two mission halls.[37] Another early initiative was the district visitor scheme, with visitors being responsible for a particular area of the town, reporting the need for clergy visits or practical help – or simply delivering the magazine.[38] The

33   HRO, 46M74/PZ1.
34   HRO, 46M74/PZ1.
35   HRO, 46M74/PZ1.
36   HRO, 46M74/PZ10.
37   Below, Anglican Church Architecture.
38   By 1873, the circulation was over 700, HRO, 46M74/PZ16.

vicar's two sisters helped with this and other work in the parish. For parishioners there were many opportunities for entertainment, learning and fundraising. One curate, Revd C.H. Lacon, a keen bellringer, started a local society of bellringers at the church in 1879.[39] This group flourished and in 1896 had the distinction of being the first ringers to include a woman in ringing a peal.[40]

In April 1871, the churchwardens' census recorded 690 people at the morning service, 296 in the afternoon and 734 in the evening. The 1882 survey showed that 514 and 549 people attended the two main services, the largest single congregations in the town.[41] Nonetheless, despite Dr Millard's efforts, the congregations were smaller than those recorded in 1851 although given the growth of Sunday schools in this period, it is likely that children were not included. Millard favoured the temperance movement, supported the SPCK Missionary Society and believed in working with fellow clergy in the town.[42] In the January 1873 issue he wrote: 'There are few parishes in which there is a greater diversity of religious opinion… there is amongst us a singular absence of bitterness and intolerance, for which God be praised.'[43]

He was an energetic incumbent, who with Francis Baigent, found time to contribute to and publish in 1889: *A History of the Town and Manor of Basingstoke in the County of Southampton*.[44] A valuable source for local historians ever since, it includes transcripts of documents in the Magdalen College library and church records, some of which are no longer extant. In June 1890, by this time a canon of Winchester Cathedral, Dr Millard gave notice of his intention to retire, due to age and ill health. Leaving by the end of the year, he died in Oxford in 1894.[45] The clerestory lights were glazed with stained glass in his memory and a brass memorial plaque in the church was dedicated by the bishop in April 1896.[46]

Millard's successor, Revd Henry R. Cooper Smith was inducted in January 1891, but did not move into the rectory until October. He was unmarried but his sisters lived with him.[47] He continued the work of his predecessor with a proper provision of services and groups for spiritual development. He was also involved in social concerns, missionary work and particularly in education and work with young people.

The 1903 census of churchgoing recorded attendance at St Michael's as 594 in the morning and 563 in the evening, with 51 attending St Andrew's mission church in Reading Road in the evening and 58 the May Street mission.[48] After a relatively short

39   HRO, 46M74/PZ27.
40   Noted on peal board in belfry.
41   Above, Table 11.
42   HRO, 46M74/PZ13; *RM*, 10 Oct. 1868.
43   HRO, 46M74/PZ16.
44   F.J. Baigent and J.E. Millard, *A History of the Ancient Town and Manor of Basingstoke in the County of Southampton* (Basingstoke and London, 1889).
45   HRO, 46M74/PZ43.
46   HRO, 46M74/PZ45.
47   *Census*, 1901.
48   *HBG*, 23 Mar. 1903.

ministry Revd Cooper Smith left Basingstoke in 1905. However, he had continued the programme of church outreach by establishing another daughter church, All Saints, like the two mission halls, but on a far grander scale, to cater for the expanding population in the south of the town.[49] He was also instrumental in the establishment of St John's, a purpose-built Sunday school, on the corner of Brook Street and Church Street, used as a day school from 1901.[50] As a parting gift, he donated the impressive font cover for St Michael's, which was dedicated in 1908.[51] It was one of the last designs by the well-known church architect, G.F. Bodley.

Revd Harry Boustead served as vicar from 1905 until May 1936. He was a strict high churchman, an imposing figure whom some older members of recent congregations remembered from their childhood.[52] The established life of the church, its services, educational interests, clubs and charitable interests continued as before, with the magazine for January 1909 listing, in addition to services, the meetings of: the district visitors (for 55 districts), the Guild, the Church of England Temperance Society, the Men's Society, the Church Lads' Brigade, choir practice, the Blanket club, the Dorcas Society and the Sunday schools.[53] Later, following their marriage in 1909, the Mothers' Union became a particular interest of his wife, their enrolling member. She also served as central president of the Mothers' Union between 1927 and 1933.[54]

Quite early in his ministry there occurred an event which received much adverse publicity, nationally as well as locally. It was customary in the town for the mayor and corporation to process to St Michael's soon after mayor making. Although Revd Boustead gave the sermon at this service in 1906 (when the mayor was a Congregationalist) he changed his mind the following year and wrote a highly controversial letter to the town clerk to say that the mayor (one of his churchwardens) and the corporation, yeomanry, police etc. would not be welcome because they were also attending a service at the Congregational church. The Anglican service was cancelled but went ahead the following year, despite the vicar's intolerant stance. By 1909, he had mellowed in his attitude towards the Nonconformists – who were often leading members of the corporation - and took a proper part in the service.[55] Moreover, in later years he did work with other clergy in the town. An important period of his ministry was the four years of the First World War, when the church was very supportive of soldiers billeted locally. [56]

As the population grew and housing expanded, outreach mission halls (from 1873) and the new church of All Saints (from 1902) were built.[57]

49   Below, Anglican Church Architecture: Anglican Mission Halls.
50   Above, Social Hist., Education, St John's.
51   HRO, 46M74/PZ56.
52   Pers. Comm. Mr A. Attwood, (d. 2002), and Mrs B. Godden, (d. 2019).
53   HRO, 46M74/PZ57.
54   HRO, 46M74/PZ81.
55   *HBG*, 4 Nov. 1909.
56   Above, Social Hist., First World War and its Aftermath.
57   Below, Anglican Church Architecture.

St Mary's Eastrop

Between 1800 and 1925, Eastrop remained a separate ecclesiastical parish with a tradition of evangelical churchmanship but in 1891 the central part of the civil parish of Eastrop including St Mary's transferred into the municipal borough of Basingstoke.[58] The church continued to serve as a place of worship for those who identified with the evangelical wing of the Church of England. As the *Hants and Berks Gazette* commented on Revd Crawford Hills' appointment as rector in 1906, this ensured 'a continuance of those evangelical doctrines which have been for so many years a distinguishing feature of that church, and one which has contributed not a little to its success and development'.[59]

Anglican Church Architecture

St Michael's

St Michael's church externally looked much the same in 1800 as it had in the 16th century (Fig. 41). There were, however, many internal changes during the 19th century. Expansion of the population saw work to increase the available seating. In 1839 a committee for alterations was set up with Revd Blatch as chairman to plan major improvements.[60] John Clacy of Reading, architect, oversaw the work to which the Incorporated Church Building Society gave a grant.[61] Galleries were added along the length of the aisles, new pews were introduced, with narrower side aisles. The benches in the side aisles and in the wider centre aisle provided more free seating. The south door was superseded as the main entrance by the insertion of the west door which led into the first bay of the church below the gallery, which was partitioned off as a vestibule (Fig. 42). This was described by Dr Millard in 1879 as 'closed off with stone and glass, where people wore hats and talked'.[62] The organ remained in the west gallery. The nave roof was renewed, and the floor partially repaved in black and white stone. Many monuments and grave markers were either re-sited or removed. Changes and delays meant that the work, carried out by local firm, Dewey and Nicholls, ended up costing much more than the original estimate of £1,550. The situation was saved by Revd Blatch, who contributed a third of the total amount. The roof work resulted in the loss of the armorial paintings in the arch spandrels recorded in Dukes' drawing.[63] Also at this time, the Jacobean pulpit was transferred to, and installed at, Old Basing.

Nonetheless, Dr Millard was not satisfied with the state of the church and instigated

---

58   Above, Introduction, Boundaries.
59   *HBG*, 5 May 1906.
60   HRO, 46M74/PW1.
61   The plans are held at LPL.
62   HRO, 46M74/PZ27.
63   Pencil drawing before the alterations, made into a print in 1840.

Fig. 41. St Michael's church early 19th century.

further improvements.[64] These included opening up the arch into St Stephen's chapel; revealing the timbers of the chancel roof; repaving and re-plastering the chancel; introducing stained glass windows; removing the recently installed pulpit which he considered unsightly and replacing it with another in memory of Bishop Wilberforce and instituting heating and lighting so that winter and evening services were made more comfortable. By the time he retired, every window except in the clerestories was filled with stained glass.[65] Clerestory glazing was his memorial. A curate, Revd C.H. Lacon, was instrumental in improving the churchyard and raising funds to complete the enhancement of the tower with pinnacles designed by architect T.H. Wyatt (Fig. 1),[66] whose work also included the chancel arch improvement with head-stops representing Queen Victoria and Bishop Fox. On 28 December 1885, Holy Innocents Day, a new font provided by subscription in memory of Mr Lamb was dedicated at the west end. Designed by G.F. Bodley, it was made from red sandstone from Dumfries.[67] Another addition to the church during the incumbency of Dr Cooper Smith[68] was a carved chancel screen to commemorate the Diamond Jubilee of Queen Victoria in 1897.[69]

64   HRO, 46M74/PZ27.
65   Baigent and Millard, *Basingstoke*, 91–6.
66   HRO, 46M74/PZ27.
67   HRO, 46M74/PZ37.
68   *HBG*, 2 Jan. 1886.
69   HRO, 46M74/PZ46.

Fig. 42. St Michael's interior after Victorian alterations.

Dr Boustead also introduced a scheme in 1906 for improving the church, concentrating on seating and concreting parts of the floor which were still earth and covering them with wood blocks.[70] The work was undertaken in 1910, with new choir stalls and organ dedicated in 1911.[71] A carved oak altar given in memory of Mrs Lefroy in St Stephen's chapel was dedicated in 1913, and later wooden figures of St Francis, St Clare and St Margaret, carved in Oberammergau (Garmisch-Partenkirchen, Germany), were given by her sister to complete the altar.[72] Also at this time an appeal was launched to repair the church roof, and work began on the nave and tower in summer 1913.[73]

After the First World War, two major options for commemorating the fallen were considered.[74] Dr Boustead favoured building a new church in the west of the town, where the population was increasing. The eventual choice, however, was adding a memorial chapel to St Michael's. This was designed by Sir Charles Nicholson in a style and materials which complemented the existing building.[75]

During the work to make an opening at the east end of the north aisle, two niches were discovered, originally on either side of an altar, which had been blocked up at the Reformation. Statues for the niches, designed by the architect, formed a memorial

70   HRO, 46M75/PW3.
71   HRO, 46M74/PZ61.
72   HRO, 46M74/PZ61.
73   HRO, 46M74/PZ61.
74   HRO, 46M74/PZ65.
75   HRO, 46M74/PZ66.

to Lt Leslie Ranson, who died in 1918. The chapel was consecrated in September 1920 (Fig. 43).[76] A further memorial was a Book of Remembrance with an illuminated manuscript title page, collated by Mrs Boustead and helpers. It recorded the names and details of home, school, military service, place of death and burial, and where possible, a photograph of all those in the parish who had died.

At the rear of St Michael's is Church Cottage, one of Basingstoke's oldest buildings.[77] Now listed, it has been used for many purposes, but especially from the incumbency of Dr Millard, as parish rooms and Sunday and day schools.[78]

Fig. 43. Memorial chapel, St Michael's church. © Active Shot

All Saints

As the town grew to the south, the need to serve this population with a church was increasingly recognised. In 1902 the sisters of Revd Cooper Smith bought a piece of land, formerly a cattle market, for this purpose at the junction of Southern Road and Victoria Street.[79] The vicar initially organised the purchase and erection of an iron church, costing just over £160, as a temporary measure. It was dedicated on All Saints'

76   HRO, 46M74/PZ68.
77   Hare, *Medieval Basingstoke*, 13–15.
78   M. Oliver, *Church Cottage Basingstoke* (*BAHS*, 2008).
79   HRO, 46M74/PZ51.

Day 1902[80] and could accommodate 130 worshippers.[81] In 1910–11 money was raised to extend the church westwards and add another 48 seats.[82] Fundraising was also begun to replace it with a permanent church, originally planned as a brick building to which Revd Hall, a retired clergyman living in Basingstoke, had contributed £5,000. At his request, the architect Temple Moore reworked the plans to rebuild in stone, and he paid most of the additional cost of £13,000. The resulting building is in the Late Gothic style for which Temple Moore is renowned (Fig. 44).[83] Inside, most of the colour and detail in the High Church tradition is at the east end. The rood screen, painted barrel-vaulted roof, lectern, pulpit, organ loft and Warrior chapel were all designed by him giving a very harmonious effect. The high altar reredos was designed by Mary Temple Moore.[84] Before building work began, the iron church was dismantled just after Easter 1915 and re-erected close by, serving as the parish hall when the new church was completed. Despite the war, work was undertaken by retired stonemasons past the age of military service, and the church was consecrated in September 1917.[85]

Fig. 44. All Saints church and church hall. Courtesy of Alastair Blair.

80   *HBG*, 8 Nov. 1902.
81   *HBG*, 21 Mar. 1903.
82   HRO, 46M74/PZ63.
83   G.K. Brandwood, *Temple Moore: An Architect of the Late Gothic Revival* (Stamford, 1997).
84   https://www.allsaintsbasingstoke.net/ (accessed 4 June 2024).
85   *HBG*, 29 Sept. 1917.

Amongst the many welcome gifts was the ring of bells given by John May.[86] Nine bells were installed, an unusual number allowing the ringing of a minor key octave – the suggestion of the vicar. With the senior curate serving as priest in charge, there was a change in personnel every two or three years.

Anglican Mission Halls

During the second half of the 19th century, Basingstoke's population grew rapidly, especially near the railway and the centres of industry, resulting in the need for church outreach in these areas. One such was Totterdown, east of St Michael's at the start of Reading Road, one of the poorer parts of the town with dense housing. Dr Millard particularly identified the need for schooling in this area and proposed a new school in 1871. Later that year a small school was opened in Steam Dell where open-air services had been held since 1866 by both Anglicans and Nonconformists. The recently formed St Michael's Guild,[87] assisted by two curates, organised these mission services together with a night school centre teaching young men and boys to read and write.[88] Larger premises were required and a mission hall/school was built across the road on the site of two old cottages opening in November 1873.[89] In 1876 a harmonium was given to the mission hall in memory of Frances Millard, the vicar's sister, by her friends.[90] The school became a public elementary school from 1878 to 1888.[91] The mission hall was renamed St Andrew's church in the early years of the 20th century. It remained a place of worship until 1950 and was demolished in the 1960s.

Similarly, another mission hall was set up to cater for the westward growth of the town at Newtown. After conducting a service in 1883 in Longcroft Road (later May Street), the vicar opened a subscription for building the new mission chapel on the site of an old workshop of Mr Powell's.[92] It was a simple brick building similar to other mission halls built gable end to the street with a simple bell turret and porch. Services were taken by a licensed lay reader, Dr Miller, and there was an active Sunday school,[93] which continued until all these buildings were lost to town development in the 1960s.

St Mary's Eastrop

The fabric of the ancient church of St Mary's Eastrop was almost completely rebuilt during the 19th century. First the chancel was replaced in brick with stone dressings in 1835, then in 1886 the nave was rebuilt in rough ashlar stone.[94] In 1911, during

86   HRO, 46M74/PZ65; above, Economic Hist., Brewing; Social Hist., Social Structure.
87   Above, Religious Life.
88   *HBG,* 29 May 1936.
89   HRO, 46M74/PZ16.
90   HRO, 46M74/PZ22.
91   *HBG,* 21 Mar. 1903; above, Social Hist., Education.
92   *HBG,* 29 May 1936.
93   *HBG,* 21 Mar. 1936.
94   *VCH Hants,* IV, 149.

the Revd Crawford Hills' incumbency (1906–1920), the congregation grew so large that the church could not accommodate all those wishing to attend. Consequently, it was decided to extend the nave westwards. Work, supervised by Sir T.G. Jackson, was completed in 1912 costing over £1,100 and resulting in 275 sittings.[95] The church has a wooden bell-turret covered by a tiled roof.[96]

Nonconformity

Religious Life and Buildings

Independents/Congregationalists

On 25 August 1801, those Dissenters who identified with the Independent cause, and dated their origins to the immediate aftermath of the Great Ejection of 1662, moved from a meeting house in Cross Street to 'new and handsome' purpose-built premises on the north side of London Street's eastern end.[97] With seating for 500 worshippers, they were designed in response to the large increase in the congregation which had occurred during the first ten years of Revd John Jefferson's ministry.[98]

During the 19th century the church thrived, being served by a succession of capable and committed clergymen.[99] Later ministers, Revd Reginald Thompson (1907–10) and Revd Rocliffe Mackintosh (1912–26) were, like their predecessors, inspirational preachers with sermons being a key feature of Sunday worship, especially at monthly evangelistic services introduced in the late 1880s.

Under their leadership and that of the diaconate, membership grew to approximately 300 in the first decade of the 20th century. Likewise, the Sunday school rapidly expanded, recording over 600 scholars and requiring many volunteers to perform the teaching and administrative roles. The spiritual needs of adolescents were met by establishing a Christian Endeavour Society in 1893, the first Nonconformist church in Basingstoke to do so. For adults the church ran, for many years, a Mutual Improvement Society,[100] and from 1899, a very successful Pleasant Sunday Afternoon (or Men's Own Brotherhood) Society. These reflected the congregation's

---

95　*Kelly's Dir.* (1915), 54.

96　NHLE, no. 1092578, Ch. of St Mary, Eastrop Ln (accessed 9 May 2024).

97　'Memoir of the Late Revd Joseph Jefferson of Thirsk, Yorkshire,' *Evangelical Magazine and Missionary Chronicle* (Jan. 1825), 1–7.

98　Baigent and Millard, *Basingstoke*, 544.

99　R. Ottewill, 'Ministers of London Street Independent/Congregational Church, Basingstoke, in the Nineteenth Century', *Jnl of the United Reformed Church History Society,* 10(8) (2021), 423–51.

100　R. Ottewill, 'Churches and Adult Education in the Edwardian Era: Learning from the Experiences of Hampshire Congregationalists' in M. Ludlow, C. Methuen and A. Spicer (eds) *Studies in Church History, 55: The Church and Education* (Cambridge, 2019), 494–510; above, Social Activities of Religious Organisations.

commitment to the doctrine of the institutional church, which meant sponsoring a range of affiliated organisations for meeting, not only the spiritual needs, but also the recreational and educational needs of church members. By the first decade of the 20th century, the standing of the Congregational church was such that in November 1908, Councillor William Cannon, newly appointed mayor of Basingstoke and leading churchman, indicated that it was generally regarded as the chief Nonconformist place of worship in the town.[101] Moreover, the church's influence was felt in the community at large with some of Basingstoke's leading businessmen and politicians being members. These included ironmongers and council members Thomas Maton Kingdon and his son Herbert; a draper and council member, Henry Jackson; a nurseryman and council member, Thomas Edney; and clothing manufacturers George Ames and John Mares.[102]

Beyond Basingstoke, the church was an active member of the Hampshire Congregational Union, with ministers holding the offices of evangelistic secretary and general secretary and, on occasions, hosting its half-yearly meetings. It also served as the mother church for chapels it had established in neighbouring rural communities - Mapledurwell (founded 1864), Pyott's Hill (1872), Winslade (1887), Ellisfield (1894) and Farleigh Wallop (1900).[103] Overseen by an evangelist, on the first Sunday in May, the church celebrated village Sunday signifying its commitment to Basingstoke's spiritual hinterland.[104]

During the 19th century the London Street church was enlarged and improved on various occasions to accommodate the expanding congregation and range of activities. A newly erected and spacious schoolroom was opened in August 1838.[105] In December 1839, the church reopened following repair and enlargement. This included the erection of two new galleries for the Sunday school children; the provision of approximately 150 additional sittings and ornamentation with a neat Gothic front of Bath stone, from a design by Clacy of Reading.[106]

In 1860, the building was again substantially enlarged and subsequently described as 'one of Basingstoke's outstanding buildings, with its attractive façade complete with pillars of Grecian style' (Fig. 6).[107] Interior alterations included adding a large number of spacious pews and adopting a new system of lighting which had 'a very beautiful effect.'[108] The following year, the back wall of the chapel was partly removed, enabling

101 *HBG*, 14 Nov. 1908. R. Ottewill, ' "The Chief Nonconformist Place of Worship in the Town"; London Street Congregational Church, Basingstoke, during the Edwardian Era 1901–1914', *Jnl of the United Reformed Church History Society*, 11.5 (2024), 250–76.

102 Above, Economic Hist., The Clothing Industry.

103 For a history of one chapel see R. Ottewill, 'A Perfect Little Paradise. A History of Winslade Congregational Chapel 1888–1935', *HFC Newsletter*, 56 (2011), 3–6.

104 *HBG*, 7 May 1910.

105 *HC*, 3 Sept. 1838.

106 *RM*, 28 Dec. 1839.

107 A. Attwood, *The Illustrated History of Basingstoke* (Derby, 2001), 67.

108 *RM*, 27 Oct. 1860.

an organ to be placed in a recess with seats for the choir surrounding it, thereby much improving the look of the building's interior and assisting the singing.[109] In 1872, the length of the schoolroom was increased by 12ft. and six new classrooms and an infant school room were added.

A new organ costing £285 was installed in 1876, together with a handsome new pulpit and various other improvements costing £70. This resulted in the need for further alterations since the pews and galleries were 'now sadly out of harmony'.[110] Thus, in 1882 new galleries were constructed and re-seated along with the ground floor area; a pulpit erected and Communion railings installed which harmonised with the building as a whole.[111] Attention was also given to the decorations, lighting, heating and ventilation. The total cost was approximately £1,250, of which £400 still had to be raised when the church was reopened.

Additional schoolrooms were added in 1888, in response to the 'very encouraging growth' of the Sunday school and bible classes which had resulted in conditions that were 'very trying for the teachers, and uncomfortable, if not unhealthy … [for] the scholars'.[112] The total cost, including what was still owing on the church renovation, was £950, with £800 having already been raised.[113] In 1894 the church was redecorated again, with the words 'O worship the Lord in the Beauty of Holiness' being painted over the recess for the organ, at a cost of £182 10s.[114]

London Street's commitment to the previously mentioned doctrine of the institutional church was evident in the construction of a new lecture hall in 1906–7. Situated in May Place, alongside the church, and opened in April 1907, it was intended that this facility should serve demands arising from the formation of the Boys' Brigade and future initiatives.[115] The foundations of the single storey building were such that they could accommodate the addition of two further storeys if necessary.

In 1915 electric lighting was installed in the church, schoolroom and May Place Hall. Two post-war projects were the installation of a new organ in January 1922, incorporating the best parts of the old organ and costing £1,500,[116] and new heating provision in 1923.[117]

Within the borough, in about 1872 a Congregational chapel was constructed at Worting Town End. A very simple building, it could accommodate about 90 worshippers.[118] In 1913 the premises of the Railway mission were purchased by

109 *RM*, 11 May 1861.
110 *RM,* 12 Aug. 1876.
111 *RM*, 16 Dec. 1882.
112 *RM*, 14 Apr. 1888.
113 *RM*, 29 Sept. 1888.
114 *HBG*, 9 June 1894.
115 *HBG*, 4 May 1907.
116 *HBG*, 19 Nov. 1921.
117 *HBG*, 24 Nov. 1923.
118 R. Ottewill, 'Congregationalism in Worting *c.*1840 to 1965: A Brief History', *BAHS Newsletter,* 232 (2020), 13–18.

London Street, renovated at a cost of approximately £100, and formally reopened in November as a Congregational place of worship. These premises were modernised in 1925.[119]

London Street Congregational (United Reformed from 1972) church survived the town centre redevelopment and can be visited. It is one of the iconic buildings in London Street.[120]

Countess of Huntingdon's Connexion

The Huntingdonian presence in Basingstoke was a legacy of the Evangelical Revival of the 18th century. In July 1802, a new chapel, on the site of existing premises in Wote Street, was opened for divine worship.[121] The chapel's dimensions were within the walls 55ft. by 27ft. and constituted of brick.[122] It could accommodate 600 people but in 1851 the number of sittings was only 325 (free 110; others 215).[123]

The Countess of Huntingdon's Connexion shared with Methodism its evangelical roots, adopted an Independent/Congregational form of church governance, but subscribed to the Anglican liturgy. Thus, the original trust deed required the use of the Book of Common Prayer at all services and although this requirement was eventually dropped the church continued to promote itself on the basis of its liturgical services. Moreover, a number of its ministers subsequently joined the Church of England while others served Congregational as well as Connexion churches. The fortunes of the church reflected, to some extent, their personality, preaching style and theological stance.[124] For example, Revd Dr James Barnes (1893–95) was described as 'an ardent evangelist, carrying the message of the Gospel, and … fill[ing] the Church almost to suffocation every Sunday'[125] and Revd Eustace Long (1899–1906), 'a thoughtful preacher, a sympathising Pastor, and an instructive teacher'.[126]

As well as regular Sunday services and those for special occasions, over the years the church sponsored various satellite organisations, including a Sunday school and a branch of Christian Endeavour, established in 1895. A key strand in the life of what became Immanuel Church in 1894 was music with a notable feature for many years being a performance of Stainer's Crucifixion at Eastertide. In 1922 the church was privileged to host the 100th anniversary conference of the Countess of Huntingdon's Connexion.

---

119 *Basingstoke Congregational Magazine* Vol.19 n.s. 1 (Jan. 1926). Demolished in 1960s.
120 https://historicengland.org.uk/listing/the-list/list-entry/1230843 (accessed 3 Sept. 2024); above, Introduction, Built Character, Top of the Town.
121 A.C.H. Seymour, *The Life and Times of Selina Countess of Huntingdon,* Vol. 1 (London, 1859), 393.
122 HRO, 571/1.
123 *Rel. Census,* 1851.
124 R. Ottewill, 'Born in Methodist Fervour: The Countess of Huntingdon's Connexion in Basingstoke, *c.*1755– 1915', *Proc. of the Wesley Historical Society,* 63.2 (2021), 43–57.
125 *HBG,* 13 Nov. 1931.
126 *HBG,* 13 Nov. 1931.

Fig. 45. Countess of Huntingdon's Connexion church in Wote Street after 1894.

From the mid 19th century onwards various improvements were made to the chapel. In November 1861 the re-pewed church was reopened[127] and in 1874 the distinctive new porch and tower were added (Fig. 45).[128] Three years later a new organ was installed in the gallery. New classrooms, designed by Richard Sterry Wallis, were built in 1891.[129]

Renovations took place in 1894[130] and 1911, thereby increasing the comfort and convenience of the worshippers and greatly improving the appearance of the building.[131] The cost of the latter was £250, of which £70 still needed to be raised at the time of the re-opening. In 1921, the organ was renovated. The church experienced a long, drawn-out decline, particularly after the Second World War, resulting in its eventual closure and demolition in 1969.[132] In 2024, a monument indicated where it had stood.

Primitive Methodists

Between their arrival in the 1830s and 1840s and the Methodist Union of 1932, the Primitive Methodists retained their distinctive identity, while enjoying productive

127 *RM*, 23 Nov. 1861.
128 *RM*, 19 Dec. 1874.
129 *HBG*, 5 Dec. 1891.
130 *HBG*, 24 Mar. 1894.
131 *HO*, 16 Aug. 1911.
132 Ottewill, 'Methodist Fervour', 58.

relations with other Nonconformist denominations in the town. Indeed, their ministers were often described as 'brotherly', serving not only their church and circuit but also the wider community.[133] Among them was Revd Henry Yeates (1869–73), who 'was especially gifted to stir and edify a congregation' and later returned to Basingstoke, serving as a borough councillor from 1884 to 1887.[134] In leading their church and circuit, ministers received support and encouragement from the laity, who performed key roles in church sponsored organisations from the Sunday school to a flourishing Christian Endeavour Society; from brass bands to the choir and from women's groups to a Peoples' Pleasant Hour. These cemented the loyalty of members and provided a means of reaching out to those unattached to any church. Indeed, evangelism was the theme running through much of the life of the church, with its anniversary celebrations, missions, camp meetings, concerts and entertainments.[135]

Prior to 1847 when their first small chapel was erected in Flaxfield Road, just to the west of the town centre, Primitive Methodists held their gatherings in various locations – in the open-air at Totterdown; in a courtyard at Bunnian Place, at the west end of the town and south of the railway; and in a timber yard owned by Mr Etheridge.[136] The cost of the chapel was £387[137] and it could accommodate 127. However, increases in the size of the congregation meant that on two occasions it had to be enlarged. The first was in 1864. This involved demolishing the greater part of the original chapel and building a replacement of nearly double the size at a cost of £373 3s. 8d.[138] The second enlargement in 1881 involved extending the chapel by 20ft. at the rear of the premises and adding a small classroom connected to the chapel by a lobby, which also gave access to the minister's house. The premises were also re-seated and re-lighted with provision being made for heating by hot water pipes.[139] Architecturally, the chapel remained a relatively plain and simple building. One consequence of these building projects was an ongoing debt, which in 1897 stood at £365.[140]

Debts notwithstanding, at the 1894 anniversary of the chapel it was reported that even since the previous enlargement 'they had seen the congregations overflow'.[141] Thus, by 1898 consideration was being given to the erection of a new chapel in another part of town.[142] Plans for a new church proceeded apace with over £600

---

133 R. Ottewill, 'From Flaxfield Road to Sarum Hill': The Consolidation of Primitive Methodism in Basingstoke, c. 1833 to 1923', *Proc. of the Wesley Historical Society*, 62.6 (Autumn 2020), 231–255.

134 Ottewill, 'Flaxfield Road', 240–1.

135 Ottewill, 'Flaxfield Road', 240–1.

136 Baigent and Millard, *Basingstoke*, 550–1; *HBG*, 29 Dec. 1933.

137 *HBG*, 28 July 1923.

138 *The Primitive Methodist Mag.*, 1864, 743; *RM*, 16 Jan. 1864.

139 *HBG*, 3 Sept. 1881.

140 *HBG*, 22 May 1897.

141 *HBG*, 26 May 1894.

142 *HBG*, 14 May 1898.

being raised to fund the new project.[143] A site on Sarum Hill, near the junction with Winchester Street, was purchased; the foundation stone laid in September 1901 and the new church opened in July 1902. Designed by T.E. Davidson of London, it was considered a 'creditable addition to the public buildings of the town from an architectural point of view … the red pressed facing bricks, with Portland stone dressings … [provided], in the impression of at least one competent and independent expert, one of the best examples of this class of work in the town.'[144] Moreover, with its arched windows and pointed pinnacles it reflected the influence of the Gothic Revival and represented a marked departure from the simplicity associated with the Primitive Methodists (Fig. 46). The cost was approximately £4,000 and the debt was only finally extinguished in 1923. It was demolished in July 1970.

Fig. 46. *Primitive Methodist church on Sarum Hill in 1903.*

Wesleyan Methodists

According to Revd William Ellis a particular challenge in the early days of the Wesleyan Methodist presence in Basingstoke was building the first chapel. Eventually some old cottages in Church Street were purchased and demolished, thereby enabling the erection of a chapel.[145] This move was described as being 'a considerable advantage to the architecture of the town'.[146] The site was directly opposite St Michael's. A board of trustees was formed and a fund-raising campaign launched. Plans were prepared by Mr Wonnacott but were substantially modified to ensure that the chapel could be afforded. Eventually the foundation stone was laid in June 1875. The total cost was expected to be about £1,300.[147] Officially opened in November 1876,[148] the new chapel

---

143 *HBG*, 28 July 1923.
144 *HBG*, 19 July 1902.
145 *HBG*, 3 Apr. 1920, recounting his experiences 50 years later.
146 *RM*, 26 June 1875.
147 *RM*, 26 June 1875.
148 *HBG*, 27 June 1896.

had accommodation for about 320 worshippers, plus rooms for Sunday school and other classes.

Once established, the Basingstoke Wesleyan Methodist circuit was well served by its superintendent ministers, with the town congregation having the privilege of hearing them preach more frequently than those of the other churches.[149] One example was Revd Walter Barnes (1912–15) who was renowned for the strong leadership he provided.[150]

The Wesleyans were also fortunate in having some long-serving and committed laymen such as Edward Kynaston, who served as Sunday school superintendent for many years in the late 19th and early 20th centuries, and William Higgs, the Circuit chapel secretary during the same period, who was also a member of Basingstoke school board. They enabled the church to support a wide variety of affiliated organisations, such as the thriving Sunday school; a branch of the Wesley Guild from 1897; a Mutual Improvement Association for a number of years in the late 1870s/early 1880s; a Ladies' Sewing party/meeting and Women's Bright Hour. These, alongside regular and special services and many ad hoc activities, including support for both home and overseas missions, offered spiritual and social sustenance for many within Basingstoke. Moreover, major fund-raising events, such as the British Empire Bazaar in 1903, together with the 'red-letter' celebration of the church's jubilee in 1920, provided a welcome diversion from the routine of everyday life.[151]

With respect to premises, in 1885 the Sunday school was extended since existing accommodation was totally inadequate for the increasing number of children who attended.[152] The following year the chapel was enlarged to ensure an adequate supply of free sittings and to meet the demands of those applying for sittings. In so doing, if felt necessary, 'beauty, and conformity to architectural fitness' had to be 'sacrificed … to utility, to the needs of the Church, and the requirements of the future'. Thanks to the skill of the architect, again Mr Wonnacott, the additional galleries improved the interior of the building, which now looked 'very compact, comfortable and neat'.[153]

Nevertheless, by 1900 and perhaps to keep pace with the Primitive Methodists, it was decided to replace the chapel with a far more imposing building on the same site.[154] Designed by Gordon and Gunton and completed in 1905, it was double the size of the old chapel, with seating for approximately 700. Its design drew on contemporary Gothic Revival and Arts and Crafts influences. Essentially a rectangular building with a gabled roof, its façade was broken into three bays. In the centre a kneelered gable was flanked by two turrets. Half-way up there was a wide

149 R. Ottewill, 'Cultivating the Wilderness': The Establishment of Wesleyan Methodism in Basingstoke 1870–1908', *Proc. of the Wesley Historical Society*, 65.5 (2020), 187–207.
150 *HBG*, 7 Aug. 1915.
151 Ottewill, 'Wilderness', 201–4.
152 *HBG*, 27 June 1885.
153 *HBG*, 29 Jan. 1887.
154 *Cliddesden*, 73–5.

Fig. 47. Wesleyan Methodist church, Church Street, early 20th century.

pointed arch over an intricate tracery window. Below were two further arched tracery windows flanking the entrance. On either side of this central bay were two two-storey porches with pillars and battlements. This detailed façade was faced with split flints and stone dressings, while the sides and ends were in Faversham stock brickwork and again stone dressings. The overall design was described at the time as 'infused with that modern feeling which is perhaps one of the most pleasing features in the recent revival of Gothic architecture' and 'one of the most striking architectural features of the town' (Fig. 47).[155]

Strict Baptists

The first Baptist chapel in Basingstoke was formally opened in 1868. It was of a very neat and plain appearance[156] and could accommodate 150 worshippers.[157] Situated on the east side of Church Street and a little to the south of the Market Place, it was set back from the road. Members did not generally attract a great deal of attention. Services were not advertised, and activities were infrequently reported.[158] However, one of their leading members was Thomas Burberry.[159] As well as acts of worship, they also ran a Sunday school and a young people's bible class.

Despite the general reticence surrounding their activities, one issue attracted attention in the town. This concerned the installation of an organ in the chapel in 1895. For some members, it was felt that a musical instrument was not necessary and, although one had been used from time to time, its continued use was terminated due

---

155 *HBG*, 11 Mar. 1905; the first chapel was taken down and rebuilt in Cliddesden in 1905–6 (See, *Cliddesden*, 74). The south side of Potters Lane was the southern limit of 1960s demolition. All north of it was demolished and became Festival Place.

156 *RM*, 8 Feb. 1868.

157 R. Chambers, *The Strict Baptist Chapels of England*, Vol. 1: *the Chapels of Surrey and Hampshire* (Thornton Heath, 1952), 87; *HBG*, 21 Mar. 1903.

158 R. Ottewill, 'The Strict Baptists of Basingstoke: *c*.1867–*c*.1935', *HFC Newsletter*, 75 (2021), 18–20.

159 Above, Economic Hist., The Clothing Industry.

to 'dissent and disapproval'. Over time, however, opinions changed, with the result that funds were raised to purchase an American organ.[160] The chapel and organ were still in use in 1925.[161]

Open Baptists

The establishment of an Open Baptist cause in 1908 was primarily due to the efforts of Revd Alfred Bird, an evangelist from Whitchurch who, with assistance from the Southern Baptist Association, guided the fledgling church during the first few years of its existence.[162] To serve as a place of worship the old British school building on the south side of Sarum Hill was acquired. Its adaptation only took a few weeks, resulting in a 'commodious but plain building' capable of seating 200. The purchase price was £550, and it was anticipated that the cost of the alterations would bring the total sum up to £900. At the time, £70 to £80 had been raised, with the balance being met by interest free loans.[163] At the opening ceremony on 8 June, six conspicuous stones were laid in front of the building by church members and others.[164]

The Open Baptists quickly formed a close bond with other major Nonconformist denominations in the town. Served by a succession of diligent ministers the cause thrived during the war years and into the 1920s. As well as leading the church, some ministers were active in other spheres of community life. For example, Revd Frederick West (1910–12) was an active supporter of the cause of women's suffrage.

Salvation Army

While the previously mentioned mayhem surrounding the arrival of the Salvation Army in 1880 attracted most attention,[165] once harmony had been established, parades, open-air and indoor services, with an emphasis on lively music and personal testimonies, became well respected features of Basingstoke's religious life. The Army soon integrated itself fully into the Nonconformist community. Indeed, Captain Symonds, at his farewell address in 1884, observed that during his service in the Salvation Army (about seven years) by contrast with other places where he had served, he had never received such tokens of sympathy from other religious bodies in any other place as he had in Basingstoke.[166]

For premises, between 1880 and 1883 the Salvation Army rented an old silk mill in Brook Street,[167] which was renamed the 'Salvation Factory'.[168] In 1903 the Salvationists

---

160 *HBG*, 6 and 13 July 1895.
161 R. Ottewill, 'Strict Baptists', 20.
162 R. Ottewill, 'The Open Baptists of Basingstoke: 1906–1939 Part 1: Laying Foundations', *HFC Newsletter*, 77 (2022), 2–4; Part 2 'Moving Forward', *HFC Newsletter*, 80 (2023), 20– 3.
163 *HBG*, 13 June 1908. Hope Community church is on this site in 2024.
164 *HBG*, 13 June 1908.
165 Above, Local Government, Politics and Public Utilities, Riots and Disorder.
166 *HBG*, 6 Dec. 1884.
167 *HBG*, 11 Sept. 1880.
168 *HBG*, 25 Sept. 1880.

moved to purpose-built barracks in Reading Road, which could accommodate 350.[169] Costing £600, these comprised a large plain structure with the entrance being approached through some iron gates. They were officially opened in September, with General Booth's wife contributing to the proceedings.[170] At the time of their re-opening in 1909, following internal re-decoration, the barracks were dignified by the name Temple. The occasion was attended by Alderman Edney who said he was there for no other reason than to show sympathy with the Salvation Army and appreciation of its aims and work.[171]

Quakers

In 1800 the Quakers of Basingstoke acquired a new meeting house in Wote Street, moving from premises in Brook Street. This was rebuilt in 1829 and enlarged in 1849.[172] In 1851 the meeting house had 93 sittings on the ground floor and 66 in the gallery.[173]

Understandably Quaker meetings, with their emphasis on quiet contemplation and extemporary contributions from anyone who felt moved to speak, attracted little publicity. However, since leading citizens, including members of the Wallis and Steevens families, were Quakers, their contributions to the economic life of the community were of considerable importance.[174] Most are buried in the Quaker plot at South View Cemetery.[175]

From the late 19th century onwards, deaths and defections to other denominations led to a decline in the number of Quakers. By the 1920s meetings for worship were only being held in the Wote Street meeting house on an intermittent basis.[176]

Nonconformist Missions and Halls

Both the Railway mission (1893–c.1912) and Working Men's mission (1905–1928, Fig. 10) were based in the Newtown area of Basingstoke and committed to the spiritual and temporal welfare of working men and their families. Although formally non-denominational, they derived assistance from leading Nonconformists. Like other Nonconformist causes, they held services and meetings and provided a variety of affiliated organisations for children and young people – Sunday school, Band of Hope and branch of Christian Endeavour - and a women's sewing class. The Railway mission had its own choir, and, for a time, the Working Men's mission had an

169   *HBG*, 21 Mar. 1903.

170   *HBG*, 15 Sept. 1883.

171   *HBG*, 25 Dec. 1909.

172   D.M. Butler, *The Quaker Meeting Houses of Britain*, Vol. 1 (London, 1999), 229.

173   *Religious census*, 1851.

174   Above, Economic Hist., Wallis and Steevens.

175   Above, Public Utilities, Cemeteries and Burial Board.

176   A. Deveson, R. Johnson and R. Ottewill, 'Basingstoke Quakers – from persecution to productive enterprise and beyond: Part 1 1655 to 1800', *Hampshire Studies*, 79 (2024), 165–74; Part 2 1800 to 2024, forthcoming 2025.

orchestra. Anniversary celebrations were also an important feature in the life of the missions.[177]

Initially, the Railway mission did not have a permanent home and meetings were held in various locations, including the Wesleyan schoolroom in Potters Lane and the British Workman, a coffee tavern in Potters Lane. During 1898 it moved into Longcroft Hall in May Street. Erected in 1878,[178] this was subsequently purchased for £200, renamed and enlarged so that it could also be accessed from Lower Brook Street. In 1913 the premises were sold to the Congregationalists.[179]

The Working Men's mission hall in George Street was erected in 1904–5, at a cost of £220 including the site. It was an iron building capable of accommodating 250 and described as being 'very comfortable' and presenting 'a light and attractive appearance'. The walls and roof were lined with match-boarding, and it was lit by incandescent gas fittings. New classrooms were added in 1913, to cater for the increasing number of children who attended the Sunday school.[180] It was still active in 1925 but closed in 1928, when the premises were sold to the Wesleyan Methodists.

Brethren

There is a reference to the presence of both Strict and Open brethren in a newspaper article from 1878[181] and the 1882 census of churchgoing recorded three Plymouth Brethren meeting rooms.[182] In 1903 the Plymouth Brethren premises were located at Sarum Hill and Southern Road, while a gospel hall for open brethren had been built and opened in Essex Road during the early 1880s. The 1903 survey records it as seating 140.[183] Here missions, with visiting evangelists, played an important part in the life and witness of members.[184] In its early years the hall also had a flourishing Sunday school.[185] For much of its history, it kept out of the limelight.

Roman Catholics

Until the 1870s, insofar as there was a Roman Catholic presence in Basingstoke it

---

177 R. Ottewill, 'Basingstoke's Railway Mission', *BAHS Newsletter,* 218 (Feb 2017), 13–15; R. Ottewill, 'Working Men's Mission Hall, Basingstoke, 1905 to 1928', *BAHS Newsletter,* 223 (May 2018), 13–17.

178 This was probably the Preaching Room built by the Plymouth Brethren; HRO, 58M74/135.

179 Above, Congregationalists.

180 *HBG*, 22 Nov. 1913.

181 *HBG*, 18 May 1878.

182 *HBG*, 18 Feb. 1878.

183 *HBG*, 21 Mar. 1903.

184 *HBG*, 3 Jan. 1903.

185 *HBG*, 7 June 1884.

Fig. 48. Roman Catholic church of the Holy Ghost. © Barbara Large.

was served by the parish priest from Woolhampton (Berks.) who visited the town to say mass in a private house.[186] In 1874, Fr Charles Paul came to live in the parish and oversaw the building of the first chapel, on land sold by John Burgess Soper, a Nonconformist, to Dr Crookhall, parish priest at Woolhampton.[187] Dedicated to the Holy Ghost, it was opened by the bishop of Southwark in May 1878.[188] Located at the junction of Sherborne and Burgess Roads, it could accommodate about 100 and served as a place of worship and a schoolroom. When used for educational purposes the altar with its imposing adornments was hidden from view by a screen which ran across the end of the room.[189]

By the early 1880s, although there were relatively few Roman Catholics, there were signs of 'vitality'. These included a young priest Fr Daly working hard to gain adherents, with numbers doubling over a six-month period, and engaging 'the sympathies of the young'.[190] Overall, however, numbers remained small (Table 11). Several priests followed Fr Paul, each staying a comparatively short time, and by 1897 there was no resident priest, with care of the parish reverting to Woolhampton.

In 1901, however, while waiting at Basingstoke station, Canon Alexander Scoles was stirred by the view of the ruins of the Holy Ghost chapel situated in the cemetery.

186 Fr T. Grufferty, *Holy Ghost Church Basingstoke* (Basingstoke, 1992).
187 Grufferty, *Holy Ghost Church*.
188 *The Universe*, 25 May 1878.
189 *HBG*, 22 May 1880.
190 *HBG*, 22 May 1880.

Having trained as an architect and already designed two churches, he decided to devote himself to the mission in Basingstoke and moved there in May of that year. A presbytery was built, and in May 1902 the foundation stone of a new church to his design was laid, near to the earlier chapel, now the parish room. Thanks to his generosity the Holy Ghost church was a far grander building, in the Early English style of flint with stone dressings, and large stone buttresses containing statues of John the Baptist and the patron saints of the diocese.[191] Above the front door a stone carving represents the disciples receiving the gift of the Holy Spirit. It was consecrated in September 1903.[192] Together with the adjoining presbytery, it serves as 'a contribution to local architecture which stands unique for solidity of structure and richness of adornment' (Fig. 48).[193]

Jews

Established in 1903, a Jewish congregation still met for services during the 1920s.[194] The president of the congregation was Reuben Polka.[195]

191 Stokes, *Basingstoke*, 157.
192 *HBG*, 19 Sept. 1903.
193 *HBG*, 19 Sept. 1903.
194 *Jewish Chron.*, 3 Apr.1903.
195 https://www.jewishgen.org/jcr-uk/community/basingstoke/index.htm (accessed 23 May 2023).

EPILOGUE

THIS BOOK DISCUSSES the major transformation of Basingstoke from an agricultural and market town to an industrial town between 1800 and 1925. This was accompanied by increased social activities, care for the poor, education, churches and chapels. The First World War kept Basingstoke busy producing munitions, lorries, army uniforms and serving the army camps that sprang up around the town. Peace brought problems, particularly for the town's largest employer Thornycroft, faced both by a cut off of army purchases and by a flooding of the domestic market with cheap ex-War Department lorries. 1920 saw massive layoffs in the company.

But by 1925 the mayor, Charles Bowman could celebrate recovery and the success of the town. He remarked that the town possessed great advantages as an industrial centre as it was situated on a railway junction: the LSWR (Southern Railway from 1923) took an hour to London; Southampton was 45 minutes away, while the GWR connected the town with the Midlands and the North. Bowman urged even greater progress by building more factories and more houses to relieve overcrowding. He did not think there was any town better situated as a commercial and industrial centre.[1] The interwar years saw further growth and two new factories: Kelvin Hughes (aircraft instruments) and Eli Lilly (pharmaceuticals) with the population doubling between 1921 and 1961.

From the 1960s Basingstoke was transformed again as a result of the London Overspill Agreement. New office blocks, a ring road, extensive suburbs and a massive shopping centre were built. This redevelopment destroyed not merely much of the medieval street plan of the lower town but many of the buildings that so characterised the dramatic transformation of the 19th century town: its new factories, grand chapels, some terraced houses, and other houses and shops. The factories of Wallis and Steevens, of Gerrish, Ames and Simpkins and of John Mares were all demolished as later was Thornycroft's. Between 1961 and 2021 the population rose almost fivefold.

However, the Victorian and Edwardian suburbs survived as did the historic upper town, where the site of Burberry's Hackwood Road/London Street establishment is preserved in the Gabardine Bar and his Emporium building still exists and is in use. Basingstoke in 2024 is not all 'new town'. Within the modern ring road with its many roundabouts, a mix of the old and the new survives. Basingstoke Heritage Town Trail offers 45 places dating from medieval to modern in which to explore the history of

---

1   *HBG* ,14 Nov. 1925; Bradshaw's July 1938 Railway Guide, David and Charles Reprints (Newton Abbot, 1969).

the town.[2] In London Street medieval buildings remain. The 1832 town hall is now the Willis Museum. The cricket ground dates from the early 19th century. The parish church, which was built over 500 years ago, is across Church Street from the modern shopping centre.

2   https://www.basingstoke.gov.uk/content/page/69592/Heritage%20trail%20leaflet%20 accessible.pdf, (accessed 19 Sept. 2024).

ABBREVIATIONS

Abbreviation	Full text
a.	Acre
Austen, *Letters*	Deirdre Le Faye (ed.), *Jane Austen's Letters*, 3rd edn (Oxford, 1995)
BAHS	Basingstoke Archaeological and Historical Society
Baigent and Millard, *Basingstoke*	F.J. Baigent and J.E. Millard, *A History of the Ancient Town and Manor of Basingstoke in the County of Southampton with a Brief Account of the Siege of Basing House, A.D. 1643–1645* (Basingstoke, 1889)
BC	*Berkshire Chronicle*
BG	*Basingstoke Gazette*
CCED	*Clergy of the Church of England database https://theclergydatabase.org.uk/*
Clarke, *Riots 1880–83*	Bob Clarke, *The Basingstoke Riots: Massagainians v the Salvation Army 1880–1883* (Basingstoke, 2010)
Cliddesden	Alison Deveson and Sue Lane, *Cliddesden, Hatch and Farleigh Wallop* (VCH, 2018)
Dir.	*Directory*
Dummer and Kempshott	Jennie Butler and Sue Lane, *Dummer and Kempshott, Two Chalkland Parishes* (VCH, 2022)
GWR	Great Western Railway
Ha.	Hectare
HA	*Hampshire Advertiser*
Hare, *Medieval Basingstoke*	John Hare, *Basingstoke: A Medieval Town, c.1000–c.1600* (VCH 2017)
HBG	*Hants and Berks Gazette*
HC	*Hampshire Chronicle*
Hampshire CC	Hampshire County Council
HCT	Hampshire Cultural Trust, Chilcomb House, Winchester, SO23 8RB
HER	Historic Environment Record Hampshire

HFC	Hampshire Field Club
HMI	His Majesty's Inspector (of schools)
HMS	Hampshire Museum Service
HO	Hampshire Observer
HRO	Hampshire Record Office
HRS	Hampshire Record Society before 1914; thereafter Hampshire Record Series
Kelly's Dir.	*Kelly's Directory of Hampshire and the Isle of Wight*
LPL	Lambeth Palace Library
Large, *Workhouse.*	Barbara A. Large, *Basingstoke Workhouse and Poor Law Union*, (The History Press, 2016)
LSWR	London and South Western Railway
Mapledurwell	John Hare, Jean Morrin and Stan Waight, *Mapledurwell,* (VCH 2012).
MERL	Museum of English Rural Life, Reading
Mitchell & Smith 1988	K. Mitchell and K. Smith, *Woking to Southampton* (Haslemere, 1988)
MRC	Modern Records Centre, University of Warwick
NHLE	National Heritage List for England
ODNB	*Oxford Dictionary of National Biography*
OS	Ordnance Survey
Parl. Papers	Parliamentary Papers
Pevsner, *North Hampshire*	Michael Bullen, John Crook, Rodney Hubbuck and Nikolaus Pevsner, *Hampshire: Winchester and the North* (London, 2010)
Pigot's Dir.	J Pigot, *National and Commercial Dir. London and Manchester, Hampshire section*
P.O. Dir.	*Post Office Directory Hampshire*
Rel. Census 1851	J.A.Vickers, *The Religious Census 1851* (HRS 12, 1993)
Reavell, *South View*	Debbie Reavell, *A short History of South View Basingstoke including the Holy Ghost Cemetery and the story of the ruined chapels* (Basingstoke, 2014) http://southviewbasingstoke.wordpress.com
RM	*Reading Mercury*
RO	Record Office
Slater's Dir.	*Slater's Directory of Hampshire.*
Staffs. RO	Staffordshire Record Office

Stokes, *Basingstoke*	Eric Stokes (ed. Bob and Barbara Applin), *The Making of Basingstoke: from Pre-History to the Present Day*, (Basingstoke, 2008)
TNA	The National Archives
Townsin, *Thornycroft*	Alan Townsin, *Thornycroft* (Hersham, Surrey, 2001)
VCH Hants	*The Victoria History of the Counties of England: Hampshire and the Isle of Wight*. Original Editions published 1902–11.
Vine, *London's Lost Route*	P.A.L. Vine, *London's Lost Route to Basingstoke. The Story of the Basingstoke Canal* (Stroud, 1994).
Whitehead	R.A. Whitehead, *Wallis and Steevens: a History* (Road Locomotive Society, 1983)
White's Dir.	W. White, *History, Gazeteer and Directory of Hampshire and the Isle of Wight* (London)
Yorks. N.R.	Yorkshire North Riding
Youngs, *Admin. Units,* Vol. 1	F.A. Youngs, *Guide to the Local Administrative Units of England*, Vol.1, *Southern England* (London, 1979)

INDEX

www.ingramcontent.com/pod-product-compliance
Ingram Content Group UK Ltd.
Pitfield, Milton Keynes, MK11 3LW, UK
UKHW060641141025
8378UKWH00050B/1078